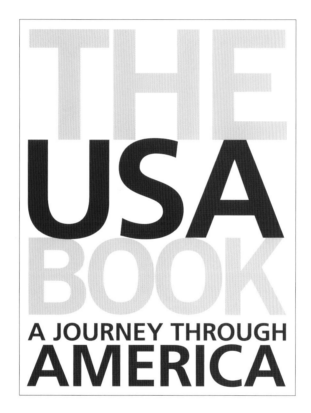

THE USA BOOK

A JOURNEY THROUGH AMERICA

CONTENTS

INTRODUCING THE USA

 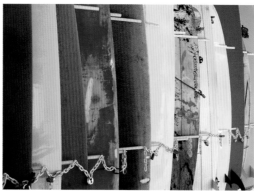 

THE PLAYWRIGHT ARTHUR MILLER ONCE SAID THAT THE ESSENCE OF AMERICA WAS ITS PROMISE. FOR NEWLY ARRIVED IMMIGRANTS AND JETLAGGED TRAVELERS ALIKE, THAT PROMISE CAN TAKE ON NEAR-MYTHIC PROPORTIONS.

The USA is a land of dazzling cities, towering redwoods, alpine lakes, rolling vineyards, chiseled peaks, barren deserts and a dramatic coastline of unrivaled beauty. And that's just one state (California).

In the other 49 states lie an astounding collection of natural and cultural wonders, from the wildly multihued tapestry of urban streets to the mountains, plains and forests that cover vast swaths of the continent. The USA is the birthplace of LA, Las Vegas, Chicago, Miami, Boston and New York City – each a brimming metropolis whose name alone conjures a million different notions of culture, cuisine and entertainment.

Look more closely, and the American quilt unfurls in all its surprising variety: the eclectic music scene of Austin, the easygoing charms of antebellum Savannah, the ecoconsciousness of free-spirited Portland, the magnificent waterfront of San Francisco, and the captivating old quarters of New Orleans, still rising from its (waterlogged) ashes.

This is a country of road trips and great open skies, where 4 million miles of highways lead past red-rock deserts, below towering mountain peaks, and across fertile wheat fields that roll toward the horizon. The sun-bleached Native American hillsides of the Great Plains, lush forests of the Pacific Northwest and the scenic country lanes of New England are a few fine starting points for the great American road trip.

The world's third-largest nation has made substantial contributions to the arts. Georgia O'Keeffe's wild landscapes, Robert Rauschenberg's surreal collages, Alexander Calder's elegant mobiles and Jackson Pollock's drip paintings have entered the vernacular of avant-garde 20th-century art. And cities like Chicago and New York have become veritable drawing boards for the great architects of the modern era. Musically speaking, the USA has few peers. From the big-band jazz that was born in New Orleans to the Memphis blues, Detroit's Motown sound, funk, hip-hop, country, and rock and roll – the USA has invented sounds integral to any understanding of contemporary music.

Cuisine is another way of illuminating the US experience. While thick BBQ ribs and sizzling meats arrive fresh off the grill at a Tennessee roadhouse, miles away talented chefs blend organic, fresh-from-the-garden produce with Asian accents at an award-winning West Coast restaurant. A smattering of locals get their fix of bagels and lox at a century-old deli in Manhattan's Upper West Side, while several states away, plump pancakes and fried eggs disappear in a hurry under the clatter of cutlery at a 1950s diner. Steaming plates of fresh lobster served off a Maine pier, oysters and champagne in a fashion-conscious wine bar, beer and pizza at a Midwestern pub – just a few ways to dine á la Americana.

But the USA isn't just about its geography, its cities or even its art and cuisine. It's also about people. The 'teeming nation of nations' (as Walt Whitman famously described it) was built on immigration and still attracts over one million arrivals per year. Representatives from nearly every country can be found inside the boundaries of the USA, adding an astounding mix of ethnicities, religions and languages to the national character.

As a collective voice, the USA has a complicated soul. In addition to the wide mix of racial and ethnic groups, it is a mishmash of factory workers and farmers, born-again Christians and Hatha yoga practitioners, literary-minded college students and tradition-bound Native Americans, beer-swilling baseball lovers and back-to-nature commune dwellers. This is a country in which regional stereotypes help Americans get a handle on their own elusive country, whether the people in question are gracious Southern belles, street-smart New Yorkers, humble Midwesterners, SoCal surfers or straight-talking Texans.

The collective identity, however, goes only so far in defining Americans. This is, after all, a country that celebrates – or rather mythologizes – feats of 'rugged individualism,' a notion well supported by the enormous ranks of the great and dastardly alike who have left their mark on the USA. This is the land of Teddy Roosevelt, John Muir, Jack Kerouac, Andy Warhol, Frank Lloyd Wright, Elvis Presley, Marilyn Monroe, Muhammad Ali and Oprah Winfrey. It is also the birthplace of Billy the Kid, Al Capone, the Dukes of Hazzard and hundreds of other real and fictional characters who contribute to that portrait of the American hero or villain heading off into the sunset.

The USA still has the ability to inspire. Although many years have passed since Martin Luther King was assassinated, his message of hope lives on. The USA is still a place where big dreamers can triumph over adversity. No one in recent history has demonstrated that more clearly than Barack Obama, the country's first African American president.

Despite this unprecedented moment in US history, change is no stranger to the American scene. Even the nation's creation was a daring paradigm shift in a world of monarchies and autocracies. A country founded as a refuge for religious tolerance by early colonists later became the world's first modern democratic republic. Over the centuries, visionary statespeople like Jefferson, Lincoln and Roosevelt have helped move the country in bold new directions. But it was courageous citizens, fighting (and sometimes sacrificing their lives) in the battle against injustice who brought about some of the USA's most profound changes – in abolishing slavery, earning equal rights for women, protecting the environment and enshrining fair wages and working conditions for laborers.

Citizens from all walks of life have participated in 'the great American experiment,' a concept that rewards bold ideas and hard work, no matter one's place in society. The results of nurturing this entrepreneurial spirit have been far-reaching. From the historic flight by the Wright Brothers to the Apollo moon landing, Americans have achieved ambitious goals. Technological revolutions beginning with Thomas Edison's lightbulb and Henry Ford's automobile manufacturing methods continue today in the pioneering work by Bill Gates, Steve Jobs, and Larry Page and Sergey Brin, whose innovations in information technology continue to have an overwhelming effect on communication and industry across the globe.

THE USA AT A GLANCE

POPULATION 303.8 MILLION | **AREA** 3.8 MILLION SQ MILES | **GROSS DOMESTIC PRODUCT** $13.8 TRILLION

YELLOWSTONE'S GRAND PRISMATIC SPRING IS ONE OF US-20'S SPOILS. ≫

THE SMITHSONIAN STUFFS A LOT IN ITS MUSEUMS. ≫

IT'S ALWAYS A FINE DAY FOR A WALK IN YOSEMITE. ≫

LONGEST ROAD

US-20 spans 3365 miles across 11 states on its coast-to-coast route from Boston, MA, to Newport, OR. In between it dawdles through Rust Belt towns, Amish farms, Plains prairie land, Yellowstone National Park and mountain hamlets before depositing road trippers on the wave-bashed Pacific shore.

BEST BEER

With more breweries (30) than any city on the planet, Portland, OR, wins the 'beervana' award. Stumble between brewpubs in watch-repair shops and old rope factories, pull up a chair by the fire and clink your fresh-from-the-vat pint of Hefeweizen, Belgian ale or ESB in gratitude to the beer gods.

BEST MUSEUM

If America was a quirky grandfather, Washington, DC's Smithsonian Institution would be his attic. Rockets, dinosaurs, Rodin sculptures, Tibetan *thangka* (banners) – even the 45-carat Hope diamond lights up a room here. The Smithsonian is actually a group of museums and they're all free.

BEST FEST

Louis Armstrong and Duke Ellington are among those who've blown their horns and tickled the ivories at the New Orleans Jazz Fest, a 10-stage bash rocking over two weekends in spring. Almost better than the music is the food: soft-shell crab po'boys, Cajun rice-and-pork sausage and white-chocolate bread pudding. Bring dancing shoes and loose-waisted pants.

BEST BEACH

Lace up tough footwear and pack water – you're going to need them for the lava trail leading to Makalawena Beach on the Big Island of Hawai'i. The payoff is huge: a series of secluded coves lapped by azure waters, white sand dunes, close encounters with turtles and excellent body boarding.

BEST HIKE

Hiking Yosemite National Park's Mist Trail is like walking into an Ansel Adams photo, where frothy white waterfalls shoot over dark granite monoliths under a stark sky. Spectacular views and cools sprays occur throughout the 3-mile round-trip to Vernal Falls (and onward to Nevada Falls).

BEST APPLE PIE

Unsheathe your fork in Mukwonago, WI, and follow your nose to the Elegant Farmer, where pies are baked in brown paper bags, a trick that makes the crust so flaky it crunches. Surrounding orchards produce the juicy Ida Reds that plump the pies to pillowlike proportions.

THANK THE COLORADO RIVER FOR CARVING SUCH A GRAND CANYON. ≫

MOUNT MCKINLEY STANDS SO TALL IT CREATES ITS OWN WEATHER. ≫

COLORADO'S BIG ADVENTURE INCLUDES OURAY ICE PARK. ≫

BUDDHIST MONKS IN PRAYER, IN SOUTHERN CALIFORNIA. ≫

BEST NATURAL FEATURE
When the earth cracks open to reveal a mile-deep, 277-mile-long wilderness of rock, glowing red-orange and purpley-pink in a kaleidoscopic sunset, that is indeed a Grand Canyon. Gawk with the masses at the South Rim or go for a hard-earned remote view on the North Rim. Either way, the Grand Canyon will knock your socks off.

BEST PLACE TO SPEND THE FOURTH OF JULY
Patriotism and partying in the city where it all began – how can you beat Philadelphia? Descendants of the men who signed the Declaration of Independence ring the Liberty Bell at 2pm; and parades, fireworks, big-name bands and Tastykakes add to the fun.

TALLEST MOUNTAIN
Rising 20,320 feet, Alaska's Mount McKinley is the highest peak in North America. The Native Alaskans who live at its flanks call it Denali (Great One). The first climbers to reach the summit did so in 1913 and many have attempted since. Only about half succeed before ferocious weather (it's colder than Everest) forces them back.

BRAVEST MENU CHOICE
Man up (or woman up) for Rocky Mountain oysters, aka Montana tendergroins, cowboy caviar or swinging beef. Common in western ranchlands where bulls are castrated (so they'll grow meatier), these fruits of labor are salvaged and then peeled, breaded and fried. The chewy nuggets are best dipped in hot sauce.

BEST ADVENTURE STATE
Skiing between the 10th Mountain Division's backcountry huts? Climbing a frozen waterfall in Ouray Ice Park? Paddling class V rapids on the Colorado River? Sand boarding at Great Sand Dunes National Park? Heli-skiing in Telluride? So much to do in Colorado, so little time.

BEST OFF-THE-BEATEN-PATH DESTINATION
Roam with the buffalo in Theodore Roosevelt National Park, through a badlands patchwork of chalky cliffs and whispering grasses. You'll likely have the place to yourself. Located in forlorn North Dakota, the park bewitches, especially when the moon's 'silvery rays' transform it into a 'grim fairy-land,' as Roosevelt himself once wrote.

BEST SUNSET
Sure, the USA's mountains, canyons and beaches offer fine places to watch the sun drop. But for sheer dramatic effect, the waterfront of Red Hook, Brooklyn, is the place to be at the end of the day. Here you'll look straight at the Statue of Liberty as the red-orange orb falls behind her mighty torch.

MOST SPIRITUAL PLACE
At the City of Ten Thousand Buddhas, deer and peacocks roam the gardens, monks and nuns pray in the misty dawn half-light and visitors admire the 10,000 hand-molded buddhas in the Jeweled Hall. That the Zen community is located amid Northern California's mountains and vineyards adds to the bliss.

ARTS & ARCHITECTURE

⌃ CHICAGO LAUNCHED THE WORLD'S FIRST SKYSCRAPER.

⌃ EVEN SKYLIGHTS HAVE STYLE AT SAN FRANCISCO'S MOMA.

⌃ WARHOL'S POP ART *MAO* AT PITTBURGH'S WARHOL MUSEUM.

From vaudeville to science fiction, Beat poets to blockbuster movies, Frank Lloyd Wright's Prairie School to Andy Warhol's pop art, the USA has put on quite a show. Geography and race continue to shape what it paints, writes and builds. And digital technology is remaking the whole shebang.

ARCHITECTURE

Architecture gave the USA its first real artistic street cred. In 1885, a group of designers in Chicago presented the pioneering skyscraper. At 10 stories it didn't exactly poke the clouds, but its use of steel framing launched modern architecture.

At the beginning of the 20th century, another Chicago architect was doing radical things closer to the ground. Frank Lloyd Wright created a building style that abandoned historical elements and references, which had long been the tradition, and instead went organic. He designed buildings in relation to the landscape, which in the Midwest were the low-slung, horizontal lines of the surrounding prairie. An entire movement grew up around Wright's Prairie style.

European architects absorbed Wright's ideas, and that influence bounced back when the Bauhaus school left Nazi Germany and set up in the USA. Here it became known as the International style, an early form of modernism. Ludwig Mies van der Rohe was the main man with the plan, and his boxy, metal-and-glass-type behemoths rose high on urban horizons. Post-modernism followed, reintroducing color and the decorative elements of art deco, beaux art and other earlier styles to the nation's sky-high designs.

Over the years, skyscrapers became fitting symbols of the USA's technical achievements, grand aspirations, commerce and modernism. Chicago's Sears Tower is the epitome – the USA's tallest building for more than 35 years.

FILM

Ever since Thomas Edison screened the first flick via a peephole Kineto-scope in 1893, the USA has been wild for movies, and its productions have dominated the global film industry.

Several genres are considered national specialties. For instance, Westerns took on mythical significance in the 1940s and '50s: good guys versus bad guys, law versus lawlessness, all duking it out on the rugged frontier. Gary Cooper, John Wayne and Clint Eastwood drew guns in many of the best ones.

Crime and gangster films moved the violence to urban locations. Film noir detectives, sometimes played by Humphrey Bogart, wore trench coats and brimmed hats while trying to figure out whodunit. Later, Francis Ford Coppola's *Godfather* trilogy (1971–90) and Martin Scorsese's *Mean Streets* (1973) and *GoodFellas* (1990) showed how mobsters do business.

Inherently cinematic and ever popular, science fiction is often just the Wild West tricked out with lasers and spaceships, but at its best it's shot through with existential dread and postmodern fears of otherness and technology. For existentialism, Stanley Kubrick's *2001: A Space Odyssey* (1968) defines the genre; for classic pulp, the original *Star Wars* (1977) sets the standard.

Blockbusters are the film industry's mainstay – multimillion dollar special-effects studio extravaganzas starring big-name actors. Increasingly though, smaller budget independent films play a role on US screens, too. US cinema-goers spend about $10 billion going to the movies each year.

LITERATURE

The 'Great American Novel' has stirred the nation's imagination for more than 150 years. And, no, it's not dead. Edgar Allan Poe told spooky short tales in the 1840s, and is credited with popularizing the detective story, horror story

ONE: NUMBER 31, 1950, BY JACKSON POLLOCK CAUSES A HEAD-SCRATCHING MOMENT AT NEW YORK'S MUSEUM OF MODERN ART. ⌃

and science fiction. Four decades later Samuel Clemens, aka Mark Twain, also made a literary splash. Twain wrote in the vernacular, loved 'tall tales' and reveled in absurdity, which endeared him to everyday readers. His novel *The Adventures of Huckleberry Finn* (1884) became the quintessential American narrative: compelled by a primal moment of rebellion against his father, Huck embarks on a search for authenticity through which he discovers himself.

The Lost Generation brought American literature into its own in the early 20th century. These writers, including Ernest Hemingway and F Scott Fitzgerald, lived as expatriates in Europe post WWI and described a growing sense of alienation. Back at home, John Steinbeck became the great voice of the West's rural and working poor in the 1930s, while William Faulkner examined the South's social rifts in dense, caustic prose.

After WWII, American writers began depicting regional and ethnic divides, experimented with style and often bashed middle-class society's values. The 1950s Beat Generation, with Jack Kerouac, Allen Ginsberg and William S Burroughs at the center, was particularly hard-core.

Today's literature reflects an ever-more-diverse panoply of voices. Toni Morrison, Amy Tan, Ana Castillo and Sherman Alexie have all written best sellers and given voice to, respectively, African American, Asian American, Mexican American and Native American issues, among many others.

THEATER

Eugene O'Neill put US drama on the map with his trilogy *Mourning Becomes Electra* (1931), which sets a tragic Greek myth in post–Civil War New England. The first major US playwright, O'Neill is still widely considered to be the best.

After WWII two playwrights dominated the stage: Arthur Miller, who wrote, among others, *Death of a Salesman* (1949) and *The Crucible* (1953), and the prolific Tennessee Williams, whose works include *The Glass Menagerie* (1945), *A Streetcar Named Desire* (1947) and *Cat on a Hot Tin Roof* (1955).

Edward Albee gave the 1960s a healthy dose of absurdism, and David Mamet and Sam Shepard filled the '70s and '80s with rough and tough guys. These days Pulitzer Prize–winner Tracy Letts writes family dramas that are often compared to O'Neill, bringing the scene full circle.

Broadway is where shows get star treatment, but away from its bright lights the country's 1500 non-profit regional theaters struggle, scrape, scrimp and ultimately breed the new plays and playwrights that keep the art vital.

PAINTING & SCULPTURE

Jackson Pollock's drip paintings, Georgia O'Keeffe's flower images, Roy Lichtenstein's comic strip–like pictures and the nostalgic works of Norman Rockwell are the different images of iconic 20-century US art. Each of these artists pushed the envelope to create something new.

In the wake of WWII, the USA developed its first truly original school of art: abstract expressionism. Pollock, Franz Kline, Mark Rothko and others explored freely created, non-representational forms. The style was so subversive, art historians have argued that the USA used it as a tool for Cold War propaganda. Evidence suggests the CIA funded traveling exhibitions of abstract expressionist works to promote US individualism and democracy overseas. Abstraction, it was hoped, would serve as an instructive antidote to the realist styles favored by Soviet regimes.

Pop art followed, where artists drew inspiration from bright, cartoony consumer images. Andy Warhol was the king (or Pope of Pop, as he's sometimes called). Minimalism came next, and by the 1980s and '90s, the canvas was wide open – any and all styles could take their place at the arts table.

MUSIC

⊼ A BLUEGRASS BAND JAMS IN NORTH CAROLINA.

⊼ TOOLS TO UNLEASH ONE'S INNER ROCKER.

⊼ GOLD RECORDS PACK THE COUNTRY MUSIC HALL OF FAME.

Of the USA's rich trove of arts, its music rocks the most influence. We mean it literally – rock and roll has fomented revolutions, both at home and abroad. In the country's social revolution in the 1960s, rock music – openly sexual, celebrating youth and dancing freely across the color line – sparked changes in civil rights and politics. Twenty-five years later, rock likewise ignited the Czech uprising against that country's repressive government. Even that rebellion's name – Velvet Revolution – supposedly came from the leaders' favorite US band, the Velvet Underground.

So rock takes center stage, but the nation's mixed tape plays blues, jazz, funk, gospel, hip-hop and country too. The USA invented all of these sounds, and they remain an integral part of the national airwaves.

BLUES

Willie Dixon said it best: 'The blues is the roots, and everything else is the fruits.' He meant that all US music starts with the blues. The blues developed in the South, out of the work songs, or 'shouts,' of black slaves and out of black spiritual songs and their 'call-and-response' pattern, both of which were adaptations of African music.

By the 1920s, Delta blues typified the sound. Musicians from Memphis to Mississippi sung passionate, plaintive melodies accompanied by a lonely slide guitar, Muddy Waters, Howlin' Wolf and Robert Johnson (who sold his soul to the devil for nimble fingers, so the story goes) among them. After WWII many headed north to Chicago, which had become a hub for African American culture and the blues. And here the genre took a turn – it went electric, with screaming guitars that laid the groundwork for rock and roll.

Blues musicians today don't sell a ton of records (or downloads, as the case may be), but Americans show up in force for blues festivals. The

biggest events take place in the delta states and Chicago (where close to 750,000 fans amass) though even small towns in Iowa, Ohio, South Dakota and elsewhere around the country sponsor homages to the primal, fret-bending form.

JAZZ

A sibling to the blues, jazz developed concurrently out of similar roots in the South. Congo Square in New Orleans, where slaves gathered to sing and dance in the early 19th century, is considered the birthplace of jazz. Here, ex-slaves adapted the reed, horn and string instruments used by the city's African American Creoles – who themselves preferred formal European music – to play their own African-influenced music. This fertile cross-pollination produced a steady stream of innovative sound.

The first variation was ragtime, so-called because of its 'ragged,' syncopated African rhythms. Next came Dixieland jazz, centered on New Orleans' infamous Storyville district and its houses of ill repute. In 1917 Storyville was shut down and the musicians dispersed (Louis Armstrong and friends went to Chicago to blow their trumpets). New York's Harlem was the Jazz Age hot spot, where Duke Ellington and Count Basie led their big bands. Miles Davis, John Coltrane and others later deconstructed the sound and made up a new one that was cool, free and avant-garde.

Like blues musicians, jazz artists don't ring up huge sales. That's not the point – it's about live performances in wee clubs and festivals where something new is created every time. 'One thing I like about jazz, kid,' said 1920s cornetist Bix Beiderbecke to a fellow player, 'is that I don't know what's going to happen next. Do you?' Fans in regional hotbeds like New York, New Orleans, Kansas City and San Francisco know the feeling.

THE BLUES AIN'T NOTHING BUT A GOOD MAN FEELIN' BAD. ≪

COUNTRY

Early Scottish, Irish and English immigrants brought their own instruments and folk music to the USA, and what emerged over time in the secluded Appalachian Mountains was fiddle-and-banjo hillbilly, or 'country,' music. 'Western' music in the Southwest was distinguished by steel guitars and larger bands. In the 1920s, these styles merged into 'country and western.' Nashville, Tennessee, became its center once the *Grand Ole Opry* began its radio broadcasts in 1925.

Something about the 'cry a tear in your beer' twanging resonated with Americans, and country music became big business. It's now the most popular commercial radio station format – there are four times as many country stations as classic rock stations on the nation's dial. The South and West remain the boot-wearin', two-steppin' strongholds. Subsequent riffs on the genre include bluegrass, rockabilly and alt country.

ROCK

Most say rock and roll was born in 1954 on the day Elvis Presley walked into Sam Phillips' Sun Studio and recorded 'That's All Right.' Initially, radio stations weren't sure why a white country boy was singing black music, or whether they should play him, and it wasn't until 1956 that Presley scored his first big breakthrough with 'Heartbreak Hotel.' In some ways, the USA never recovered from the rock and roll aftermath.

Musically, rock was a hybrid of guitar-driven blues, black rhythm and blues (R & B), and white country-and-western music. R & B evolved in the 1940s out of swing and the blues, and was then known as 'race music.' With rock and roll, white musicians (and some African American musicians)

transformed 'race music' into something that white youths could embrace freely – and boy, did they.

Rock morphed into the psychedelic sounds of the Grateful Dead and Jefferson Airplane, and the electric wails of Janis Joplin, Jimi Hendrix, Bob Dylan and Patti Smith. Since then, rock has been about music and lifestyle, alternating between hedonism and seriousness, commercialism and authenticity. Woodstock exemplified the scene in 1969.

Which brings us to today's rock festivals: Lollapalooza in Chicago, South by Southwest in Austin, and Coachella in Southern California are 'musical, cultural, community experiences,' to quote Lollapalooza, attracting fans from around the country who are willing to pay up and immerse themselves in a hip, multiday scene.

HIP-HOP & RAP

Hip-hop and rap took the 'outlaw' mantle from rock in the last few decades, rising from down-and-out areas with a vital voice. New York, Detroit and Los Angeles became spawning grounds for groups like NWA. By the turn of the millennium, the genre was the nation's second most popular music (after pop/rock).

Then, like all American music, it saw a decrease in sales. Some say it's because of rap's glorification of consumerism, misogyny and drug use; others say it's just going through growing pains as it changes. The development of cheaper and simpler music recording programs has given rise to thousands of bedroom producers who make their own sounds – not just for rap, but rock, Latin, Cajun, krunk, punk and all the rest.

Stay tuned for the new revolution.

FOOD & DRINK

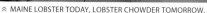

≫ MAINE LOBSTER TODAY, LOBSTER CHOWDER TOMORROW.

≫ GRAPES AWAIT STOMPING AT A VINEYARD.

≫ THE SECRET'S IN THE SAUCE, SOUTHERN BBQ PROS SAY.

When *Betty Crocker's Cookbook* lists tandoori chicken next to tuna-noodle casserole, you know US cuisine has reached the point where it defies easy description. We can agree on a few nationwide classics though: breakfast bacon and eggs; a hamburger or sandwich for lunch; for dinner, beef, pork or chicken – probably fried, broiled or barbecued and served with potatoes; and a thick slice of pie for dessert. These dishes top tables pretty much everywhere, but the beauty of US fare is the ethnic and regional riffs that create new flavors and traditions.

For more on US cuisine, turn to the state sections throughout this book.

NEW ENGLAND

New England claims to have the nation's best seafood, and who's to argue? The North Atlantic Ocean churns up clams, mussels, oysters and huge lobsters, along with shad, bluefish and cod. This bounty stirs into a mighty fine chowder, for which every seafood shack up the coast has its own secret recipe that's put to the test during summertime chowder fests and cook-offs. The clambake, in which shellfish are buried in a pit fire with foil-wrapped corn, chicken and sausages, is another tradition. Fried clam fritters and lobster rolls (lobster meat with mayonnaise served in a bread bun) appear on most menus. Then there are the specialties New Englanders don't have to fish for – maple syrup from the region's forests, cranberries from Massachusetts, and Vermont's cheeses and ice cream (for which Ben & Jerry's sets the sweet standard).

MID-ATLANTIC

From New York down through Maryland, the Mid-Atlantic states share a long coastline and a cornucopia of apple, pear and berry farms. New Jersey wins prizes for tomatoes, New York's Long Island for potatoes. Chesapeake Bay's blue crabs make diners swoon, as do Pennsylvania Dutch Country's heaping plates of chicken pot pie, noodles and meatloaflike scrapple. Of course it's New York City that dominates the scene: a 24/7 gateway to a world of cuisines. Got a craving? New York City will satisfy it, from a slice of New York–style pizza (thin crust, lightly sauced and foldable) to a Jewish-deli pastrami sandwich, Jamaican jerk chicken to Ukrainian *varenyky* (dumplings). Wines from New York's Hudson Valley, Finger Lakes and Long Island help wash it all down. The vintages here are no joke, with many achieving international status.

THE SOUTH

The South is where good eatin' reaches epic proportions, and belt loosening becomes a necessity. Local dishes mix Anglo, French, African, Spanish, Caribbean and Native American ingredients and customs, and if your lips don't smack at the results, you'd better check your pulse. Slow-cooked BBQ is one of the top stokers of regional pride; there are as many meaty and saucy variations as there are towns in the South. Southern fried chicken and catfish pop out of the pan crisp on the outside and moist inside. Fluffy hot biscuits, corn bread, sweet potatoes, collard greens and – most passionately – grits (ground corn cooked to a cereal-like consistency) accompany Southern plates, all butter-smothered.

For the crème de la crème, pull up a chair at a Louisiana table. The state stands out for its two main cuisines: Cajun food is found in the bayou country and marries native spices like sassafras and chili peppers to French home cooking; Creole food is more urban, centered in New Orleans, where zippy dishes like shrimp rémoulade, crabmeat *ravigote* and gumbo (soupy

stew of okra and chicken, shellfish and/or sausage) have eaters dabbing their brow. Southerners drink sweet iced tea or, when the occasion calls for something stronger, bourbon (the USA's only native spirit and by law made only in Kentucky, though Tennessee whiskey tastes similar).

THE MIDWEST & GREAT PLAINS

This is farm country, where folks need a lot of sustenance to get their work done, so they fire up the meat and potatoes and get on with it, no fuss required. The region is tops for serving US classics like pot roast, meatloaf, steak and pork chops; add walleye, perch and other freshwater fish to menus in Great Lakes states. BBQ sizzles on many a grill, especially in Kansas City. And Chicago stands tall as the region's – and nation's – foodie star; critics recently crowned it the USA's best restaurant city. Perhaps the heartland's greatest gift to the nation's cuisine is beer. Cities here have long been known for suds crafting thanks to their German heritage. Today 80% of domestic beer comes from the region, including big names like Budweiser and Miller, and lots of slurpable microbrews too.

SOUTHWEST

One word sums up the scene here: *hot*. As in red and green chile pepper hot. The powerful little plant simmers in traditional sauces that embolden meat, eggs and just about everything else. You can thank the Spanish and Mexicans: they controlled the region's territories until well into the 19th century and shaped the cuisine. First, the Spanish brought cattle to Mexico. Then the Mexicans adapted the meat to their own corn-and-chile-based gastronomy to make tacos, tortillas, enchiladas, burritos and chimichangas, all mainstays of today's Southwestern fare. Steaks and

BBQ, especially in Texas, also beef up local menus. Beer is the drink of choice with dinner and a night out.

THE WEST

California is the West's cuisine king, owing to its vastness and various climates. It's truly the USA's most bountiful source of fruits and vegetables, and a melting wok for Asian flavors. In the 1980s, California chefs like Alice Waters of Berkeley's Chez Panisse and Wolfgang Puck of Beverly Hills' Spago pioneered 'California cuisine' by incorporating only the best local ingredients into simple yet delectable preparations. Chefs today have a lot that's local to work with: seafood, like wild salmon, Dungeness crab, oysters and halibut; excellent produce year-round; and artisanal products like cheese, bread, olive oil and chocolate. About 90% of US wine comes from California, with vineyards growing throughout the fertile Napa, Sonoma, Mendocino and Santa Barbara valleys.

The Pacific Northwest draws on the traditions of local Native Americans, whose diets center on game, seafood – especially salmon – and foraged mushrooms, fruits and berries. Seattle spawned the modern international coffeehouse craze with Starbucks. And Portland, god bless it, has more microbreweries than any city in the world, making it a 'beervana' for suds lovers.

It's probably no surprise the cowboy states eat beef; stirred in are Russian, Basque and other immigrant tastes. Far-flung Hawaii takes advantage of local Pacific fish like mahimahi, wahoo and opakapaka, while at tradtional luaus, locals cook kalua pig in a pit on hot stones under palm leaves. Alaska cuisine is also Pacific-plucked, and centers on salmon, halibut and king crab.

WEIRD & WONDERFUL

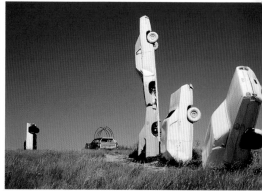

▲ MURALS MADE OF – GUESS WHAT – DECORATE THE CORN PALACE.   ▲ A CONTESTANT MUD-FLOPS AT THE REDNECK GAMES.   ▲ ENGLAND HAS STONEHENGE, NEBRASKA HAS CARHENGE.

Enormous balls of twine, toilet museums, beer-can houses, UFO watchtowers – the USA is rich in kitsch. It has devoted entire cities, such as Las Vegas, to the art form. But most of the quirks rise from the nation's backyards and back roads – wherever there are folks with passion, imagination and maybe a little too much time on their hands. Here's a sample of what you might find.

WORLD'S LARGEST

Ah, supersize. America's reverence of all things gigantic was around long before a certain fast-food company co-opted the word. Biggest chair, largest catsup bottle – you name it, the USA has got it.

Behold the 'world's largest ball of twine.' You'd think there would be just one mondo string orb, but it turns out that several vie for the prize. Darwin, MN, claims the 'largest built by one person': Francis A Johnson wrapped a 17,400-pound whopper on his farm over the course of several years. In Cawker City, KS, Frank Stoeber decided he could outdo the Minnesota ball but died before finishing. So his townsfolk took up the cause. Each August they host a twine-a-thon to add to Stoeber's baby, and to date they've amassed an 18,000-pound behemoth. Thus, Cawker declares the 'largest ball of twine built by a community.' Then there's the giant string ball at Ripley's Believe It or Not in Branson, MO – but purists say it's a pretender to the throne because it's made of lightweight nylon string, not real twine. Recently, a gent in northern Wisconsin said he'd rolled a 19,000-pound Goliath... and the battle of the balls continues.

Naming the 'world's largest wooden nickel' is no easier. Iowa City sports one that's 16 feet 3 inches in diameter and weighs around 4000 pounds; it's on display in a local field. But San Antonio, TX, says *it* has the largest wooden nickel. Though the Texas coin measures a mere 13 feet 4 inches and weighs only 2500 pounds, it's *double-sided* – a crucial difference because that's the way real wooden nickels are printed. So take that, Iowa.

We're not even going to get into all the 'biggest chickens' that peck around the country. Suffice it to say the critter hulking over the town of Marietta, GA, with the movie star looks of a poultry Godzilla, deserves to win the prize. The skyscraping bird (with a rolling eyeball and moving beak) looms over a KFC restaurant.

OUTSIDER ART

Gallery shmallery – anyone can be an artist. Just get creative and use whatever materials are handy. Like beer cans. A retired railroad company employee in Houston, TX, flattened 50,000 cans – many of which he and his friends drank over the course of 18 years – to create the Beer Can House. It's aluminum siding 12 ounces at a time, as they like to say, and people come from miles around to pay homage.

Old Plymouths, Fords, Chevrolets and Cadillacs have found new life at Carhenge, in a lonely field at Alliance, NB. A local artist arranged the stony-gray painted vehicles in a circle in the exact placement of the monoliths at England's Stonehenge. Even the number of cars he used matches the number of stones at the English site. At sunset, from a distance, the likeness is good enough to fool a druid.

And let's see, what would folks in Mitchell, SD, have on hand to use as art? The Corn Palace answers that. Artists cover the local Moorish-style community hall with new murals each year, using 275,000 ears of corn. Who knew cobs could depict such moving scenes of covered wagons and pioneer life?

THE ALIENS OF ROSWELL, NM, HAVE BEEN TRYING TO PHONE HOME FOR 60-PLUS YEARS. ⌃

MUSEUMS

Sometimes Americans take their offbeat passions, amass them in a building, slap up a sign and call it a 'museum.'

Such is the case of the family of plumbers in Worcester, MA, who've opened the American Sanitary Plumbing Museum. It contains their vintage toilet collection so visitors can get the scoop on all that's happened since the flush replaced the chamber pot. And, yes, it's the butt of many a joke.

Locals in Felton, CA, say bigfoot roams the surrounding Santa Cruz Mountains. To prove it, they've opened Bigfoot Discovery Museum, filled with old newspaper articles, videos and audio tapes of the hulking primate. Don't forget to pick up your bigfoot coloring book.

Austin, MN, is mighty proud of being the birthplace of SPAM, the peculiar canned meat. The town's SPAM Museum shows visitors how the blue tins have fed armies, become a Hawaiian food staple and inspired legions of haiku writers.

ODDBALL EVENTS

Any excuse for a party will do (and we mean *any*).

April's Interstate Mullet Toss is not about the short-in-front/long-in-back haircut. It's about dead fish. Locals gather on the Florida–Alabama border at Perdido Key and throw mullets (a one-pound indigenous fish) as far as they can across the state line. Not surprisingly, a pub organizes the raucous beach event.

In a similar vein, the folks of Prairie du Sac, WI, hold a Cow Chip Throw in early September. More than 800 competitors fling dried manure patties across the grazing fields. The record is 248 feet (cow doo has better velocity than mullet, for which the record is 189 feet).

Pesky bugs are big fun from north to south. Cuyuna, MN, hosts wood-tick races each June, in which small bloodsucking creatures try to outrun each other on a wooden board. Walcott, AR, hosts an annual Mosquito-Calling Contest and 'mosquito recipe' swaps in August.

July's Summer Redneck Games provide more good times down south. Locals in East Dublin, GA, poke good-hearted fun at the stereotype with events like the Mud-Pit Belly Flop, Hubcap Hurl and Armpit Serenade. Bring your best overalls and banjo.

ALL THINGS ALIEN

The truth is out there, and you can find it at places like the UFO Watchtower in Hooper, CO. The area is reputedly a window to other worlds, and you can hang out, have a drink and maybe see a spaceship. Or get married – the tower's owner is ordained.

Alien corpses and crop-circle exhibits fill the far-out UFO Museum in Roswell, NM. The town is the alleged site of a 1947 spaceship crash, and it markets its extraterrestrial history with pride. Bulbous alien heads glow atop downtown lampposts, and July brings the alien costume parade and motorcycle rally.

Meanwhile, wee Riverside, IA, is ready and waiting for its otherworldly encounter. As the future birthplace of Captain James T Kirk – who will be born in Riverside on March 22, 2228, according to *Star Trek* lore – the little farming town pulls in Trekkies who come to gawk and buy their tube of Kirk Dirt.

SPORTS

≫ BASKETBALL MADNESS SWEEPS THE COUNTRY COME MARCH.

≫ TEAM SPIRIT ISN'T ALWAYS PRETTY IN GREEN BAY.

≫ BASEBALL REMAINS THE NATIONAL PASTIME.

You can talk all you want to about arts, politics, religion or any of those other admirable pursuits. What really draws Americans together, sometimes slathered in blue body paint or with foam-rubber cheese wedges on their heads, is sports. It provides social glue, so whether one is conservative or liberal, married or single, Mormon or pagan, come Monday at the office he or she is chatting about the performance of their favorite team.

Sports fandom is a year-round commitment. In spring and summer there's baseball nearly every day. In fall and winter, a weekend or Monday night wouldn't feel right without a football game on, and through the long nights of deep winter there's plenty of basketball to keep the adrenaline going.

It's true some citizens actually *play* sports. Local communities host basketball, softball, even dodgeball, leagues. But if Americans join a league it's more likely to be of the 'fantasy' type. It's estimated that 16 million adults in the USA, aged 18 to 55, play fantasy sports, which entails not only minute statistical analysis of favorite players but also shelling out the cash to back up one's picks. Some reports say fantasy sports have morphed into a multibillion-dollar industry.

Tailgating may not generate as much money, but it's no less vital to the scene. Tailgate parties erupt pre- and postgame in stadium parking lots, when fans bring portable grills and fire up BBQ feasts with friends and family.

BASEBALL
Despite some ridiculously high salaries and lingering steroid rumors, baseball remains the USA's national pastime. It might not command the

same TV viewership (and subsequent advertising dollars) as football but, hey, baseball has 162 games over a season versus football's 16. Besides, baseball has nothing to do with TV – it's all about the live version. There's nothing better than being at the ballpark on a sunny day, sitting in the stands with a beer and hot dog, and indulging in the seventh-inning stretch, when the entire park erupts in a communal sing-along of 'Take Me Out to the Ballgame.'

Traditional rivalries remain heated throughout the season. The New York Yankees like nothing better than to clobber the Boston Red Sox (and vice versa). During the crosstown classic series, the Chicago Cubs thrive on pummeling the Chicago White Sox (and vice versa). Historic enemies the San Francisco Giants and LA Dodgers once had a brawl where they smacked each other with bats. And no matter who's playing in the World Series, it still delivers excitement and unexpected champions each October.

The most storied ballparks are Chicago's Wrigley Field and Boston's Fenway Park, both beautiful in a historic kind of way and smack-dab in the middle of bar-filled urban neighborhoods. Newer stadiums attract crowds with gimmicks like an on-site swimming pool (Arizona's Chase Field), carousel and Ferris wheel rides (Detroit's Comerica Park) and sushi sold from the concession stands (Los Angeles' Dodger Stadium).

More than 3 million kids play Little League baseball across the country, so the love of the game starts young.

FOOTBALL
Football has successfully tackled the rest of US sports. It's big, it's physical, it makes the most money. With the shortest season and least number of games of any of the major sports, every match takes on the emotion of an

epic battle. Football is played in fall and winter in all manner of rain, sleet and snow. Green Bay's Lambeau Field wins the prize for coldest game ever: -13°F (-25°C) with a wind chill of -43°F (-42°C) in 1967.

Different teams have dominated different decades: the Pittsburgh Steelers in the 1970s, the San Francisco 49ers in the 1980s, the Dallas Cowboys in the 1990s and the New England Patriots in the 2000s. The league's oldest rivalry is between the Chicago Bears and Green Bay Packers, who've been knocking the stuffing out of each other since 1921.

But it's not just pro football that's crazily popular. College football – and even high school football in Southern states like Texas – enjoy an intense amount of pomp and circumstance, with cheerleaders, marching bands, mascots, songs and mandatory pre- and postgame rituals. Rivalries at this level – Ohio State/Michigan, Auburn/Alabama, Florida State/Florida – are even more intense than in the pros.

The rabidly popular Super Bowl is pro football's championship match, held in early February. Few spectacles compare. It's estimated the event costs the nation $800 million in lost workplace productivity as employees gossip about the game, make bets and shop for new TVs online. The bowl games (ie Rose Bowl, Orange Bowl etc) are college football's title matches, held on New Year's Day and thereabouts, also to much fanfare.

BASKETBALL

While popular on street courts and in high school gyms from coast to coast, pro basketball lags behind pro football and baseball in the public consciousness. After peak fandom in the 1990s, it's lost some of its mojo. Still, teams like the Chicago Bulls (thanks to the lingering Michael Jordan effect), Detroit Pistons and Cleveland Cavaliers (home of Lebron James, aka

the new Michael Jordan) are among those that draw big crowds.

College basketball also draws millions of fans, especially every spring when March Madness rolls around. This series of play-off games starts with 65 college teams and whittles down quickly to the Final Four, who compete for the championship. The games are widely televised – and bet upon (this is when Las Vegas bookies earn their keep). Like the Super Bowl, it's a workplace diversion – especially in the Midwest, where it's estimated that 27% of people have bet on March Madness games at the office.

Women play basketball college and pro levels, and it's not uncommon for certain college women's teams to outdraw the men's.

OTHER SPORTS

The National Hockey League has fervent fans, mostly concentrated in northern, cold-weather cities across the USA and Canada. Perhaps because of the sport's regional nature, it gets less national airplay than pro football, baseball or basketball. Major League Soccer is the USA's newest pro sport, with play starting in 1996. Alas, it remains on the fringe of the national scene, with several of its 15 teams still not turning a profit. Nascar revs up lots of car-racing fans, particularly in the Southeast, where it originated. And then there's golf, horse racing and bass fishing – all with big-money tournaments, TV deals and frenzied fans clamoring to be part of it.

RELIGION

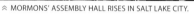
⌃ MORMONS' ASSEMBLY HALL RISES IN SALT LAKE CITY.

⌃ A CATHOLIC ICON GRACES A STORE SHELF.

⌃ JEWISH CHILDREN READ HEBREW IN BROOKLYN, NY.

When the Pilgrims came ashore, fleeing their European homeland because of religious persecution, they were adamant their new country would be one of religious tolerance. They valued so highly the freedom to practice religion that they refused to make their Protestant faith official state policy, and forbade the government from doing anything that might privilege one religion or belief over another. Freedom of religion has remained the law ever since.

Today, Protestants are on the verge of becoming a minority in the country they founded. Numbers have declined steadily, from about two-thirds of residents in the 1980s to 51% currently, according to the Pew Research Center. Catholics represent about 24% of the country, with the denomination receiving a boost from Latino immigration. Those practicing the main non-Christian religions – Islam, Buddhism, Hindu, Judaism – have grown collectively to represent nearly 5% of the country. Mormons comprise about 2%.

The remaining slice of the pie – and one of the fastest-growing categories – is 'unaffiliated.' These are Americans who say they have 'no religion'; the proportion has grown to 16%. Some in this catch-all category disavow religion altogether (around 4%), but more nurse spiritual beliefs that simply fall outside the box.

Americans are fluid regarding religion. Not only do they switch religions frequently, but 37% are married to someone with a different religious affiliation.

PROTESTANTISM

The founding fathers' religion branched out into a wide swath of denominations. Today, they fall under two main headings: evangelical Protestantism, of which Baptists form the biggest contingent; and mainline Protestantism, which includes groups such as Lutherans, Methodists and Presbyterians.

Evangelicals have the greater number of worshippers, and that number has actually grown. Baptists account for one-third of all Protestants and close to one-fifth of the nation's total adult population. Their numbers are strongest in the South.

Anabaptists are remotely related, and though their numbers are small (they account for less than 0.3% of Protestants), they are well known culturally due to their Amish members. The Amish famously shun modern conveniences such as electricity and motorized vehicles, and lead simple lives, often as farmers. Mennonites share a faith similar to the Amish, but they embrace modern amenities. The largest Amish/Mennonite communities are gathered in Ohio, Pennsylvania and Indiana.

The long-established mainline denominations are where the Protestant decline is seen most vividly. Mainline worshippers are likely to keep decreasing in number, too, since the average age of practitioners is older than in all other faith groups. This affects Presbyterians and Methodists, who spread throughout the country, and Lutherans, who concentrate in the Dakotas, Minnesota and Wisconsin as a result of those states' German and Scandinavian heritage.

Megachurches span both evangelical and mainline traditions (though they're more likely to be evangelical). A growing trend, they've been called 'behemoths of belief': attendance of 20,000 people at services is not uncommon. More than 1200 megachurches (ie those with attendance of 2000 or more weekly) exist across the country, with the two most mega located in Houston, TX.

A PARISHIONER READS THE HOLY WORD ON HIS CHURCH'S STEPS. ⌃

CATHOLICISM

While Catholics have experienced the greatest membership loss of any denomination, this has been offset with the immigration of new members from other Catholic countries such as Mexico and elsewhere in Latin America. Latinos currently account for one in three adult Catholics, and since Latino families tend to be younger and have more children than other US population segments (Latinos' median age is 27.6 compared with 36.6 for the overall population), Catholic numbers are set to rise.

Currently, New England is the country's most Catholic region, and the numbers trickle down to the Mid-Atlantic states. New York City holds the nation's largest Catholic church – St Patrick's Cathedral – which shoots up its neo-Gothic spires on 5th Avenue and has a *pieta* statue three times the size of Michelangelo's in Rome. Rhode Island is the most Catholic state, with 64% of residents worshipping in the tradition, and Baltimore is the country's oldest archdiocese, established in 1789.

States that are home to large numbers of Latinos, including Texas, California, Florida and Illinois, also have high rates of Catholicism. Churches here often conduct their masses in Spanish. And throughout the country, Catholics continue their strong tradition of education – there are more than 8000 Catholic primary and secondary schools in the USA, teaching nearly 2.3 million children (including 14% who are not practitioners of the religion).

OTHER RELIGIONS

Jews comprise the largest portion of the USA's non-Christian-religion followers, with 1.7% of the population. Reform Judaism claims the most members, followed by Conservative and then Orthodox Judaism. The New York City metro area, south Florida and Los Angeles all have large Jewish communities. New York City also has the world's largest synagogue: Temple Emanu-El on the Upper East Side has more than 10,000 members.

Buddhists are the next largest group, capturing 0.7% of the US population. Their numbers span Zen, Theravada and Tibetan traditions. The West Coast has the largest communities, in part because of the high number of Asians who live there. But three-quarters of US Buddhists are converts who were born in the USA. The golden-statue-filled City of Ten Thousand Buddhas in Northern California, and Hsi Lai Temple outside Los Angeles, are two of the largest worship sites.

Muslims represent 0.6% of the US population and form the nation's most racially diverse tradition, with a following that's 37% white, 24% African American and 20% Asian. Muslim Americans cluster in the New York, Chicago, Detroit and Los Angeles metro areas.

Hindus represent 0.4% of the population. Large communities live in New York and New Jersey, and in Chicago, Washington, DC, and Atlanta.

The homegrown Mormon Church, today called the Church of Jesus Christ of Latter-day Saints (LDS), accounts for about 2% of the US population. The group is headquartered in Utah, where 60% of residents are Mormon, though substantial populations also live in surrounding states like Idaho, Wyoming, Nevada and Arizona. Mormons are the faith with the largest families: more than 20% of Mormon adults have three or more children living at home.

Jehovah's Witnesses are another local religion and make up 0.7% of the US population. While the group is based in Pennsylvania, followers live all over the country. It has the lowest retention rate of any religion, with only 37% of those raised as Jehovah's Witnesses still identifying as such.

Other traditions include Christian Orthodox religions (which 0.6% practice); New Age faiths (0.4%); and Native American spirituality (less than 0.3%).

GOVERNMENT & POLITICS

⌃ IT'S HATS OFF AT THE REPUBLICAN NATIONAL CONVENTION.　　⌃ THE SUPREME COURT GIVES CASES THE ULTIMATE GAVEL BANG.　　⌃ DEMOCRATS, REPUBLICANS AND THOSE IN BETWEEN MIX IN DC.

Thomas Jefferson had it figured out from the get-go. On July 4, 1776, at the birth of the United States of America, he laid out the tenets for a new form of government on a piece of parchment titled the Declaration of Independence. It went like this:

We hold these truths to be self-evident: That all men are created equal; that they are endowed by their Creator with certain unalienable rights; that among these are life, liberty, and the pursuit of happiness. That to secure these rights, governments are instituted among men, deriving their just powers from the consent of the governed.

Of course, years of revolution intervened before Jefferson and his colleagues sat down to the real job of governing. And when they finally did, they discovered the nation's loose confederation of states, squabbling and competing like hens at a grain bucket, were hardly 'united.' So the founders gathered again in 1787, and in Philadelphia they drafted the Constitution.

It provided for separate executive, legislative and judiciary arms of government, with various checks and balances between them. The document was far-reaching, but it wasn't finished yet. In 1791 the first Congress added a Bill of Rights: 10 amendments, including things like freedom of speech, of religion and the right to bear arms, designed to protect citizens and states against the federal government's power. The final document was remarkably prescient: the fact that it has been amended only 17 more times since the Bill of Rights (for a total of 27 amendments) proves it.

Here's the system that keeps this heaving, changing country governed.

THE PRESIDENT

The US president is head of state, chief of the executive government and commander in chief of the armed forces. The president's term is four years, and (since 1951) no person can be elected president for more than two consecutive terms. The country holds presidential elections in early November and inaugurates the successful candidate on January 20th of the following year. The president appoints the heads (called secretaries) of the 15 executive departments that form the Cabinet.

The president is not elected directly, but by an electoral college in which each state has the same number of votes as it has representatives in Congress (which relates to its population) plus the number of its senators (always two per state). California, the most populous state, has 55 electors, while the seven least-populous states have three each. The people vote for their choice of presidential candidate, and the candidate with the most votes in a state gets all that state's electoral college votes (except in Maine and Nebraska, which divide the electoral vote). So if 51% of Florida voters choose Candidate A, then he or she gets all 27 of Florida's electoral college votes, and Candidate B, with 49% of the popular vote, gets nothing. The candidate with the majority of electoral college votes becomes president. This system leaves open the possibility that the candidate who wins the popular vote can still lose the election – which happened to Al Gore against George W Bush in 2000.

CONGRESS

The legislative arm of government is Congress, comprising the Senate, with two senators from each state, and the House of Representatives, with 435 members in varying numbers from each state, depending on population. All budget, tax and revenue laws must originate in the House of

A SIGHT THAT WOULD MAKE THOMAS JEFFERSON TEARY: PATRIOTIC BALLOONS FLOAT OVER THE CAPITOL. ⌃

Representatives, while the Senate has special powers in respect to foreign relations, senior government appointments and impeachment. The Speaker of the House is the leader of the majority party, not a neutral chairperson as in the British system. After a bill is passed by Congress, it can be vetoed by the president, but the presidential veto can be overturned by a two-thirds majority in both houses, which allows it to become law.

House members serve two-year terms and senators serve six-year terms. Elections are held every two years for all representatives' seats and approximately one-third of the senators. Every four years, these coincide with presidential elections, when the turnout is between 50% and 60% of eligible voters. In non-presidential election years, voter turnout is about 35%.

POLITICAL PARTIES
US politics is dominated by two main parties. The Republicans, nicknamed the Grand Old Party (GOP) and symbolized by an elephant and the color red, are traditionally more conservative, opposed to big government and for states' rights. The Democrats, symbolized by a donkey and the color blue, are generally more liberal and favor a more active role for the federal government. In general, the Republicans hold sway in the Plains and Southern states ('red' states), while the Democrats lock in the east and west coasts ('blue' states). In some states ('swing' or 'battleground' states) neither party dominates. Smaller parties like the Green Party and America's Independent Party are insignificant in terms of their elected representation, but in a close election they can be important in diverting votes away from the major parties.

The parties are not as monolithic as in other political systems, and there are conservative Democrats and progressive Republicans. Members of Congress do not vote strictly on party lines. It's common for the president

to be from one party while both houses of Congress have a majority from the other party. In this situation of 'divided government,' there is generally a limited output of new legislation and an increase in presidential vetoes.

JUDICIARY
The highest judicial authority is the US Supreme Court, whose nine justices are appointed for life by the president, with the advice and consent of the Senate. The Supreme Court can overrule any federal or state law or executive action that violates the Constitution. Beneath it are 13 federal courts of appeal, 94 US district courts and various special courts.

STATE & LOCAL GOVERNMENT
The USA has a federal system; powers not delegated to the federal government by the Constitution are retained by the states. Each state has its own constitution and a government that generally mirrors that of the federal government. The governor is the state's chief executive, and a state senate and a house delegation enact state laws (Nebraska alone has a unicameral state government, ie it has no senate). The state police and court system enforce the laws. Among other things, states are responsible for education, criminal justice, prisons, hospitals, administration of elections, commerce regulation and highway maintenance. They now do many of these things in cooperation with the federal government, especially for funding purposes.

The states are divided progressively into counties, boroughs, parishes, cities, towns, school districts and/or special districts that provide services like police, sanitation, schools and so on. Local government units often combine to administer a large urban area as a single unit, as in the five boroughs of New York City.

ENVIRONMENT

⌃ THE MOUNTAIN MAJESTIES OF GRAND TETON NATIONAL PARK, WY.

⌃ DEATH VALLEY'S MESQUITE DUNES KEEP BLOWIN' IN THE WIND.

⌃ SMATHERS BEACH SPREADS ITS PEARLY SAND IN KEY WEST, FL.

You can travel far and wide in this world seeing endless deserts and epic mountains, reptile-filled swamps and caribou-trampled tundra. Or you can see the same things in the USA.

Never underestimate this country's vastness, or how wild its wild places are. Covering some 3.8 million square miles (an area smaller than only Russia and Canada), the country provides a lot of ground that's eye-popping and jaw-dropping. The national and state park systems protect much of it, along with the bears, bison and other beasts who call it home.

LANDSCAPE

To get the lay of the land, start in the north at the nation's watering hole. The largest expanse of fresh water on the planet, the Great Lakes are the tap for about 90% of the USA's water supply.

To the east, the rugged, ancient Appalachian Mountains parallel the Atlantic Coast. The strip of land between the range and the water holds the country's most populated region, particularly the Washington, DC-to-Boston corridor. Further down the coast, things get wetter and warmer, until the swamps of southern Florida and bayous around the Gulf of Mexico.

West of the Appalachians sprawl the vast interior plains. They're not just pancake flat, but pancake-run-over-by-a-truck flat. The eastern plains are the nation's breadbasket, roughly divided into the northern 'corn belt' and the southern 'cotton belt.' Going west, the farmland slowly gives way to cowboys and ranches in the semiarid, big-sky Great Plains.

Then suddenly, the young, jagged Rocky Mountains pop up, a complex set of tall ranges that runs all the way from Mexico to Canada in clumps

that please skiers greatly. Drop over the Rockies to the Southwest and the desert opens its jaws. It's much more than the average sage-and-cacti scene, with parts of the region – like the Grand Canyon – cut to dramatic effect by the Colorado River.

After this comes the USA's third major mountain system: the southern, granite Sierra Nevada and the northern, volcanic Cascades, which both parallel the Pacific Coast. America's last primeval forests grow in the Pacific Northwest and, to the south, everything grows in California's Central Valley, one of the most fertile places on earth. Meanwhile, the entire coastline from San Diego to Seattle is celebrated in song and legend – a stretch of sandy beaches, redwoods and steep, fog-mantled cliffs.

There's more in the non-contiguous USA. Alaska reaches all the way to the Arctic Ocean and contains tundra, glaciers and 17 of the country's 20 highest peaks. Hawaii, more than 2000 miles west of the mainland, adds a string of volcanic, bamboo-forested islands to the mix.

PARKS

In places like the kaleidoscopic chasm of the Grand Canyon and the otherworldly, pink-red cliffs of Utah's Zion, the USA's national parks are where nature offers up its masterworks. More than a quarter of the USA falls under some kind of federal protection or stewardship. That's a lot of public land, and nearly all of it can be visited.

The love affair started in 1864, when a 10-square-mile portion of Yosemite Valley was set aside as a state park. Then in 1872, President Ulysses S Grant designated 2 million acres as Yellowstone National Park, the first such large-scale preserve in the world. The National Park Service (NPS) was off and running.

MAMA BEAR ON THE ALERT FOR ANY DANGER TO HER BABY BEARS IN ALASKA. ⌃

Today the NPS manages 391 areas, totaling 84 million acres and touching almost every state and territory (Delaware and the Northern Marianas are the exceptions). Its 58 parks are the NPS's crown jewels, but the organization's properties go well beyond: the NPS also watches over national preserves and national monuments. The former are like national parks but with hunting and mining permitted, while the latter are places of historical or scientific interest (think Statue of Liberty or Muir Woods).

Then there are the slew of battlefields, military parks, historical parks, historic sites, lakeshores, seashores, recreation areas, scenic rivers and trails – even roads like the Blue Ridge Parkway come under NPS purview. To give you an idea of the scope involved, the NPS' largest property is Wrangell-St Elias National Park and Preserve in Alaska, spanning 13.2 million acres, while its smallest is Thaddeus Kosciuszko National Memorial in Pennsylvania, which takes up a mere 871 square feet.

The areas vary wildly in visitor numbers, too. The most popular national park is the Great Smoky Mountains, where 9.4 million people crowd annually. The Grand Canyon, Yosemite and Yellowstone follow right behind. On the other hand, Isle Royale – a forlorn island-park in Lake Superior, home to wolves and moose – attracts just 16,000 people per year. Other sublime places to escape the masses are parks like far-flung Big Bend in Texas; Lassen Volcanic, steaming in northern California; and Theodore Roosevelt, under North Dakota's lonely prairie sky.

State park systems operate in ways similar to the NPS and protect many additional unspoiled areas.

WILDLIFE

An ark's worth of creatures shares the local lands and waters. Grizzly bears are among the most commanding: males can stand up to 9 feet tall, weigh 1400 pounds and consider 500 square miles home. Successful conservation efforts, particularly in the Greater Yellowstone Region, have increased the population in the lower 48 states to around 1200, and Alaska remains chock-full of grizzlies, with upwards of 30,000. Black bears are smaller and reside nearly everywhere.

The home where the buffalo roam spans Yellowstone, Grand Teton and Badlands National Parks. Wolves and moose tramp through the northern Rockies, Alaska and the Midwest's North Woods. Though an icon of the Southwest, coyotes are found all over, sometimes even in cities (one recently loped into a Chicago sandwich shop during the lunchtime rush). America's one big-cat species goes by several names – mountain lion, cougar, puma and panther – and licks its chops mostly in the West, though a panther population lives in southern Florida, too. Alligators slither throughout the southeast's wetlands.

In the ocean, gargantuan gray, humpback and blue whales migrate annually along the Pacific Coast, while humpback and North Atlantic right whales swim off New England's coast. Orcas lurk around the San Juan Islands in Washington.

Some 800 bird species fly over the USA. The bald eagle, the nation's symbol since 1782, is the only eagle unique to North America. It's made a remarkable comeback from a low of 417 breeding pairs in 1963 to more than 9750 pairs today (that's in the lower 48; another 30,000-plus live in Alaska). Their resilience, and the nation's efforts to help them, are what ecology is all about.

EXPLORATION & INNOVATION

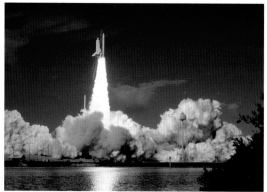

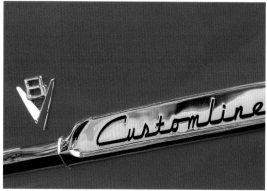

≈ SPACE SHUTTLE *DISCOVERY* ROCKETS INTO ORBIT.　　≈ HENRY FORD'S KNOW-HOW MADE CARS FOR THE MASSES.　　≈ A SAN FRANCISCAN NAMED LEVI STRAUSS INVENTED BLUE JEANS.

Think Big. It's not written on the nation's currency or anything, but it is the USA's unofficial motto. The very size of the country has inspired its citizens from the beginning. What's on the other side of those mountains? What's down that river? People needed ingenuity, ambition and confidence to find out.

THE VOYAGE WEST

Meriwether Lewis and William Clark set the explorers' bar high when they went out West. President Thomas Jefferson had just spent $15 million for a chunk of land from France in the Louisiana Purchase, and while he was thrilled to double the nation's size, Jefferson had no idea what he'd got in the bargain. Wooly mammoths? Volcanoes? Those were some of his guesses. He procured $2500 from Congress and dispatched Lewis, Clark and their team of nearly four dozen men to get the lay of the land.

The Corps of Discovery, as the group was called, displayed serious American know-how. They set out from St Louis in May 1804, paddled and trekked through uncharted territory and reached Oregon's coast in late 1805. With the help of a Shoshone Indian woman named Sacagawea, along the way they collected data on plants, animals, landscapes and native peoples, before returning home by September 1806. That's 8000 miles in 2.5 years, with the loss of only one member (to appendicitis).

Lewis and Clark's voyage sparked the country's imagination, but it took a few decades before settlers got up the gumption to follow. In 1841 the first wagon trains rattled along the Oregon Trail from Missouri to the coast. Promises of gold, free land and the chance to start something new enticed hardy folks, and within 25 years roughly 400,000 people had made the 2000-mile journey.

While these expeditions were bold and literally groundbreaking for the colonists, they wreaked havoc on Native Americans. Many were killed in battles against settlers and others were pushed to undesirable lands.

TELEGRAPHS TO BLUE JEANS

Not everyone headed into the wilderness to blaze a trail Lewis-and-Clark style. Several Americans made equally important discoveries from home. The mid to late 19th century was a golden age for US invention.

Take Samuel Morse and his telegraph, on which he tapped out the first message in 1844: 'What hath God wrought?' It only traveled from Washington, DC, to Baltimore, but it meant long-distance communication was now possible, shrinking time and space – a godly act, indeed.

Thomas Edison is the patron saint of inventors. This self-taught man of humble means racked up 1093 patents for his creations. The phonograph, the lightbulb, the movie camera and a heap of telephone components all sprung from his whirring mind, though he claimed 'genius is 1% inspiration, 99% perspiration.'

Next to Edison, Henry Ford looks like a slacker with just 161 patents, but he too revolutionized American life with his innovations. Ford didn't invent the automobile, as many people mistakenly believe; rather, he perfected assembly line manufacturing and became one of the first industrialists to use mass production. The result was the Model T in the early 1900s, the first car the USA's middle class could afford to own. As Ford himself pointed out, 'the great multitude' now had access to the nation's 'great open spaces.'

Inventions such as reapers, threshers, combines and steel-blade plows aren't as exciting as cars and lightbulbs, but they industrialized agriculture

THE TELEPHONE WAS JUST ONE OF THOMAS EDISON'S 1093 PATENTS. ⌃

and enabled US commerce to surge in the 1800s. On the other hand, the coffee pot (Benjamin Thompson, 1806), toilet-paper roll (Seth Wheeler, 1871) and blue jeans (Levi Strauss and Jacob Davis, 1873) may not have fueled the economy, but they're important US contributions to the world nonetheless.

And the big ideas continue. Since 1790 the US Patent Office has granted close to 8 million patents; applications currently hover around 450,000 per year.

THE FINAL FRONTIER
It didn't take long for the USA's innovators to set their eyes on the skies.

The Wright Brothers started the flight revolution in 1903. They didn't invent the airplane per se, because flying machines had already been gliding around for almost a century. What Wilbur and Orville did was develop the first controlled aircraft with a motor, so pilots could fly from point A to point B instead of willy-nilly through the air. The brothers got their lofty ideas while repairing bicycles in their Dayton, OH, shop. They successfully launched their contraption in Kitty Hawk, NC.

With that taken care of it was time to go higher. President John F Kennedy pledged to put a person on the moon before the end of the 1960s – and promised that the USA would be the first nation to do so. Few thought it was possible and even fewer had any idea how to go about it. But the Eisenhower government had formed NASA in 1958 and by 1961 US astronauts had been lifted into space. Eight years later, the incredible happened. Neil Armstrong and Buzz Aldrin landed on the moon on July 20, 1969, and walked over its cratered surface – a feat so fantastical some people in remote corners of the globe and at home in the USA still don't believe it.

Space exploration pushed onward from there. Today the Hubble Telescope looks deep into the cosmos, the International Space Station orbits the earth with a full-time staff, and Mars rovers patrol and send images from the red planet.

STILL INNOVATING
US corporations developed much of the computer industry's early technology. In 1964 IBM introduced the first mass-produced operating system; in 1965, Digital made the first minicomputer; and a Department of Defense programmer sent the first email in 1971. Then Bill Gates, Steve Jobs, and Larry Page and Sergey Brin took the baton for the next generation: Microsoft, Apple and Google have changed the way people work, learn and interact across the industrialized world.

US minds also gave the world its first video game, in 1971's 'Computer Space,' in which a rocket ship shot at evil flying saucers. The developers formed the company Atari the following year and released the beloved, faux table-tennis game 'Pong.'

On a more serious note, US advances in science and medicine – from vaccines (polio, Hepatitis B) to oral contraceptives to the artificial heart – have saved countless lives and brought meaningful changes to others.

Perhaps John F Kennedy summed up American innovation best when he said: 'The American, by nature, is optimistic. He is experimental, an inventor and a builder who builds best when called upon to build greatly.'

Americans think big, in other words.

THE USA
BY REGION

« PLAYERS WAIT TENSELY IN THE DUGOUT.

« FULL OF HOT AIR AT THE ALBUQUERQUE INTERNATIONAL BALLOON FIESTA.

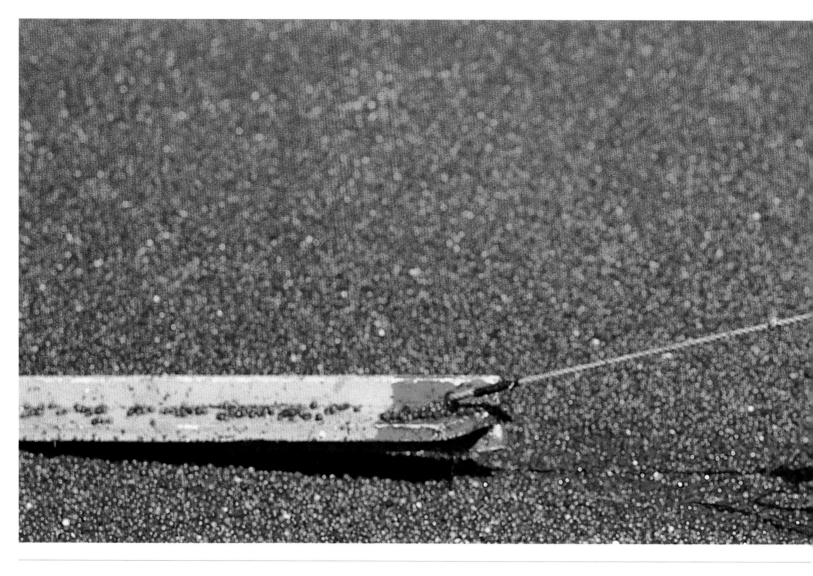

NEW ENGLAND

A MUSE TO ARTISTS AND REVOLUTIONARIES ALIKE, NEW ENGLAND BLENDS HISTORIC SETTLEMENTS WITH GORGEOUS COASTAL AND MOUNTAIN LANDSCAPES – ALL BROUGHT VIBRANTLY TO LIFE BY THE USA'S MOST FLAMBOYANT DISPLAYS OF FALL FOLIAGE.

THE NEW ENGLAND STATES

- ○ Connecticut
- ○ Maine
- ○ Massachusetts
- ○ New Hampshire
- ○ Rhode Island
- ○ Vermont

WADING THROUGH A CRANBERRY BOG AT HARVEST TIME IN MASSACHUSETTS. ⌃

New England's allure begins with the land. From Maine's piney shoreline to Massachusetts' shifting dunes, the White Mountains' granite majesty to the soft lushness of the Berkshires and Greens, Connecticut's rolling farmland to the watery vastness of Narragansett Bay, it's hard not to be drawn in by New England. Enhancing these varied landscapes, strongly defined seasons create dazzling visual effects: blazing maples and white-barked birches juxtaposed against crisp blue skies; pumpkin patches and cranberry bogs; granite ledges draped in new-fallen snow; branches glinting in traceries of ice; sprays of forsythia; and trees bursting with the first shoots of pale new leaves so welcome after the long winter.

Such natural splendor invites year-round outdoor exploration. Following the 'leaf peepers,' who invade New England each fall to admire the changing colors, are skiers who crowd Vermont for the best snow east of the Rockies, and ice climbers who flock to New Hampshire's sheer outcrops. In spring and summer rafters hit the rapids of northwestern Connecticut and surfers try to avoid getting bashed against Rhode Island's famous cliffs, while in Maine, fishing enthusiasts pit themselves against lakes, streams and the Atlantic coastline, and vacationers of all ages build sand castles on Cape Cod's endless beaches.

Completing this picture are New England's white-steepled churches and old brick home-steads, red barns and covered bridges, light-houses and stone walls, lobster traps, general stores and entire villages and urban centers that have managed to keep their original character. Boston, the region's largest city, and one of the country's oldest, combines a plethora of historic attractions with a youthful heart. Throughout the region farmers' love for the land has, over time, enhanced the landscape's native beauty, seen in lush green pastures, dirt roads lined with ancient maples, and harvest-time farm stands, whose pumpkins, gourds and corn – all native foods – echo the colors of the turning leaves. It's this blending of nature, architecture and agriculture that gives New England its irresistible charm.

Humankind's presence in New England stretches back to the end of the last ice age, and its Native American cultures have been many and diverse. Europeans reached these shores perhaps as early as Leif Ericsson (about 1000 years ago), and British settlement started at Popham, ME, in 1607. Although that colony failed, the British (Pilgrims) returned 13 years later. In churchyards across New England, ancient slate tombstones splotched with lichen and engraved with winged death's heads spell out these early immigrants' names. Joining this English matrix came Dutch sailors, French explorers, African slaves and Portuguese fishing-folk; each group left a mark on the region's culture.

New England's early prosperity was built on Atlantic trading ports, whaling harbors and mill towns, which hugged its many riverbanks. In the late 1700s the region jumped full-bore into the Industrial Revolution and more newcomers arrived, French Canadians, Irish and Italians prominent among them. The lumber and textile mills have long since fallen upon hard times, and farming, fishing and quarrying struggle for survival, yet the New Englanders' inventive spirit has stepped in to preserve and revitalize their heritage. Places like the Massachusetts Museum of Contemporary Art fill factories long abandoned, artisanal cheesemakers and organic farmers rely on farmers markets and CSAs (community supported agriculture) to reshape the agricultural economy. Tourism, high-tech and service industries help take up the slack.

Creative spirits and independent thinkers have always been drawn to New England. The first – Pilgrims, Puritans, Shakers, Quakers and Jews – came seeking religious freedom. As religious exiles from Massachusetts began founding new colonies in Connecticut and Rhode Island, a region-wide notion of independence took root, culminating in the American Revolution and the region's leading role in the abolitionist movement. Academic and artistic creativity also flourished: the Ivy League colleges began with Harvard nearly four centuries ago, and countless painters, writers and great thinkers have found their inspiration here.

In the 21st century, New England remains an eclectic mix of strong-minded individuals, from laconic old-timers and crusty libertarians to artists, environmentalists and gay activists. While retaining elements of staid traditionalism, New England continues to champion progressive social change and innovative thinking, as it has since the Revolutionary War. The communal vision of settlers banding together in a harsh land runs clear from the Mayflower Compact to the town meetings still held today, where issues from road paving to presidential impeachment get publicly debated. Even amid change, New England's spirit lives on.

TEXT GREGOR CLARK

THE MID-ATLANTIC

THE MID-ATLANTIC'S HISTORIC URBAN CENTERS CLUSTER AT THE COAST, ITS BEACHES CATERING TO THE WEEKEND NEEDS OF MANY OF THE REGION'S 52 MILLION LOCALS. INLAND LOOM MOUNTAIN PEAKS, HIKING TRAILS AND A MORE DOWN-HOME FLAVOR.

THE MID-ATLANTIC STATES

- Delaware
- Maryland
- New Jersey
- New York
- Pennsylvania
- Washington, DC

BEYOND THE BROOKLYN BRIDGE MANHATTAN'S SKYLINE BEGINS TO LIGHT UP. ⌃

Most people around the Mid-Atlantic seem to be in a hurry to get somewhere else. The USA's most densely populated region is crammed into 99,500 square miles (about the size of Britain). The web of interstates and, especially, toll roads and bridges that connect Washington, DC, with the five states (New York, New Jersey, Pennsylvania, Delaware and Maryland) all get choked with city dwellers. Some are commuting while others are racing to weekend getaways – at New Jersey's and Delaware's surprising beaches, Pennsylvania's Brandywine Valley or Amish communities, the antique shops of New York's Hudson River Valley, and Maryland's yacht (and crab cake) scene on the upper Chesapeake Bay (the latter is home to 3600 plant and animal species).

The mix of Mid-Atlantic locals makes up one of the nation's most ethnically diverse regions, particularly in the cities. Slightly fewer than three in four residents are white, while 16% are African American and 10% are Hispanic. Locals frequently hop state lines but few identify themselves as 'Mid-Atlantic,' preferring their state or national identity. Some of the reasons for this stubborn distinction date to colonial rivalries that didn't necessarily stop in 1776. William Penn (namesake of Pennsylvania) had no love lost for Lord Baltimore (of Maryland). They bickered over their borders until land was parceled out, eventually leading to the existence of Delaware, the nation's first state. New Jersey and New York, meanwhile, have long haggled over a few tiny rocky islands in New York Harbor that might have been ignored if not for their occupants, including a certain Statue of Liberty.

The biggest urban centers of the Mid-Atlantic region, huddling close to the coast, weigh as heavily in national lore as they do in travel itineraries. New York City – hailed by many (especially its residents) as the world's greatest – briefly served as the first US capital before that institution moved to DC, while the colonial roots of Rocky Balboa's hometown, Philadelphia, remain in the city's Independence Hall and cracked Liberty Bell. New Jersey fielded many key revolutionary battles, and Pennsylvania's Gettysburg was the stage for a one-of-a-kind speech from Abe Lincoln after the tide of the Civil War turned in the north's favor. Baltimore's history will forever be linked with gloomy author Edgar Allan Poe.

Though the region's interstates seem perpetually jammed there is elbow space to be found. Particularly further inland, where things get decidedly less urban; a land of roly-poly hills and green forests, and country-style cobblers replacing the cities' tiramisu. The angular New York State stretches towards two Canadian borders: rolling past Catskills valleys and the Finger Lakes to meet Ontario at blue-collar Buffalo and the triumphant (and cheesy) Niagara Falls; and rising to Quebec, north of the stunning Adirondacks. It was in New York's Catskills, at Bear Mountain, that the first steps of the legendary 2158-mile Appalachian Trail – ultimately connecting Maine with Georgia – were taken in 1923. Meanwhile, western Pennsylvania feels separate from the eastern Pennsylvania Dutch roots: here the hills give way to a declining population and dying steel towns like the Russian-American one devastatingly shown in *The Deer Hunter* (1979). Delaware – the only state *east* of the Mason-Dixon line – is hard to pin down, with both properly painted colonial buildings and wild southern-fried stock-car races. Meanwhile back roads in Maryland's Cumberland Gap, occupying the state's mountainous western paw, hint at the rustic Appalachia looming in nearby West Virginia.

Action moves by season: to the seashore in summer, the ski slopes of Pennsylvania's Poconos or New York's Adirondacks in winter, to forest drives past trees of gold, red and rust in fall. The Mid-Atlantic never slows down. As the center of American politics, communications and finance – thanks to New York and DC – it can't afford to.

TEXT ROBERT REID

THE SOUTH

ALMOST EVERYONE HAS A PRECONCEIVED NOTION ABOUT THE SOUTH, INVOKING THE CIVIL WAR, GRAND HISTORIC TRADITIONS, SOUTHERN ACCENTS AND HOSPITALITY, SLAVERY AND THE CIVIL RIGHTS MOVEMENT. BUT THE SOUTH IS ABOUT SO MUCH MORE.

THE SOUTHERN STATES

- Alabama
- Arkansas
- Florida
- Georgia
- Kentucky
- Louisiana
- Mississippi
- North Carolina
- South Carolina
- Tennessee
- Virginia
- West Virginia

LOUISIANA'S AVENUES OF TREES MANAGE TO APPEAR SWAMPLIKE, DESPITE BEING FAR FROM THE GROUND. ⊼

The South is still closely tied to its history, arguably more so than any other region. If you mention 'the war,' everyone knows exactly which one. Some older folk still reminisce about storing their canned jellies in the springhouse, quilting bees with Mama, slaughtering the family pigs, or hearing about their relatives' memories of the Civil War.

What constitutes 'The South' has been evolving for over 400 years, ever since the USA's first European colonies were settled here (even before Massachusetts). Most agree upon the geography of the Deep South (Louisiana, Alabama, Mississippi, Georgia and South Carolina), which slowly radiates to incorporate Arkansas, Tennessee, North Carolina, Virginia, Kentucky and West Virginia. Florida is technically part of the South but has an identity of its own, especially below the I-4 corridor.

Because of favorable growing conditions, the South quickly became an agricultural power-house in the late 1600s and Southern colonies were some of the wealthiest for over a century. To this day, there's a palpable nostalgia across some parts of the South for the gilded repre-sentation of Southern culture from this era, for example the way it is evoked in *Gone With the Wind* (the novel was released in 1936; the film 1939).

The most profitable yields came from labor-intensive crops like tobacco, rice and cotton, which required unending amounts of back-breaking work. While small farmers in the country's north owned slaves up until the 19th century, it was in the Southern plantations that the 'peculiar institution' of slavery became entrenched as the most shameful period in US history. Although slavery seems to many like a distant memory, it reverberates to this day: in 2007 it was discovered that the great-grandfather of minister and activist Reverend Al Sharpton was once owned by relatives of long-serving South Carolina Senator Strom Thurmond.

The Civil War began in 1861 when vast cultural differences between the North and South, differences that went beyond slavery, erupted. Afterwards, decades of Reconstruction, an economic shift from a plantation culture to industrial factories and mills, and government-sponsored racism through Jim Crow laws, took a heavy toll on the South.

Statistically, times have been tough for the South, especially in the Deep South and Appalachian states like West Virginia. According to the US Census, many of the states with the highest concentrations of poverty, obesity, infant mortality and violent crime are in the South. Don't expect change to come too soon; government intervention is frowned upon in these parts.

But the statistics hide another side of the South, where politeness is next to godliness and where one's commitment to family, land and church is foremost. Although some think these values were only part of the past, many see the South as changing and adapting in a positive direction.

The Civil Rights movement in the 1960s started a sea change in the South, as did urban expansion. African Americans could openly vote for the first time in the South's history, and educational and occupational opportunities changed the urban landscape. In 2008, three relatively wealthy and well-educated border states – Virginia, North Carolina and Florida – turned blue to vote for Democrat Barack Obama.

Over the past 40 years, the trickle of migrating Yankees has become a flood. Several of the USA's fastest-growing foreign-born populations are in Southern states. You're now as likely to find a Thai joint in Durham, NC, as you are shrimp and grits in Mobile, AL. Agriculture and industry still rule in the countryside but knowledge-based industries such as technology and pharma-ceuticals have bloomed in the cities. Walmart, one of the largest companies on the planet (it vies for top spot with Exxon Mobil) is head-quartered in Bentonville, AR, and has over 2 *million* employees worldwide.

The landscape of the southeastern United States is as varied as its people. The mountains of Tennessee have little in common geographically or socially with the beaches of Florida, the bayous of Louisiana or the flat urban sprawl of Northern Virginia. In between are ancient mountains, rolling hills, marshy swamps and flat plains. The diversity of wildlife is astounding; there are over 100,000 species of flora and fauna in the southern Appalachians alone. However, whether you're at a gallery opening in downtown Chattanooga or gearing up at a hunting camp in rural Mississippi, Southern manners are still an art form.

TEXT ALEX LEVITON

THE MIDWEST & GREAT PLAINS

THE LOOSELY DEFINED MIDWEST REGION AND ITS NEIGHBOR THE GREAT PLAINS MAY SEEM LIKE FLYOVER STATES OF FLAT FIELDS, FACTORY TOWNS AND WIDE-GIRTHED LOCALS WHO SAY 'YUP' OR 'ALRIGHTY THEN.' BUT THIS AREA HAS SOME SURPRISES.

THE MIDWEST & GREAT PLAINS STATES

- Illinois
- Indiana
- Iowa
- Kansas
- Michigan
- Minnesota
- Missouri
- Nebraska
- North Dakota
- Ohio
- Oklahoma
- South Dakota
- Wisconsin

ENDLESS PLAIN – A GOLDEN MIDWEST HARVEST SCENE. ⌃

No one really knows where the Midwest begins and ends – New Yorkers think it starts somewhere in eastern Pennsylvania, Californians might stretch it to Boise – but that doesn't stop most people who've never been from having a ready-made impression. One of a land of corn-fed locals sticking to speed limits in pickups, pancake-flat horizons of waving wheat dotted with grain elevators, and dead-end rust belt towns with closed factories and US flags. A place flown over or driven through, with eternal cries of 'are we there yet?' coming from the back seat.

The funny thing is, that's not half wrong. But the Midwest – 'real America,' some say – is far from a bore. Its 13 states combine two spirited regions that, at 891,600 square miles, outsize France, Germany and Spain combined. The Great Lakes states (Ohio, Indiana, Michigan, Illinois, Wisconsin, Minnesota) look toward inland sea-sized lakes, an Ice Age gift to weekend trippers. The Great Plains states (for our purposes: Missouri, Iowa, North and South Dakota, Nebraska, Kansas, Oklahoma) stretch out on more or less endless rolling fields that were once prehistoric seafloors.

So, the land is pretty flat but it's not all flat. Roads rise and twist along the Mississippi River, including Wisconsin's gorgeous Great River Road (Hwy 35), across Missouri's bumpy, forested Ozarks, which spill into Oklahoma along Route 66, and through South Dakota's gold-filled Black Hills. Visitors who make it to Michigan's Upper Peninsula can hike steep lakeside cliffs. Even a detour from Kansas' mind-numbing I-70 weaves along the subtle but underrated Flint Hills, which spread southwest of Kansas City. When the Midwest does flatten out, goofball roadside attractions – like Nebraska's Carhenge (a 34-car Stonehenge parody) or South Dakota's 275,000-ear Corn Palace – are there to revive imaginations.

City-wise, the Midwest is far from a one-note dullsville dominated by Chicago's world-famous skyscrapers and architecture. Just north, surprising Milwaukee is becoming more than just the home of Pabst, with a new Harley-Davidson Museum, the stunningly modern Milwaukee Art Museum, and good microbrews in the Historic Third Ward warehouse district. Detroit, meanwhile, may still look like a bomb victim, but its music halls steadily foster a fresh mix of new rock and rap. Minneapolis' Uptown and Northeast are hipster magnets, and up-to-date Kansas City's historic African American neighborhood 17th and Vine sure does a mean BBQ. Plus there are atmospheric college towns – such as Madison, WI, Lawrence, KS, and Bloomington, IN – that give an alternative to the frequently conservative mindset, with quaint historic downtowns where pedestrian-power rules.

Midwesterners make up the emotional median of the country – can-do folk with an underrated sense of irony, whose pace is a world apart from the East Coast rush or West Coast rootlessness. Folks here live bunched together or spread way out: Chicago has more than 12,000 people per square mile, while North Dakota has fewer than 10. Many carry Scandinavian, German and Irish surnames dating from centuries-past ancestors, but they are far from all white (well, only 86% are white). Midwesterners are also Native Americans (Oklahoma has the country's biggest population per capita), African Americans and, more recently, Latin Americans. Traditional religious communities still exist too, such as Ohio's Amish Country or Iowa's Amana Colonies.

Midwesterners are friendly, just not always to each other. All sorts of thorny issues ignite interstate rivalries around here. Michigan has been ticked at Ohio since losing Toledo to that state in the 1830s (not to mention Ohio State's annual romps over Michigan's football teams of late), while the bloody origins of Kansas–Missouri tensions lie in conflict between abolitionist Jayhawkers and the slave owners of 'Little Dixie.' Even quiet South Dakota openly mocks its northern twin whenever North Dakota considers changing its name to 'Dakota.' Which is often enough.

That doesn't detract from the locals' charms. Writer and Illinois native Dave Eggers swears locals are so nice that if your car breaks down on the side of a highway, you'll not only get quick help, but '*every car* will stop.' That self-perception – along with the fact that Midwest farms feed the country with grain, corn, soybean, hogs and beef – swells into a mighty big sense of regional pride.

TEXT ROBERT REID

THE SOUTHWEST

LIKE A CHIPOTLE CHICKEN ENCHILADA SERVED WITH SWEET TEA, THE SOUTHWEST IS A LIVELY MIX OF NEW WEST, OLD SOUTH AND HISPANIC CULTURES – SEASONED WITH STUNNING SCENERY AND ICONIC WILD WEST HISTORY.

THE SOUTHWEST STATES

- Arizona
- New Mexico
- Texas

THE ROCK LAYERS OF ARIZONA'S VERMILION CLIFFS NATIONAL MONUMENT ARE THE RESULT OF MILLIONS OF YEARS OF EROSION. ⌃

You've seen the iconic American Southwest on the silver screen: John Wayne and Wild West baddies rode here, through sage-and-pinion scrub brush, past false-front wooden towns and over rocky and rugged scenery. In *National Lampoon's Vacation,* Chevy Chase had just one of countless film families that vacationed at the Grand Canyon. And no less than 14 movies have been made about Texas' Alamo. The Southwest's major sights are well known: ghost towns and remnants of the Old West, Native American pueblos and cliff dwellings, Spanish missions and stupendous displays of nature's wilder side. But the Southwest is also about laid-back urban areas, artsy little towns, great live music and a varied landscape worth exploring.

Some define the southern parts of Utah and Colorado as 'Southwest'; many others would put Texas in a category all its own. But more than anything else, the uniting factor in Arizona, New Mexico and Texas is a strong Spanish accent. To a greater or lesser degree, each state's ethos is a mix of Anglo, Mexican and Native American cultures. The Spanish first arrived in the mid-15th century, searching for gold. They set up missions to convert the Native Americans and colonized their new territory. Mexico won independence in 1821, and within 50 years the territory that comprised today's three Southwest states was under US control.

To this day large Mexican American populations have a strong influence – apparent in the area's cuisine. An enchilada might come stuffed with Sonoran *carne seca* (dried spiced beef) in Arizona, wrapped in a blue corn tortilla in New Mexico or topped with a vibrant red chile-and-tomato sauce in west Texas. The two western states were harbingers of Southwest cuisine, which brought chipotle peppers (smoked jalapeño peppers sometimes marinated in a rich tomato sauce called adobo) to the world. This area also features a few Native American dishes. Texas is a bit more south than west, and has small cafés that serve heaping portions of chicken-fried steak (batter-dipped-and-fried pounded flank steak) and barbecued brisket.

The Southwestern states are loosely connected in a geologic sense as well. Arizona's stunning red rock and sculptural sandstone, carved into canyons big and small, creates otherworldly vistas – nature's own artwork. The Colorado Plateau continues into the mesas of northern New Mexico. To the south, forested mountains stay snow covered throughout winter, as do the ranges in western Texas. Further into Texas the land gets more diverse – tall piney woods sprout in the far east, while on the southern Gulf Coast sand and palm trees prevail. All three have semi-arid to desertlike climes, where succulents and cacti grow. National parks like Saguaro and Grand Canyon in Arizona, and Big Bend in Texas, showcase these natural beauties. In New Mexico, the federal government also protects treasures of human construction, like the Ancestral Puebloan Gila Cliff Dwellings.

Wherever you go in the Southwest, even in the biggest cities, a laid-back attitude pervades. Rarely will a pair of cowboy boots and a button-down shirt be out of place, even in the finest restaurants. Phoenix, Houston and Dallas all have populations over the million mark and are modern, sprawling metropolises, but it's the smaller cities that hold the real appeal. Turquoise shops and boutiques inhabit 19th-century buildings in Tucson's historic district. Adobe-filled Santa Fe is full of artistic character and characters, with galleries and museums galore. Snow bunnies haunt the affluent mountain town of Taos. Austin bills itself as the nation's live-music capital, and it has the bands and bars to back up the claim. San Antonio's River Walk fiestas to a distinctly Mexican beat.

Outside the cities, the Old West spirit lives on at dude ranches, gunfight reenactments (remember the Alamo, and the OK Corral…) and through Native American craft markets. A pinch of old, a dash of new – it's all part of the spicy recipe for today's Southwest.

TEXT LISA DUNFORD

THE WEST

AT THE FAR EDGE OF THE CONTINENT, THE WEST IS A STATE OF MIND. HERE THE USA'S INDIGENOUS TRADITIONS AND PIONEERING SPIRIT LIVE ON, FROM THE ROCKY MOUNTAINS TO THE PACIFIC COAST AND EVEN TO FAR-FLUNG ALASKA AND HAWAII.

THE WEST STATES

- Alaska
- California
- Colorado
- Hawaii
- Idaho
- Montana
- Nevada
- Oregon
- Utah
- Washington
- Wyoming

FOAM AND FOOTSTEPS – AN ALMOST-DESERTED VIEW OF THE GOLDEN GATE BRIDGE. ⌃

In the West, wide-open ranges and cattle country are cut by jagged chains of mountain peaks, wild river systems, the country's deepest canyons, and harsh deserts that nearly swallow entire states. This untamed land is where wild grizzly and black bears, moose and wolves still roam. A network of conservation areas protect diverse and fragile ecosystems, including those in awesome Yellowstone and Yosemite National Parks.

In the early 1800s, Lewis and Clark explored the country between the Mississippi River and the Pacific Ocean while being guided by the Shoshone tribeswoman Sacagawea. It wasn't until the California gold rush of 1849 that thousands of pioneer settlers began arriving in the West. Just 20 years later a transcontinental railroad was completed, with the driving of a golden spike into Utah Territory in 1869. Manifest Destiny – the belief that this nation was preordained by God to expand 'from sea to shining sea' – seemed unstoppable.

During the nation's ruthless westward expansion, indigenous peoples were trampled on, fought against, stripped of their lands and often killed. Conflicts with Native Americans had always been part of New World colonial rule, from the times of the earliest Spanish conquistadores through domination by the newly independent republic of Mexico starting in the 1820s. After the 1848 Treaty of Hidalgo ended the Mexican–American War, the US federal government took the reins. Many tribal peoples were rounded up and forced onto reservations, while more desirable farm and ranch land was sold off to new settlers.

Part of the West today is still a land of 'cowboys and Indians,' where rodeos and tribal powwows are woven into the fabric of everyday life. For ethnic diversity, look first to California, a hotbed of global immigration. Over 100 different native languages are spoken in the Golden State's biggest metro areas. More than half of California's residents share Latino and/or Asian ancestry. Hawaii also has a richly mixed Pan-Asian population. Other Western states are predominantly white with small but significant minority populations. Utah is a stronghold of the Mormon religion, with over half of its residents belonging to that church.

Urban sprawl has gobbled up much of what was once the wide-open frontier. The famous directive 'Go West, young man!' still holds sway over the modern American imagination. Western states boast some of the fastest-growing, most-crowded metro areas in the USA, such as Los Angeles and Las Vegas. At the same time, the region hides some of the most remote and wild places in the entire country, from the sparsely populated deserts of California and Nevada to the uninhabited Northwestern Hawaiian Islands and the wildernesses of Alaska, where the population density averages just one person per square mile.

While ranching and mining are economic mainstays in the mountainous interior of the West, high-tech innovation leads the way in California's Silicon Valley and elsewhere along the Pacific Coast, including in Portland and Seattle. Meanwhile, in fertile inland valleys, agriculture is the primary industry: in California you'll find the garlic, artichoke, almond, avocado, citrus, raisin and date capitals of the world, to name just a few. The coastal states also have prized wine-growing regions. Drilling for oil and natural gas is another huge moneymaker, with renewable energy production such as solar and wind power gaining ground. Many Western states also rely heavily on tourism: Nevada, with its casino gambling; Colorado and Utah for skiing; and coastal California for its sunny beaches and, of course, Disneyland.

What the future holds for the US West depends on how long its natural resources can hold out against a burgeoning population, especially as the effects of global warming begin to hit home. Water is the key to the future. Environmental and political headaches arise from water's scarcity during periods of drought, the necessity of large-scale irrigation for farms, bitter contests over states' rights to major river ways and the diversion of water from rural regions to ever-more-thirsty metro areas. In spite of water shortages, many residents of the US West remain, for the most part, as optimistic as their 19th-century pioneer predecessors. The West still appears to hold out the mythical possibility that anyone can strike it rich here. There's gold in them thar hills, doncha know.

TEXT SARA BENSON

BEST ROAD TRIPS

Snaking across the USA, this fragile ribbon of concrete pavement first connected Chicago with Los Angeles in 1926. Along the way sprouted lightning-bug towns with neon signs, motor courts, diners and drive-ins.

Nicknamed the 'Mother Road' by John Steinbeck in *Grapes of Wrath*, Route 66 was popularized during the Depression, when dust bowl migrants drove west in beat-up jalopies painted with 'California or bust' signs. Post WWII, middle-class motorists got their kicks along Route 66 but, after gradually being bypassed by the interstate system, the highway was decommissioned in 1984.

Driving 66 today means seeking blue-line highways and gravel frontage roads. Start with the skyscrapers of Chicago, then cruise through downstate Illinois farm towns. Cross the Mississippi River into St Louis, where the Gateway Arch stands. Route 66 bounds across the Ozark Plateau, dipping into Civil War history and passing folk icons like the Black Madonna shrine.

Only 13 beautifully preserved miles of Mother Road pass through Kansas, where the 1925 Eisler Bros general store still stands. Oklahoma claims nearly 400 miles of Route 66: lazy stretches of highway pass Native American battlefields and a motel where Elvis once slept, taking in Tulsa's art-deco architecture and cowboy-flavored Oklahoma City.

Route 66 speeds across the hard-baked plains of the Texas Panhandle, with its sprawling cattle ranches and flat landscape, punctuated by utility poles, windmills and the 1930s Tower Conoco Station & U-Drop Inn. Don't miss the Devil's Rope Museum of barbed wire in McLean or the Cadillac Ranch outside Amarillo. New Mexico's Route 66 gives you a taste of the Southwest: timeless adobe houses, chile-spiced cooking and a rich ethnic mix, including Native American nations and the descendants of Spanish conquistadores.

Arizona has the longest stretch of original Mother Road. Curve through the Painted Desert and Petrified Forest into Holbrook, where you can sleep in a concrete teepee at the Wigwam Motel. Old-fashioned Williams offers steam-train excursions to the Grand Canyon, while in the historic mining town of Oatman, wild burros run amok in the streets.

Ah, California. Here the crashing waves of the Pacific await at the end of the 2200-mile-long Mother Road. After running a gauntlet of Mojave Desert ghost towns and dusty railway whistle-stops, Route 66 dives into LA's urban sprawl, dramatically ending at the ocean's edge in coastal Santa Monica.

⌃ SLOWPOKE SIGHTS LIKE THIS ELK CITY, OK, MUSEUM UNFURL ALONG ROUTE 66.

In coastal California, the beautiful and torturously winding Pacific Coast Hwy (PCH) hugs the ocean from San Diego, heading north past Los Angeles to San Francisco and beyond.

Officially speaking, PCH refers only to a short stretch of Hwy 1 through Orange County in Southern California, but many argue that it extends north along Hwys 1 and 101 all the way to the Oregon border.

Whatever its actual boundaries, the PCH is a footloose, fancy-free road trip that requires little planning. Oceanfront motels, sandy beaches and seafood shacks serving Neptune's bounty – fish tacos, lobster and old-fashioned cioppino stew – are everywhere along the route. When the sun sets at the end of each day of coastal cruising, just bed down in the next beach town.

Start in laid-back, surf-style San Diego, just a few miles from Tijuana, Mexico. See where Marilyn Monroe cavorted in *Some Like It Hot,* at the peninsular Hotel Del Coronado. Soak up the sea views at the Point Loma lighthouse, then cruise north along the coast past eclectic beach towns into Orange County ('the OC'). Be swept away by the rich-and-famous lifestyles of arty Laguna Beach, or hang ten in Huntington Beach, aka 'Surf City USA.' Detour inland to Mission San Juan Capistrano, the best-preserved of California's Spanish 18th-century colonial churches.

Motor into LA for people watching on the Venice Beach boardwalk and to ride Santa Monica Pier's solar-powered Ferris wheel. Wind dreamily north along the movie star–studded Malibu coast to Santa Barbara's signature Mediterranean-style buildings and wine country. Revel in the retro Americana of Pismo Beach, then join the crowds at the San Luis Obispo farmers market and take a tour of the museumlike splendors of Hearst Castle.

Trek north along the remote Big Sur coast, a forested haunt of artists, beatniks and hippies. After passing posh Carmel-by-the-Sea and maritime Monterey, take a break in wild Santa Cruz, another surfing mecca, before curving north to San Francisco Bay. The iconic Golden Gate Bridge stands as the gateway to Northern California's redwood coast.

At Point Arena climb to the top of the lighthouse, then linger overnight in Mendocino, whose Victorian village charms have it looking more like Cape Cod than California. Near Eureka, commune with the world's tallest trees in Redwood National and State Parks, beyond which the rugged, wild beaches of Oregon and Washington look mighty tempting – for those with more time to spare.

⌃ CLIFFS, CRASHING WAVES AND FOG DELIGHT ON THE BIG SUR COAST NEAR CARMEL, CA.

ROUTE 66
HISTORIC JOURNEY

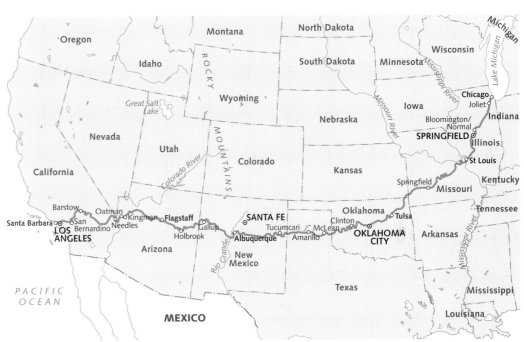

PACIFIC COAST HIGHWAY
ALONG THE COAST

NATIONAL PARKS OF THE WEST
CALIFORNIA TO MONTANA

THE GREAT RIVER ROAD
ALONG THE MISSISSIPPI

HERE 1475 FT ABOVE THE OCEAN THE MIGHTY MISSISSIPPI BEGINS TO FLOW ON IT'S WINDING WAY 2552 MILES TO THE GULF OF MEXICO

TAKE A PIT STOP AT MUSHROOM ROCK IN DEATH VALLEY NATIONAL PARK. ⚐

This 3000-plus-mile nature lover's road trip zigzags through California, Nevada, Arizona, Utah, Colorado, Wyoming and Montana, and will take anywhere from a month to an entire summer. Begin sometime in the spring. If you are lucky, the winter rains will have brought out the wildflowers in Southern California's Joshua Tree National Park. If not, stick around for a day or a week; the camping and rock climbing are amazing.

From Joshua Tree, head north to Kings Canyon National Park. While not as dramatic as its rocky-faced neighbor Yosemite National Park, Kings Canyon is a great place for desolation angels to find their little corner of Zen.

After a few low-key days, head further north to Yosemite, arguably one of the most beautiful wilderness areas in the world. This nearly 1200-square-mile park is almost the size of Rhode Island, and despite the 3.5 million visitors that come every year, it's easy to find some Sierra solitude outside the din of the main valley attractions. Exit Yosemite over Tioga Pass so you can catch a glimpse of the spectacular domes of Tuolumne Meadows before you head toward the vast desert of the American West.

Take Hwy 395 south, which passes through Death Valley National Park – the hottest, driest, lowest and arguably loneliest spot in the USA – on your way to the Grand Canyon National Park. Spend at least a few days here before heading up to the less-trafficked wilderness of Utah. There are four national parks in Utah that are definitely worth visiting: Zion, Bryce Canyon, Canyonlands and Arches. It's possible to spend a week or a month in each park and not get bored, but be sure to be out of there by June, when the summer heat sparks up and hiking during the day becomes nearly impossible.

With the coming summer, head toward the cool blue skies of the Rocky Mountains – first stop Rocky Mountain National Park in Colorado.

After you've had enough of elk, moose and sky-bound Colorado peaks, head north through Grand Teton National Park to Yellowstone. America's first national park, Yellowstone is home to geysers, grizzlies, moose, elk, wolves and more open space than even Teddy Roosevelt, the Rough Rider–turned-president who was essential in preserving the area, could have imagined: 3468 square miles of it.

From there it's northward still to Glacier National Park, where rocks have been moved over passing millennia to form spectacular cliffs, creating a visceral, intoxicating end to a summer of adventure.

MINNESOTA'S HUMBLE ITASCA STATE PARK SPAWNS THE EPIC RIVER AND ITS ROADWAY. ⚐

The Great River Road traces the meanderings of the Mississippi River, from the pine forests of northern Minnesota to the palmetto-fringed coast of the Gulf of Mexico. The road – actually a series of linked highways – covers more than 2000 miles and skirts the edges of 10 states. It hugs levees, crosses bridges, becomes Main Street in small river towns and encounters a number of large cities. Driving its entire length affords the motorist a dissected view of the nation's heartland.

Ideally, such a trip begins where the river itself begins, at Minnesota's Lake Itasca State Park. Here it is possible to wade through a knee-high stream and say you walked across Old Man River. Downstream St Paul and Minneapolis are worth an overnight stop for live music, a baseball game, or to sleep on board a tugboat B&B.

Wisconsin's riverside towns are pleasant pictures of small-town America, set amid rolling hills and historic sites where settlers once fought Native Americans in the Black Hawk War. From there, river and road plunge into the cornfield monotony of Iowa and Illinois.

Mark Twain, chronicler of the Big Muddy's steamboat days, grew up in the Missouri town of Hannibal, which has become a natural, if touristy, pilgrimage stop. St Louis honors its history as gateway to the Wild West with its magnificent Gateway Arch. Ride to the top for an endless view of the river and the plains.

When you reach Memphis, TN, you've arrived in the South, where good times and warmer climes await. Graceland, Elvis' extravagant bachelor pad, is not to be missed. Neither is Sun Studio or the city's outstanding down-home BBQ joints.

The Mississippi Delta, in Arkansas and Mississippi, still feels like the home of the blues, thanks in equal parts to the lively Clarksdale music scene and the neglected, dragged-down feel of the region. Vicksburg, MS, trades on its Civil War history with its fascinating museums and battleground. Natchez, with its magnificent mansions, is still dreaming the dream of antebellum splendor.

More plantations and history line the River Road in Louisiana, but the real draw at this point is the *bon temps* of New Orleans where, Katrina be damned, you can still hear live jazz, drink Sazerac cocktails, consult with a voodoo priestess or even ride a steamboat on the Old Man himself.

The West has always been the direction Americans look to for fresh starts, so it's appropriate that one of the USA's oldest scenic highways runs down the nation's original western edge. In colonial days the backbone of the country, and the furthest limit of westward expansion, was the Appalachians. One stretch of these mountains, glimpsed in the hazy cerulean distance, is known as the Blue Ridge. Running down this escarpment is a 469-mile highway, which cuts over deep forests, quick streams, white rivers and mountains buttered with laurel, galax, fir, oak, dogwood, hickory and buckeye.

The Blue Ridge Parkway both traces a route through and is the name of the narrowest national park in the world (and the longest national park in the USA). Because the parkway runs parallel to the highway (which can only be accessed via side roads), you can experience a great American road trip without encountering billboards, McDonald's and suburban sprawl – something difficult even in the vast open areas of the West.

If heading north to south, start at Mile 0: Rockfish Gap, VA, near the heart of one of the USA's most enduring, distinctive regional cultures – the Mountain South. As you jaunt down the ridge you'll trace by soda-fountain towns that got lost in the 1950s, abutting hillside communities that could be stuck in the 1850s.

About 50 miles south of Mile 0 detour west to Lexington, VA, a town that encompasses one of the last bastions of Southern military-aristocracy – to whit, the Virginia Military Institute and Washington and Lee University (where you can see the tomb of Robert E Lee and his horse, Traveller). There are few more evocative Southern academic sights than young cadets jogging past students deconstructing Faulkner.

One of the USA's great homegrown music genres, bluegrass, was born here. See the fiddle, banjo and mandolin played as they should be, in front of appreciative audiences of locals whose families produced the likes of June Carter Cash, in towns such as Floyd and Galax, only a little way off the parkway.

In North Carolina, Mount Mitchell is the highest point east of the Mississippi. Towns like Asheville give a welcome break from road rigors with their associated arts scene and to-die-for BBQ, while Daniel Boone's trace marks the spot where the eponymous frontiersman made his first forays into the back of beyond, the great land that lay beyond the first US frontier.

⌃ THE BLUE RIDGE PARKWAY AMBLES OVER HILL AND DALE IN NORTH CAROLINA.

Start where the Pilgrims did, at the tip of Cape Cod. After navigating Provincetown's labyrinth of colorful streets, cycle through the dunes to some of New England's best swimming beaches, or head offshore on a whale-watching expedition.

Next, head 'up-Cape,' past clam shacks and cranberry bogs to Hyannis for the ferry ride to Nantucket. Whaling capital of the world for nearly a century, Nantucket's harbor still struts its stuff with an ensemble of pre-1850 buildings that constitute America's largest National Historic Landmark. Island-hop to Martha's Vineyard, where you can catch the sunset against the multicolored sediments of Aquinnah Cliffs or wander Edgartown's streets in search of celebrities and fried clams.

Get your land legs again on the 3.5-mile Cliff Walk in Newport, RI, where the outlandishly large homes of the Vanderbilts, Astors and other high-society families perch atop wave-battered bluffs while surfers and yacht racers brave the waters offshore.

Follow in the steps of revolutionaries on Boston's historic Freedom Trail, from the Old North Church to Bunker Hill. Then don your pointy hat and hit Salem, where a bevy of witchy attractions re-creates the darker side of 17th-century Puritan life, and the Peabody Essex Museum counters with a dazzling collection of artifacts brought from overseas by early American merchants.

Crossing north into New Hampshire, don't blink or you'll miss the state's 18-mile coastline. Several sandy beaches invite you to dip your toe in the Atlantic, and Portsmouth, one of New England's best-preserved historic seaports, begs for a stroll.

Across Piscataqua River in Maine, rockier shores await. Stop to indulge your taste buds in cosmopolitan Portland's Old Port, then follow the jagged shoreline eastward into some of coastal New England's most classic scenery. At Bath, get a feel for shipbuilding traditions old and new at the Maine Maritime Museum. Browse the antique shops in Wiscasset, detour down to Pemaquid Point Lighthouse, discover the coves and islands around Camden aboard a full-rigged windjammer, or climb to the top of Mount Battie for ocean views that just won't quit.

Wrap up your trip in Acadia National Park, crown jewel of the Maine coast. Established in 1916, Acadia preserves a mix of fishing villages and raw natural beauty. Here you can take your pick of exhilarating or relaxing pursuits: scale the granite heights of Cadillac Mountain, spread a towel on Sand Beach, explore miles of traffic-free carriage roads, or head into Bar Harbor for lobster and a pint of wild-blueberry ale.

⌃ EXLORE LIGHTHOUSE-DOTTED LANDSCAPES, SUCH AS CASTLE HILL LIGHT, IN NEWPORT, R

BLUE RIDGE PARKWAY
MILES OF MOUNTAINS

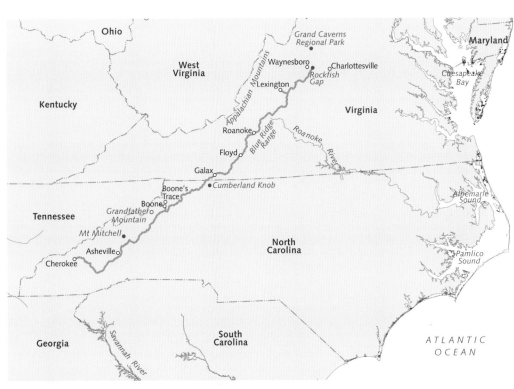

COASTAL NEW ENGLAND
CAPE COD TO BAR HARBOR

THE STATES

AT MOST DINERS YOU'LL RECEIVE A SLICE OF LOCAL CULTURE WITH YOUR PIE.

THE DAY-GLO ARCHES OF LOWER ANTELOPE CANYON RISE ON NAVAJO LAND NEAR PAGE, AZ.

ALABAMA

ALABAMA IS THE DEEP END OF THE DEEP SOUTH, WITH SIGNIFICANT CIVIL RIGHTS HISTORY, HEARTY SOUTHERN COOKING, BIBLE-THUMPING CITIZENRY AND NATURAL SPLENDORS RANGING FROM APPALACHIA TO THE GULF COAST.

≈ HENS STRUT THEIR STUFF WHILE A WOMAN COLLECTS THEIR EGGS ON A FREE-RANGE FARM.

- **Etymology of the State Name** Derives from the Alabama, or Alibamu, tribe
- **Nickname** The Heart of Dixie
- **Motto** *Audemus jura nostra defendere* (We dare defend our rights)
- **Capital City** Montgomery

- **Population** 4.6 million
- **Area** 52,419 sq miles
- **Time Zone** Central
- **State Bird** Yellowhammer
- **State Flower** Camellia

- **Major Industry** Manufacturing
- **Politics** Red state in 2008
- **Best Time to Go** September to December – for weekend college-football games

HISTORY IN A NUTSHELL

The land that is now Alabama was home to many Native American tribes, including Alibamus, Chickasaws, Choctaws and Creeks. Alabama was part of the Mississippi Territory before being admitted to the Union in 1819 as the 22nd state. The rich soil of middle Alabama attracted cotton planters, who eventually brought in more than 400,000 slaves. Montgomery was the first capital of the Confederacy, though only for a few months. After the Civil War, Alabama began to industrialize, with the founding of Birmingham, a steel-producing center, in 1871. Rosa Parks' bus protest took place in Montgomery in 1955 and Martin Luther King Jr was based in the city throughout the Civil Rights era.

LANDSCAPE

Progressing down from the north, Appalachia gives way to forested highlands and the 'Black Belt' lowlands that flatten out before the state dead ends at the Gulf Coast. The northern part of the state is rugged, with waterfalls, canyons and mountain lakes interspersed with dense forest. The Black Belt, an area that was once carpeted with cotton plants, has gently rolling hills that are richly soiled and ideal for farming. Thanks to the Florida Panhandle, Alabama has just 53 miles of coast, but it is a rich mix of marshes, bays and white-sand beaches. The state's highest point is Cheaha Mountain (2407 feet) in the Talladega National Forest.

NATURAL BEAUTY

In the USA, only California and Florida can boast greater ecological diversity than Alabama. The state is home to 300 varieties of wildflower and the oldest forests east of the Mississippi. Forests of pine, oak, hickory and maple cover about two-thirds of the state. Some of the state's best hiking trails meander through the Sipsey Wilderness, a protected parkland of primeval forest, gorges and waterfalls. Comparable splendor can be found at the Little River Canyon, a 700-foot-deep gorge that features 60-foot Little River Falls. On the Gulf Coast, Dauphin Island and Bon Secour National Wildlife Refuge attract huge numbers of migrating birds in spring and fall. Alligators lurk in the swamps north and east of Mobile.

A CLASSIC SOUTHERN MEAL OF FRIED CHICKEN, MASHED POTATOES AND GREEN BEANS.

PEOPLE

Alabama's population is 71% white and 26% African American. The remainder is divided mostly between Hispanics, Asians and Native Americans. The ratio of African Americans continues to decline (it peaked at around 45% before the Civil War) as Alabama's population increases and African Americans depart for other parts of the country.

CULTURE & TRADITIONS

Clever folks call Alabama the 'buckle' of the Bible Belt. About 90% of the state's population professes faith in Christianity. Baptists outnumber all other denominations. Alabamians also get behind their college football teams (Auburn and the University of Alabama at Tuscaloosa) and avidly follow Nascar. Hunting, fishing and hiking are also popular. Mobile, once colonized by French Catholics, still celebrates Mardi Gras: it's not as flashy as in New Orleans, but Mobilians will proudly tell you they have been doing it longer – since 1703.

CUISINE

Alabama restaurants typically feature traditional Southern fare, such as fried chicken, corn pone, chicken and dumplings, sweet potatoes and buttered beans. Alabamians are also partial to tomato sandwiches and fried green tomatoes. Mobile shares New Orleans' fondness for oysters and Creole cuisine. Largemouth bass is abundant in local waters, and Alabama suffers

no shortage of farmed catfish. The state also enjoys a plenitude of fresh fruit such as Chilton County peaches and berries, and pecans and peanuts. Naturally, peach cobbler and pecan pie are popular. Rattlesnake meat is the featured delicacy at the Rattlesnake Rodeo, in the town of Opp. The town of Luverne hosts the World's Largest Peanut Boil on Labor Day Weekend.

TRADEMARKS

- ○ Bible Belt
- ○ Freedom marches
- ○ Rebels (or 'rebs')
- ○ Alabama, the country rock group
- ○ Crimson Tide (University of Alabama football)

ECONOMY

Cotton is a thing of the past. Alabama's economy is primarily concerned with the production of iron, steel, coal, paper, chemicals, plastics, textiles and automobile assembly. Poultry, soybeans and acquaculture are the state's biggest agricultural goods. Still, Alabama is among the poorest states, with an income per capita of around $20,000.

URBAN SCENE

Industrial Birmingham (population 229,000) wasn't founded until after the Civil War. It lacks Antebellum charm but makes up for it with fine Southern dining and direct access to Appalachian

rivers and trails. Its Five Points South historic district attracts all types for nightlife and people watching. Montgomery has a slower, more provincial feel. Both cities make a commendable homage to the Civil Rights Era – in Birmingham's illuminating Civil Rights Institute and Montgomery's moving Civil Rights Memorial.

REPRESENTATIONS

- ○ 'Alabamy Bound'; Al Jolson warbled this Tin Pan Alley hit on Vaudeville stages
- ○ *To Kill a Mockingbird* (1960); Harper Lee's novel is a much-loved depiction of small town Alabama life
- ○ 'Alabama' (1972); Neil Young pointed a righteous finger at the state with this song
- ○ 'Sweet Home Alabama' (1974); Lynyrd Skynyrd's Southern rock reply to the Neil Young song

DID YOU KNOW?

- ○ Winston County, in northwestern Alabama, declared itself neutral during the Civil War
- ○ Wikipedia was founded by a native Alabamian – Jimmy Wales of Huntsville

ALABAMA LEGEND

Add the Welsh Prince Madoc to the number of explorers to reach America before Columbus. The Welsh claim he reached Alabama in 1169, and local Cherokee legend corroborates that white people built stone forts along the Alabama River.

TEXT TOM DOWNS

⌃ CLIMBERS BOULDERING IN LITTLE RIVER CANYON TAKE A SUN-SPLASHED BREAK.

⌃ MARTIN LUTHER KING JR MONUMENT AT SELMA.

ESSENTIAL EXPERIENCES

- ○ Getting emotional at Montgomery's Civil Rights Memorial
- ○ Touring gator-infested swamps north of Mobile
- ○ Contemplating space travel in Rocket City (aka Huntsville)
- ○ Hiking through Sipsey Wilderness' ancient forest
- ○ Admiring rural folk art at Anton Haardt Gallery in Montgomery
- ○ Eating fried green tomatoes at Birmingham's Irondale Cafe

MAP REF // PAGE 5 S11

⌃ GOOD THING THERE ARE NO ALLIGATORS, JUST FERNS AND FOREST IN THE GREEN-GLOWING SIPSEY WILDERNESS.

CIVIL RIGHTS LEADER JAMES ARMSTRONG CUT DR KING'S HAIR, TOO, AT HIS BIRMINGHAM BARBER SHOP. »

ROOMS WITH A VIEW NEAR FORT MORGAN ON THE BEACH-DAPPLED GULF COAST. »

ALASKA

BIG, BOLD AND WILD – THERE ARE FEW PLACES IN THE WORLD, AND NONE IN THE USA, WITH THE UNSPOILED WILDERNESS, MOUNTAINOUS GRANDEUR AND IMMENSE WILDLIFE THAT ALASKA POSSESSES.

- **Etymology of the State Name** The Aleut word 'Alyeska,' meaning 'the great land'
- **Nicknames** Final Frontier, Last Frontier
- **Motto** North to the future
- **Capital City** Juneau
- **Population** 683,480
- **Area** 656,425 sq miles
- **Time Zones** Alaska, Hawaii-Aleutian
- **State Bird** Willow ptarmigan
- **State Flower** Forget-me-not
- **Major Industry** Oil
- **Politics** Red state in 2008
- **Best Time to Go** July to August – 20-hour days and pleasant temperatures

HISTORY IN A NUTSHELL

Alaska's vast natural resources were first exploited by the Russians, who established the first European settlement in 1772 and subsequently decimated the sea otter population. In 1867 Russia sold Alaska to the US for $7.2 million; soon after, the Klondike Gold Rush (1897) drew attention to the remote territory. After Japan attacked Alaska during WWII, the US military rushed to build the Alaska Hwy, and in 1959 the territory became the USA's 49th state. In 1968, Prudhoe Bay, North America's largest oil field, was discovered and ushered in Alaska's latest boom: oil production.

LANDSCAPE

Simply put, Alaska is big. The state is a fifth of the size of the lower 48, and has the third longest river in North America, 17 of the country's 20 highest peaks and a glacier larger than Switzerland. Its climate and landscapes range from a temperate rainforest in the Southeast to the rugged Alaska Range and the treeless North Slope where Arctic winters are one long night.

NATURAL BEAUTY

Less than 1% of Alaska is developed. The rest remains untrampled by civilization's heavy footprint and includes the country's largest national parks: Wrangell-St Elias and Gates of the Arctic. Visitors are awed by tidewater glaciers that discharge icebergs the size of small houses and above which rise mountains and peaks. At 20,320 feet, Mount McKinley is North America's highest peak and a stunning scene on a clear day. In Southeast Alaska and Prince William Sound those mountains and glaciers are surrounded by towering Sitka spruce and hemlock; trees so tall it's hard to see the tops of them. And scattered throughout this massive place is the greatest concentration of wildlife in the USA: brown bears that tip the scales at up to 1500 pounds, salmon that choke streams during the summer and bald eagles by the thousand.

PEOPLE

The largest state in the USA is the most sparse, with a density of only 1.2 persons per square mile (compared to Manhattan's 70,000 per square mile). Alaskans are urban (74%) and white (70%), and 42% of them live in Anchorage. Native Alaskans (including the Athabascan, Eyak, Haida, Tlingit, Tsimshian, Aleut, Alutiiq, Inupiaq, Yuk'ik and Cup'ik people) represent less than 16% of the population.

CULTURE & TRADITIONS

Regardless of why they arrived, most residents remain because of the Great Outdoors. Hunting and fishing is not just a passion in Alaska: living off the land by what one shoots or catches is still widely practiced (PETA is a four-letter word here). In the summer when the days are long, Alaskans hike, cycle, climb mountains, kayak glacier-filled fjords or visit the Alaska State Fair. Winter is for catching up on sleep, the mending or the office job.

TRADEMARKS

- Midnight sun – in Barrow the sun doesn't set for 84 days
- Igloos – Native Alaskans once used them as temporary shelters but now they just return home on their snowmobile
- Kodiak bear – the largest land carnivore can stand 10 feet and weigh up to 1500 pounds
- Giant vegetables – with 20-hour days, cabbages can tip the scales at 90 pounds at the Alaska State Fair.
- Northern lights – the atmospheric phenomenon is Alaska's greatest light show
- Sarah Palin – Alaska's first woman governor, and former White House aspirant
- Oil – the lifeblood of Alaska

CUISINE

Alaska's cuisine is all about wild seafood. Alaskans don't grow much but they catch more salmon, halibut and king crab than any other state. You'll see salmon in streams, on ice at markets, in your chowder at the lunch counter and being slathered with tangy sauces at every salmon bake.

BALD EAGLES, LOOKING EVERY BIT THE MAJESTIC NATIONAL SYMBOL IN ALASKA'S KATMAI NATIONAL PARK. »

ECONOMY

Oil fuels Alaska's boom-and-bust economy. Nearly 90% of the state's general fund revenue comes from taxes on oil production and when the price of a barrel is up, as it was in 2008, Alaska is flush with cash. When it isn't, there are serious budget problems in Juneau. Commercial fishing is the state's second-leading industry; Alaska accounts for 56% of the total catch in the USA. Wages are high in Alaska – its median household income of $64,333 is the country's fourth highest – but so is the cost of living.

URBAN SCENE

Anchorage is the Athens of Alaska. Almost half of the state's residents live in the city or the surrounding area, allowing Anchorage to dominate Alaska culturally and politically. It has the best museums, the finest restaurants and the liveliest nightlife, yet is surrounded by wilderness – seeing a moose in this city of 278,700 people is a common occurrence.

REPRESENTATIONS

○ *Coming into the Country* (1977), by John McPhee; this timeless classic is arguably the best portrait of Alaska ever written

○ *Into the Wild* (1996), by Jon Krakauer; a best-selling account of a young man's journey (and end) in the Alaskan wilderness

○ *The Deadliest Catch* (2005–); the hit reality TV show where fishing crews endure the icy Alaskan seas for a fortune in king crab

DID YOU KNOW?

○ Alaska is almost as close to Tokyo (3520 miles) as it is to New York City (3280 miles).

○ In 1914, the temperature hit 100°F (38°C) at Fort Yukon. In 1971, it dropped to -80°F (-62°C) at Prospect Creek.

○ Because of the international date line, Alaska has the furthest points north, west and *east* in the USA.

ALASKA LEGEND

Nome's most unlikely resident was Wyatt Earp. He arrived in 1899 after hearing about the city's gold rush, but not as a prospector. Earp headed to Alaska to 'mine the miners.' The noted gunslinger immediately built the Dexter, a luxurious, two-story saloon in the middle of a tent city, only a block from the red-light district. After offering gambling and liquor for two years, Earp left Nome with, as legend has it, $80,000 – a fortune at that time.

TEXT JIM DUFRESNE

NATIVE ALASKAN CHILDREN KEEPING WARM. ⌃

⌃ YEARLING BROWN BEARS PLAY AT HALLO BAY, KATMAI NATIONAL PARK.

ESSENTIAL EXPERIENCES

○ Gazing at the reflection of Mount McKinley in Wonder Lake

○ Soaking with locals at the Tenakee Hot Springs bathhouse

○ Watching giant icebergs tumbling from Childs Glacier near Cordova

○ Tipping back a beverage with the brewmaster at Kodiak Island Brewing Company

○ Strapping on crampons and hiking the frozen surface of Matanuska Glacier

○ Photographing bears catching salmon at Anan Creek near Wrangell

○ Hooking a giant halibut in Homer

MAP REF // PAGE 4 D14

ICEBERGS AND CLOUDS FLOAT AROUND PORTAGE GLACIER RECREATION AREA, NEAR ANCHORAGE. ⟫

THE EYES HAVE IT AT TOTEM BIGHT STATE HISTORICAL PARK. ⟫

ON TOP OF THE WORLD ON PYRAMID PEAK IN WRANGELL-ST ELIAS. ⟫

ARIZONA

A MICROCOSM OF THE US SOUTHWEST, ARIZONA HAS IT ALL: OLD-WEST GHOST TOWNS, THE RUGGED BEAUTY OF CANYONS AND RED ROCK, ANCESTRAL PUEBLOAN CLIFF-DWELLINGS – AND A UNIQUE AZ-MEX CUISINE.

⌃ AN ELDER FLASHES HIS TRADITIONAL JEWELRY IN MONUMENT VALLEY NAVAJO TRIBAL PARK.

- **Etymology of the State Name** Possibly from a corruption of the Aztec word *arizuma* (silver bearing) and the Pima Indian word *arizonac* (little spring place)
- **Nickname** Grand Canyon State
- **Motto** *Ditat deus* (God enriches)

- **Capital City** Phoenix
- **Population** 6.3 million
- **Area** 114,006 sq miles
- **Time Zone** Mountain
- **State Bird** Cactus wren

- **State Flower** Saguaro cactus flower
- **Major Industries** Tourism, mining and manufacturing
- **Politics** Red state in 2008
- **Best Time to Go** September to October – after the heat and before the northern snows

HISTORY IN A NUTSHELL

The Aztec, Hohokam and Salado were ancient forebears of today's Native Americans. They lived on the land that became Arizona for more than 1000 years before Spanish explorers set up missions starting in the mid-1500s. The capture and exile of Apache warrior Geronimo in 1886 ended the period of Indian Wars during which the US governments struggled for control of the land. Railroad and mining interests expanded until Arizona became the 48th state, in 1912. Though marginalized, Arizona's Native American tribes – including the Navajo, Hopi and Tohono O'odham – continue to play a strong cultural role. Scarcity of water is the hot-button topic in the very dry, yet fast-growing state.

NATURAL BEAUTY

One beautiful natural vista seems to overshadow the next in Arizona: the colossal red buttes and mesas in Monument Valley, the army of cacti with upheld arms at Saguaro National Park, the stratified rock spires of Chiricahua National Monument… Of course the ever-changing light playing on the ochre-, red- and dust-colored layers of the mile-deep Grand Canyon is this state's overwhelming spectacle.

DID YOU KNOW?

- Arizona has more species of hummingbirds than any other place in America.
- In Arizona, only the Navajo Nation, in the north of the state, observes daylight savings time.

LANDSCAPE

The northernmost section of Arizona is part of the rugged Colorado Plateau; here between 5000 and 8000 feet is the time-worn beauty of the Grand Canyon. Starting in central Arizona, a series of forested mountain ranges with cool climes (Humphrey's Peak is highest at 12,633 feet) diminishes in height towards the south. These ranges alternate with arid basins, often blazing hot (above 100°F/38°C), that contain the state's largest cities, and desert flora like the iconic saguaro cactus that are part of the Arizona-Sonoran desert.

GIVE RATTLESNAKES A BRAKE, WARNS THIS ROAD SIGN NEAR CAREFREE. »

THE OLD WEST LIVES (SANS GUNFIGHTS) AT THE COPPER QUEEN HOTEL SALOON IN BISBEE. »

PEOPLE

Although Arizona has one of the highest concentrations of Native Americans, that group makes up only 5% of the state's population. The Navajo Nation accounts for roughly half of that number. Much larger is the 26% minority of Hispanic origin. The influence of Mexican-American heritage is strongest in the southern part of the state. Correspondingly, the largest religious affiliation is Catholicism (25%).

CULTURE & TRADITIONS

The Native American legacy in the state is positive and negative. You'll hear of racism, poverty and how ancestors were forced onto reservations. But Puebloan adobe architecture also inspires housing and Hopi kachinas (brightly painted spirit-messenger dolls) and Navajo pottery are widely sold. The Navajo reservation is the state's largest and maintains many of the old traditions. Visitors can eat fry bread (deep-fried dough) with stew or see native dances and chants at a powwow. Ceremonies are something different entirely; they're sacred and usually private, as is the topic of religion.

CUISINE

'Southwest cuisine,' a blend of Mexican-, Spanish- and Native American-inspired dishes, is as popular in Arizona as it is in New Mexico. You might find top chefs experimenting with lobster-stuffed chiles or duck tacos. Mexican food here is usually of the Sonoran variety – tortillas are made from wheat, not corn, and carne seca (dried, spiced beef) is used as a filling for burritos, enchiladas and chimichangas (a deep-fried burrito). On or near a reservation you might try a Navajo taco: fry bread folded and stuffed with beans, cheese, chiles and meat; sometimes it's made as a breakfast sandwich with eggs and cheese instead.

TRADEMARKS

○ Grand Canyon

○ OK Corral

○ Sunshine

○ Retirees

○ Cacti and citrus trees

○ John McCain

ECONOMY

Arizona has an economy bigger than that of Ireland. The median household income is $43,696, roughly even with the national average. The government is the largest single employer; Walmart comes in second. Roughly 44% of Arizonans are employed in service industries, and 11% have jobs connected with mining and extraction.

URBAN SCENE

A sprawling modern city of relaxed sophistication, Phoenix is where a local can practice their swing on more than 230 golf courses during the day and attend an opera or hit a nightclub at night. The greater metropolis is actually a collection of 21 cities (and 3.3 million people). In smaller Tucson (population 526,000), the interplay of Native American, Spanish and Anglo cultures is much more evident than in its modern, big-sister city. Mexican restaurants, turquoise jewelry shops and artsy boutiques fill 19th-century buildings in historic neighborhoods.

REPRESENTATIONS

○ Zane Grey; this renowned Western novelist was much inspired by his beloved Arizona

○ John Ford; turned many of Grey's books into films, often shooting on location in Arizona

○ Monument Valley; featured in numerous big name films, including 2001: A Space Odyssey (1968), Easy Rider (1969), Thelma & Louise (1991) and Forrest Gump (1994)

ARIZONA LEGEND

Everyone's heard about the shoot-out at the OK Corral. In 30 seconds Wyatt Earp, his brothers and Doc Holliday outgunned the Clanton Gang and law prevailed in the western mining town of Tombstone, right? Yes, but the fight took place not in the corral, but in a 15-foot-wide alley nearby. Virgil Earp, the eldest brother, was marshal, not Wyatt, and the event was more like an arrest gone awry than a personal settling of scores. Other than that, so many stories have been told (and fraudulent memoirs published), it's hard to tell how much truth movies like Wyatt Earp (1994, starring Kevin Costner) preserve.

TEXT LISA DUNFORD

ESSENTIAL EXPERIENCES

○ Rafting the Colorado River through the majestic Grand Canyon

○ Picking a lemon off a nearby tree

○ Being dwarfed by red rock buttes on a drive through Monument Valley

○ Cruising out to the desert to see the tips of the long, whiplike ocotillo plant's branches in bloom after a summer shower

○ Having your chakras aligned and aura photographed at a new-age shop in Sedona

RICHARD SMITH // ALAMY

⌃ A COOL POOL IN SUN CITY, TUCSON, MAKES WORKOUTS MORE FUN.

MAP REF // PAGE 4 G10

THE MITTENS AND MERRICK BUTTE CAST LONG SHADOWS OVER MONUMENT VALLEY. ⊼

A PRICKLY PEAR CACTUS IN FULL PROTECTIVE GEAR IN SEDONA. ⊼

ARKANSAS

THE 'NATURAL STATE' NICKNAME MIGHT NOT SEEM VERY APPROPRIATE FOR THE FLAT, FERTILE COTTON FIELDS OFF THE MISSISSIPPI DELTA, BUT IT ALL BECOMES CLEAR ON THE BACK ROADS OF THE GORGEOUS OZARKS AND OUACHITAS TO THE NORTH AND WEST.

≫ IT'S TIME TO HARVEST ON A LOCAL COTTON FARM.

- **Etymology of the State Name** French pronunciation of a Quapaw word meaning 'people of the south wind'
- **Nicknames** Natural State, Razorback State
- **Motto** *Regnant populus* (The people rule)
- **Capital City** Little Rock
- **Population** 2.8 million
- **Area** 53,182 sq miles
- **Time Zone** Central
- **State Bird** Mockingbird
- **State Flower** Apple blossom
- **Major Industries** Agriculture, tourism, Walmart
- **Politics** Red state in 2008
- **Best Time to Go** April to June, September to October – to miss the bulk of summer heat and visitors

HISTORY IN A NUTSHELL

Caddo, Osage and Quapaw had permanent settlements here when Spaniard Hernando de Soto visited in the mid-1500s. After the 1803 Louisiana Purchase, Arkansas became a US territory, then the 25th state in 1836, with many slaveholding landowners moving in to plant cotton. Reconstruction after the Civil War was difficult, but was aided in 1870 with the expansion of railroads. Racial tension peaked in 1957, when the federal government intervened to enforce the integration of Arkansas schools. Though Bill Clinton hails from Hope, local politics are better represented by a recent presidential hopeful, ultra-conservative Republican Mike Huckabee.

LANDSCAPE

Arkansas' flat east Delta stretches to far-off horizons, while rocky, forested cliffs rise and roll in the Ozark and Ouachita mountains of the north and east. Highest point Mount Magazine stands at 2753 feet. Notable rivers include the Mississippi, which lines the east border, and the Arkansas, which cuts east from Oklahoma. Others feed many artificial lakes, such as Bull Shoals in the north. The soil sees 45 to 55 inches of rainfall annually. January highs sit around freezing; humid days in July reach 95°F (35°C).

NATURAL BEAUTY

Many back roads of Arkansas are gorgeous – particularly through the Arkansas River Valley (at towns such as Pine Bluff) or the Ozarks (eg the Victorian town of Eureka Springs) – but perhaps the best way to see Arkansas is by boat. The 150-mile Buffalo National River cuts through 500-foot sandstone cliffs in the Ozarks, home to caves and waterfalls.

PEOPLE

Arkansas is about 82% white; many living in the Ozarks have German and British ancestry. The state's African American population accounts for 16% of the state, mostly living in Little Rock and more agricultural areas of the south and east. The Latin American population has grown by 50% in a decade. Arkansas is proudly part of the Bible Belt (nearly nine in 10 are Christians).

INNER TUBING IS ANOTHER WAY TO SOAK UP THE RECREATION AT HOT SPRINGS NATIONAL PARK.

CULTURE & TRADITIONS

Blues and country music owe a nod to down-home family sing-alongs: Johnny Cash, Conway Twitty, Howlin' Wolf, Sonny Boy Williamson, Ronnie Hawkins and Glen Campbell all hail from Arkansas towns. Jim Bowie, who got himself shot to pieces in the Alamo, was famed for his 'Bowie knife,' which was supposedly designed by an Arkansan and is now called an 'Arkansas toothpick.' The northeastern town of Walcott gets a bit cheeky over summer pests, with its annual Mosquito-Calling Contest and 'mosquito recipe' swaps.

REPRESENTATIONS

o *I Know Why the Caged Bird Sings* (1969); Maya Angelou's account of how she handled tough times growing up in Arkansas

o 'Five Feet High and Rising' (1959); a Johnny Cash song about the dangers of the Mississippi

o Black Oak Arkansas (of Black Oak, AR); this band plays endless overlapping guitar solos and southern-fried rock

o 'The Night They Drove Ol' Dixie Down' (1969); The Band were mostly Canadians but their drummer was the feisty, raspy-voiced, real-deal Arkansan, Levon Helm, who sang this song of the South

CUISINE

Arkansas' dinner plates keep mindful of the state's neighbors. Southern and Creole specialties from Louisiana (corn bread, crawfish boils, raccoon…) find their way into the east and south of the state; in the southwest, near Texas, BBQ rises in importance, while central and northern lakes provide the catfish for fish fries. Up in the Ozarks, watch for black-pot (Dutch oven) cook-offs, enough of a tradition to warrant an Arkansas Dutch Oven Society.

ECONOMY

Favorable tax brackets have lured some big-name companies to set up shop here, notably Walmart and Tyson Foods. Much of the state's money comes from agriculture (hogs, eggs, chicken, rice, cotton) and food processing, though tourism is a big player too – contributing $4 billion to the state's nearly $90 billion gross domestic product. Salaries are another story; the state's median household income ($38,100) is the country's third-lowest.

TRADEMARKS

o Ozark Mountains

o Walmart's HQ in Bentonville

o Little Rock's Central High School (for its role in desegregation in 1957)

o Johnny Cash

o Bill Clinton

URBAN SCENE

Attractive Little Rock, with its roads rising over hills, sits on the Arkansas River. Visitors can take 'Bill Clinton Tours,' which go to the Old State House, where he celebrated both his presidential victories, and the William J Clinton Presidential Center. West of downtown, Hillcrest is a bohemian neighborhood, and the Heights (just north) has ritzier restaurants and shops. Along the Arkansas River, the River Market District is an arts-and-entertainment area with many dining choices.

DID YOU KNOW?

o Arkansas is the only place in North America that mines diamonds – a fact paid tribute to by the diamond-shape design in its flag and a huge diamond floating over a natural scene on the 2003 Arkansas quarter.

o Davy Crockett, the coonskin-cap wearer of Alamo fame, likened Arkansans to being 'half-horse, half-alligator' – he meant it in a good way.

ARKANSAS LEGEND

If you're hiking by a southwestern creek or lake and get approached by a hulking 7-foot, 800-pound, hairy hominid beast – that may or may not attack you – you're not the first. The so-called Fouke Monster, a Sasquatch of sorts outside Texarkana, was supposedly spotted many times in the early 1970s, and was documented by Arkansan director Charles B Pierce in the classic 1973 docu-drama *The Legend of Boggy Creek*, which cost about $160,000 to make and earned $22 million. Please report your sighting to the dead-serious Texas Bigfoot Research Conservancy.

TEXT ROBERT REID

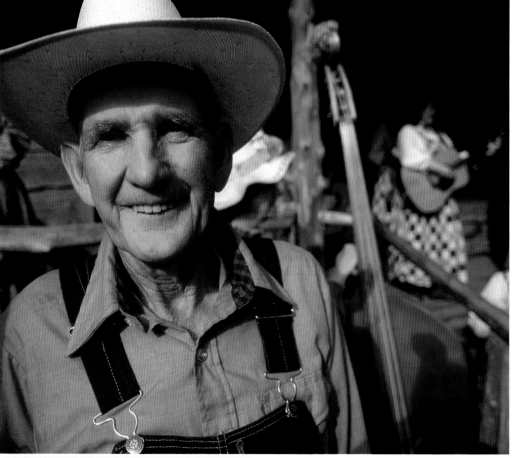

⌃ GETTING READY TO JAM AT THE OZARK FOLK CENTER, MOUNTAIN VIEW.

ESSENTIAL EXPERIENCES

o Soaking those aching bones in the hot waters of Hot Springs

o Canoeing down the Buffalo National River

o Boating on the weekends at Table Rock Lake

o Inhaling the air at the William J Clinton Presidential Center

o Driving Ozark back roads, the likely original home of those Beverly Hillbillies

o Calling out for a pig ('woo pig sooie!') with the mass of Razorback fans in Fayetteville

MAP REF // PAGE 5 P10

THE LITTLE MISSOURI RIVER FLOWS PAST THE ALBERT PIKE RECREATION AREA IN OUACHITA NATIONAL FOREST. ≫

THE BOY FROM HOPE, AR, BECAME THE USA'S 42ND PRESIDENT. ≫

A FARM NEAR BATESVILLE ADDS TO THE STATE'S BIG BUSINESS OF AGRICULTURE. ≫

CALIFORNIA

ONLY ALASKA AND TEXAS ARE BIGGER THAN THE GOLDEN STATE, WHICH LOOMS EVEN LARGER IN POP CULTURE'S IMAGINATION – YES, THERE ARE PALM TREES, PACIFIC BEACHES AND MOVIE STARS, BUT ALSO A CUTTING-EDGE URBAN SCENE, HIGH-TECH INNOVATION AND A LIFE-BRINGING WAVE OF ETHNICALLY DIVERSE IMMIGRANTS.

≈ GUESS WHAT'S BLOOMING AT THE ANTELOPE VALLEY POPPY RESERVE.

- **Etymology of the State Name** Spanish, possibly for a fictional paradise
- **Nickname** Golden State
- **Motto** Eureka! (I have found it)
- **Capital City** Sacramento
- **Population** 36.5 million
- **Area** 163,707 sq miles
- **Time Zone** Pacific
- **State Bird** California quail
- **State Flower** California poppy
- **Major Industry** Technology
- **Politics** Blue state in 2008
- **Best Time to Go** August to November – warm, dry 'Indian summer' days and vineyard grape harvests

HISTORY IN A NUTSHELL

When Spanish conquistador Juan Rodríguez Cabrillo sailed up in 1542, Native Americans were thriving. In 1769 the Spanish military returned to establish missions from San Diego to Sonoma. After Mexico won independence in 1821, Alta California was divided into land grants called ranchos. The USA assumed control in 1848, the same year gold was discovered at Sutter's Creek. California was soon flooded by miners and pioneer settlers, and in 1850 became the 31st state.

LANDSCAPE

California is larger than the UK. It straddles the San Andreas Fault, one of the world's major earthquake zones, and the north–south Sierra Nevada mountain range stretches for over 400 miles through the state's belly. Mount Whitney (14,495 feet) is the USA's highest non-Alaskan peak. Many of California's coastal areas enjoy a Mediterranean climate, while east of the Sierra Nevada lie arid deserts. Forested mountain areas, especially in the north, are snow-bound in winter, while the beaches of Southern California (SoCal) catch sunshine year-round.

NATURAL BEAUTY

Yosemite Valley is such a scenic treasure that it jump-started the national park system in the 19th century. California claims the largest known living trees (giant sequoias), the earth's oldest (bristlecone pines) and the tallest (redwoods). Marine life includes elephant seals and migratory whales. California lies along the Pacific Flyway, a prime spot for observing migratory birds. Endangered California condors still fly along the Big Sur Coast and at Pinnacles National Monument.

TRADEMARKS

- Hollywood
- Disneyland
- Beaches and surfing
- Golden Gate Bridge
- Vineyards and wineries
- Hippies
- Arnold Schwarzenegger (aka 'The Governator')

POINT BONITA POKES INTO THE PACIFIC APPROACHING FROM MARIN HEADLANDS ROAD. »

THE GOLD TEAM DISCUSSES STRATEGY AT MANHATTAN BEACH'S SURF FESTIVAL VOLLEYBALL TOURNAMENT. »

PEOPLE

California's population is ethnically diverse. One out of every four Californians was born outside the US, almost 40% speak a language other than English at home, and more than half have Asian or Latino ancestry. More Catholics live here than in any other state, and more Mormons reside here than anywhere else outside of Utah. California also has significant Jewish, Buddhist and Muslim communities. New-age belief systems vary, from neo-paganism to the controversial Church of Scientology.

CULTURE & TRADITIONS

Californians pride themselves on being health-conscious and environmentally aware. Smoking indoors in public is a no-no, recycling is the norm and more new hybrid cars are registered here than in any other US state. Socially speaking, Californians are a very relaxed bunch, influenced by the laid-back surf-and-sand beach lifestyle, and informality is the norm. According to locals, the biggest cultural divide is between SoCal and Northern California (NorCal). The former is still a bastion of movie stars but also an incubator for the arts, while the latter is more about Silicon Valley millionaires than hippies and beatniks these days.

DID YOU KNOW?

- Only one out of every four Californians has ever tried surfing.

- 63% of Californians admit to having hugged a tree.

- The highest temperature ever recorded in the Western Hemisphere was at Death Valley: 134°F (57°C) on July 10, 1913.

CALIFORNIA LEGEND

For one month during 1846, revolutionaries declared California an independent nation. After the US annexed Texas from Mexico, the Mexican government had issued orders to expel all foreigners from California. Some settlers revolted, taking over the Spanish colonial presidio (fort) in Sonoma and raising the Bear Flag. Although the new nation lasted only until the US declared war on Mexico, the state flag still proclaims California the 'bear flag republic.'

CUISINE

Fresh agricultural bounty – from fertile valleys, fruitful vineyards, orchards and the sea – puts local, organic and seasonal cooking first. An increasing number of ecoconscious 'locavores' eat only food that was grown within 100 miles of their homes. California's multicultural population means that anything might appear on dinner plates here – French cassoulet to Spanish paella, Moroccan stews to Burmese curry, Southern soul food to Oaxacan mole sauces. California is also the birthplace of the fast-food burger joint, a tradition carried out today by beloved In-N-Out Burger.

REPRESENTATIONS

- *My First Summer in the Sierra* (1911), by John Muir; inspirational nature narrative by pivotal California conservationist

- *Chinatown* (1974), directed by Roman Polanski

- *American Graffiti* (1973), directed by George Lucas

- *Dharma Bums* (1958), by Jack Kerouac; classic Beat Generation novel

- *Vertigo* (1958), directed by Alfred Hitchcock

- *The Graduate* (1967), directed by Mike Nichols

- David Hockney's 20th-century California modern paintings

- *Californication* (1999); introspective post-punk rock album by the Red Hot Chili Peppers

ECONOMY

If California were an independent country, its economy would rank as the eighth-largest in the world, comparable with Italy. Industry is comfortably diversified, led by high-tech and scientific research and development, followed by agriculture. Tourism and the media and entertainment industry are also economic pillars, and foreign trade with Asia, Europe, Mexico and Canada is an economic boon. Housing in this increasingly crowded state costs almost double the national norm, even though Californians' incomes are only 10% above the US average.

URBAN SCENE

California's truly great cities embrace the Pacific coast: surf-style San Diego, dating from 18th-century Spanish colonial times; metro Los Angeles, actually a mosaic of dozens of independent cities; and foggy, romantic San Francisco, a bohemian enclave north of high-tech Silicon Valley. Smaller coastal towns are made for lingering: Mediterranean-style Santa Barbara, with its red-tiled roofs and palm trees; wacky Santa Cruz, overrun with surfers and modern-day hippies; and Mendocino, a Victorian-era village set on dramatic rocky headlands.

TEXT SARA BENSON

ESSENTIAL EXPERIENCES

- Watching pro surfers battle monster waves at Mavericks, near Santa Cruz

- Cycling across San Francisco Bay on the Golden Gate Bridge

- Sipping and spitting in a Sonoma County winery

- Climbing Half Dome in Yosemite National Park

- Driving through a (still alive!) redwood tree

- Discovering what 'hot as hell' really means in Death Valley

⌃ SOMEONE'S GETTING A BELLYFUL AT LA TAQUERIA IN SAN FRANCISCO.

MAP REF // PAGE 4 D9

FILMMAKERS SHOT PART OF *STAR WARS* AT DEATH VALLEY'S OTHERWORLDLY MESQUITE SAND DUNES. »

NAPA VALLEY GRAPES – A FUTURE SMOOTH CHARDONNAY. »

IF A DUCK CAN GET A STAR ON HOLLYWOOD'S WALK OF FAME, MAYBE I'M NEXT. »

COLORADO

MORE THAN 300 DAYS OF SUNSHINE ILLUMINATE THIS RUGGED STATE, WHICH IS AN ADVENTURE TRAVELER'S DREAM, COMPLETE WITH ROCKY PEAKS, RAPID RIVERS AND SNOW SO FLUFFY THE LOCALS CALL IT CHAMPAGNE POWDER.

⌃ ASPEN TREES WATCH AS A MOUNTAIN-BIKE TEAM RACES BY.

- **Etymology of the State Name** Named after the Colorado ('color red' in Spanish) River
- **Nicknames** Centennial State, Colorful Colorado
- **Motto** *Nil sine numine* (Nothing without providence)

- **Capital City** Denver
- **Population** 4.9 million
- **Area** 104,100 sq miles
- **Time Zone** Mountain
- **State Bird** Lark bunting

- **State Flower** Rocky Mountain columbine
- **Major Industries** Tourism, tech and military
- **Politics** Swing state (blue in 2008)
- **Best Time to Go** June to August – best for wildflowers, hiking and rooftop beer drinking

HISTORY IN A NUTSHELL

People first moved into Colorado about 13,000 years ago. Plains Native Americans such as the Cheyenne and Arapahoe rumbled across the state's eastern Great Plains, while in the mountains, the Ute reigned supreme. Along the Colorado Plateau, the Pueblo people created their homes up in the rocks, most notably in cliff dwellings at Mesa Verde, now a National Park. A series of wars and treaties saw Colorado pass from US hands to Spanish and Mexican hands and back again. The state remained a frontier backwoods until 1858, when the discovery of gold along the South Platte River triggered the Pike's Peak Gold Rush. Colorado proved to be rich in mineral resources, and was rewarded with statehood in August 1876, the 38th state to join the Union. The state hosted the Democratic National Convention in 1908 and again in 2008.

LANDSCAPE

Most people think of Colorado as a lush land, but the majority of the state is actually semi-desert. Its signature topography is the Rocky Mountains, which stretch through the middle of the state in a studded spine of alpine lakes, 14,000-foot snow-crusted peaks (known locally as 14ers) and more pine and aspen trees than you could count in a lifetime. To the east, the Great Plains roll out like a big velvet carpet, while to the west, the Colorado Plateau is a harsh desert land highlighted by topsy-turvy towers, mesas and canyons.

REPRESENTATIONS

- *The Shining* (1980); Kubrick's version wasn't actually filmed here, but the Stanley Hotel in Estes Park apparently inspired Stephen King's novel
- *Cliffhanger* (1983) and *Dumb and Dumber* (1994); both partially filmed in Colorado's snow country
- *The Real World* (2006–07); the 18th season of MTV's 'reality' show took place in Denver
- Cowboy poetry

YOUNG COWBOYS SIZE UP THE COMPETITION AT A STEAMBOAT SPRINGS RODEO. »

CLIFF PALACE AT MESA VERDE, THE PUEBLO PEOPLE'S SKY-HIGH ANCESTRAL PUEBLOAN RUINS. »

NATURAL BEAUTY

Nature's never-ending game is played in vast open areas, where elk, moose, deer and buffalo pray to make it through the snowy winter, as large predators – coyote, lynx, mountain lion and bear – head out to hunt. This is also a place where wild horses run free, where the Black Canyon of the Gunnison cuts so deep into the earth it can be seen from space; where sand dunes pile up in the south and west, and entire mountainsides collapse to reveal their jagged granite interiors. And in wild protected areas like Rocky Mountain and Great Sand Dunes National Parks people witness the ebb and pull of these natural forces.

PEOPLE

There are growing numbers of Asian and African Americans in this ever-diversifying state. Hispanics and Hispanos (the descendants of early Spanish settlers) comprise the largest minority in the state. Just over 10% of Coloradans speak Spanish at home. It is also home to many evangelical groups, with more than 65% of the state's population claiming Christian affiliation. The second-largest city, Colorado Springs, is the home to many large conservative Christian organizations like Focus on the Family.

CUISINE

Nobody should leave the state without trying Rocky Mountain oysters (buffalo testicles). Other game dishes like deer and elk are also popular. Then of course there's the bevy of nationally recognized microbrews, such as New Belgian, Avery and Left Hand.

CULTURE & TRADITIONS

The frontier culture that forged this state from silver and gold continues today, and the people of Colorado are proud of their independent spirit. A Hispanic influence is seen throughout the state, and it's the only place you'll see bumper stickers that proudly proclaim 'native' status. Of course, this remains John Denver country: you can still head over to the stock show to buy a horse, and businessmen wear cowboy hats without a hint of irony. But who can complain when Coloradans are some of the healthiest people in the USA?

TRADEMARKS

- John Denver and his 'Rocky Mountain High'
- Champagne-powder skiing
- Coors beer and about a million microbrews
- Adventure sports
- Denver Broncos and The Rockies
- Norad (North American Aerospace Defense Command), the Air Force Academy

ECONOMY

Tourism makes up a big part of Colorado's economy, as do the high-tech and telecommunications industries, with companies like Google and Verizon setting up operations here. Throughout the state are signs of the feared military-industrial complex, seen at Peterson Air Force Base, at the Air Force Academy and at Fort Carson. There are also still farmers and ranchers, as well as a truckload of resources, from timber to minerals to oil, that cowboy-hatted folk are itching to get out of the ground.

URBAN SCENE

Denver is the state's only true urban center. It has a cosmopolitan scene and is becoming more sophisticated by the day. There are great public-art exhibits, along with theater, graffiti and even a handful of punks that won't give up on that whole break-dancing craze. College towns like Boulder and Fort Collins have good arts scenes, as do many of the smaller mountain towns.

DID YOU KNOW?

- Colorado's highest mountain is Mount Elbert (14,440 feet), and Denver, 'Mile High City,' is actually 5280 feet above sea level (though the mapmakers may have fudged 'just a little').
- Woody Allen's *Sleeper* was filmed in Colorado: you can still see the 'mushroom' house on I-70 but the 'orgasmatron' is no longer functional.

COLORADO LEGEND

One of the most famous survivors of the *Titanic*, the 'Unsinkable' Molly Brown, moved to Leadville, CO, at 18, pre-*Titanic* and back when everybody knew her as Margaret. Brown married a man who would make huge riches with the Ibex Mining Company and, with wealth and power behind her, became a champion of women's rights, education and historic preservation. Her legacy lives on in movies and musicals about her life. She was played by Kathy Bates in 1997's *Titanic*.

TEXT GREG BENCHWICK

ESSENTIAL EXPERIENCES

- Climbing a lung-busting '14er' like Long's Peak (for the smokers, there's always the cog railway that goes to the top of Pike's Peak outside Colorado Springs)
- Scrambling around ancient cliff dwellings at Mesa Verde National Park
- Charging off a cornice into knee-deep powder
- Rafting on the Arkansas River
- Having a Coors at a Colorado Rockies Baseball Game
- Wearing a cowboy hat to a rodeo (they'll never know you're from New Jersey)
- Hiking up to Crater Lake at the Maroon Bells near Aspen

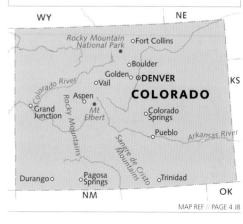

⌃ WILDFLOWERS CARPET THE GROUND TO MOUNT PRINCETON IN CHAFFEE COUNTY.

MAP REF // PAGE 4 J8

HIKERS FEEL THE BURN AS THEY TRAMP THROUGH GREAT SAND DUNES NATIONAL PARK. ⟰

JOHN HYDE // PHOTOLIBRARY

THE DENVER ART MUSEUM'S BOLD HAMILTON BUILDING EVOKES THE PEAKS OF THE ROCKY MOUNTAINS. ⟰

AN ICE CLIMBER PICKS THROUGH A GLISTENING CAVE. ⟰

CONNECTICUT

CONNECTICUT WEARS MANY FACES: FROM WEALTHY BEDROOM COMMUNITIES A STONE'S THROW FROM NEW YORK CITY, TO HISTORIC YANKEE SETTLEMENTS ALONG NEW ENGLAND'S MIGHTIEST RIVER, TO THE MULTICULTURAL CITIES OF NEW HAVEN AND HARTFORD.

≪ UNFURLING THE SAILS AT MYSTIC SEAPORT'S MARITIME MUSEUM.

- **Etymology of the State Name** From *quinnitukqut,* an Algonquian term meaning 'at the long tidal river'
- **Nicknames** The Constitution State, The Nutmeg State, Land of Steady Habits
- **Motto** *Qui transtulit sustinet* (He who transplanted still sustains)

- **Capital City** Hartford
- **Population** 3.5 million
- **Area** 5543 sq miles
- **Time Zone** Eastern
- **State Bird** Robin

- **State Flower** Mountain laurel
- **Major Industries** Insurance and financial services, manufacturing
- **Politics** Blue state in 2008
- **Best Time to Go** May to October – to appreciate Connecticut's lush greenery

HISTORY IN A NUTSHELL

Home to the Pequot and Mohegan tribes (both nearly wiped out in the 17th century), Connecticut made it onto European maps in 1614 when Adriaen Block sailed up the Connecticut River. In the 1630s religious refugees from Massachusetts settled along the river (including at Hartford and New Haven). Moves toward self-governance of these 'river towns' started in 1639 and culminated in the chartering of Connecticut Colony in 1662. Connecticut joined the Union on January 9, 1788, as the fifth state.

LANDSCAPE

The Connecticut River cuts the state roughly in half, emptying into Long Island Sound to the south. Aside from the lowlands adjoining the two waters, Connecticut's terrain is undulating, reaching its highest point at Mount Frissell (2379 feet, though the peak, in Massachusetts, is 2454 feet). The climate is temperate by Northeastern standards, with mean statewide temperatures of 70°F (21°C) in summer and 27°F (-3°C) in winter, cooler in the northwestern highlands and milder along the coast.

NATURAL BEAUTY

Connecticut's back roads, passing deciduous forests, farms and old stone walls, are among the prettiest in New England. The Housatonic River valley in northwestern Litchfield County is especially lovely, offering camping and outdoor recreation along the Appalachian Trail and in Housatonic Meadows State Park. Also appealing are the state parks of the lower Connecticut River valley, the Long Island Sound shoreline in southeastern Connecticut and the rolling farm country of the Quiet Corner in the northeast.

PEOPLE

Italian Americans constitute nearly one-fifth (18.6%) of the population, second only to Rhode Island. Irish Americans (16.6%), African Americans (10.2%) and Latinos (11.2%, especially Puerto Ricans) also figure prominently; cities such as Hartford and New Haven are particularly diverse. Protestants outnumber Catholics 48% to 34%, while about 3% of the population is Jewish.

GIRLS AT WESTOVER BOARDING SCHOOL TAKE PART IN A 'MOVING UP' CEREMONY. ⌃

IS THE NEXT NOBEL LAUREATE OR PULITZER PRIZE WINNER AMONG THESE YALE GRADS? ⌃

CULTURE & TRADITIONS

Nutmeggers (Connecticut residents) are reserved, but their more gregarious side is on show at community events like the annual Essex Shad Bake. This June tradition celebrates Connecticut's state fish by nailing hundreds of shad fillets secured with strips of pork onto oak planks, then roasting them around a bonfire.

TRADEMARKS

- Wealthy suburbs
- Preppies
- Martha Stewart
- Insurance companies
- Skull and Bones Society (based at Yale)

CUISINE

For a slice of culinary Connecticut, head to New Haven. The local Italian community is famous for *apizza* (ah-*beetz*), a thin-crusted brick oven–fired pizza best enjoyed with clams and garlicky white sauce. Another New Haven classic is Louis' Lunch Wagon, which claims to have invented the 'Hamburg steak sandwich' in 1900; it still serves burgers the old-fashioned way, broiled vertically in an ancient cast-iron stove and slapped between two slices of toast. Another everyday Connecticut treat is the hot Italian sandwich known as the 'grinder.'

ECONOMY

Connecticut has the USA's highest income per capita and third-highest median household income, but income distribution is widely skewed. Greenwich and other 'Gold Coast' towns are among the USA's richest communities, while just up the interstate, Hartford is one of the nation's poorest. Insurance and finance (think The Hartford!) are the cornerstones of Connecticut's white-collar economy, which got its start providing marine insurance in the 1700s. Precision metalworking, transportation, aerospace and military manufacturing are also important.

DID YOU KNOW?

- Frank Sinatra liked New Haven pizza so much that he often had it delivered to New York City, two hours away.
- Scoville Memorial Library (established 1803) in Salisbury was the first free public library in the USA.

URBAN SCENE

Bridgeport is Connecticut's largest city, but the state's most interesting urban scene is in New Haven, home to a wide-ranging mix of ethnic communities and cultural attractions, such as the Long Wharf and Schubert Theaters, the Peabody Museum of Natural History, and the Yale University Art Gallery and Yale Center for British Art. The capital city of Hartford is noteworthy for its historic Old State House, the former homes of Mark Twain and Harriet Beecher Stowe, and acclaimed arts venues, such as the Wadsworth Atheneum and Bushnell Performing Arts Center.

REPRESENTATIONS

- *Ah, Wilderness!* (1933); playwright Eugene O'Neill's comic re-imagining of his Connecticut adolescence
- *The Stepford Wives* (1972); Ira Levin's surreal horror tale of women turned to zombies in the fictional town of Stepford, CT, was twice adapted for the screen (1975 and 2004)
- *The Ice Storm* (1994); Rick Moody's tragicomic portrayal of dysfunctional family life in 1970s suburban Connecticut was filmed in 1997
- *Amistad* (1997); Steven Spielberg movie about a 19th-century slave mutiny and subsequent trial in Connecticut courts

CONNECTICUT LEGEND

The Charter Oak, seen on Connecticut's state quarter, was an ancient tree near Hartford, long prized by the Native Americans who timed the planting of corn to coincide with the development of its leaves. On Halloween 1687, the tree assumed legendary status for Connecticut colonists. The British, wanting to centralize control over New England under a single government in Boston, had decreed that the New England colonies were to 'make surrender of their Charter.' Connecticut governor Robert Treat, loath to give up the self-determination enjoyed for the past quarter-century, refused. British emissary Sir Edmund Andros came to Hartford backed by British troops and an assembly was convened to hand over the charter; but at the critical moment all the candles mysteriously blew out, allowing the colonists to spirit the charter away and hide it within the massive oak. Although the tree blew down in a violent storm in 1856, its legendary symbolism lives on.

TEXT GREGOR CLARK

ESSENTIAL EXPERIENCES

- Going eye to eye with sharks at the Mystic Aquarium
- Rafting down the Housatonic River or crossing it on the picturesque West Cornwall covered bridge
- Cruising past Goodspeed Opera House, Gillette Castle and other classic Connecticut River edifices aboard the Essex Steam Train and Riverboat
- Touring beautiful 17th-century Stonington and its lighthouse museum
- Enjoying a slice of pizza with white clam sauce on Wooster St, New Haven

MAP REF // PAGE 5 X5

« CANCAN ALONG TO THE GOODSPEED OPERA HOUSE, IN EAST HADDAM.

CADETS CELEBRATE COMMENCEMENT AT THE US COAST GUARD ACADEMY IN NEW LONDON. »

HEAVY ARTILLERY PROTECTS THE HALL OF FLAGS »
AT THE HARTFORD STATE CAPITOL.

TREES AROUND LAKE WARAMAUG GO OUT IN A BLAZE OF GLORY EACH FALL. »

DELAWARE

DELAWARE IS MAINLY KNOWN FOR BEING UNKNOWN BUT IT'S ALSO PRETTY AS A PICTURE, POSSESSING TWEE TOWNS, GOLDEN ATLANTIC COASTLINE AND A CULTURE THAT JUMBLES EASTERN SHORE DUCK HUNTERS AND CRAB TRAPPERS WITH CLASSIC BLUE COLLAR 'BURBS AND SOME OF THE USA'S OLDEST MONEY.

≫ A SUNNY BELT OF BEACHES BRUSHES DELAWARE'S EASTERN EDGE.

- **Etymology of the State Name** Named for Thomas West, the Baron de la Warr and governor of colonial Virginia
- **Nicknames** Small Wonder, First State
- **Motto** Liberty and independence
- **Capital City** Dover
- **Population** 864,760
- **Area** 2489 sq miles
- **Time Zone** Eastern
- **State Bird** Blue hen
- **State Flower** Peach blossom
- **Major Industries** Poultry, chemicals, military services
- **Politics** Blue state in 2008
- **Best Time to Go** May to June, September to October – temperate and comfortable

HISTORY IN A NUTSHELL

The Susquehanna and Lenni Lenape nations were the original inhabitants of the Delaware River watershed. While claimed by the British, the Dutch settled the area at Zwaanendael (Valley of the Swans), near modern-day Lewes, in 1631. That colony was wiped out by native peoples and replaced by Swedish settlers in 1638, who were then reconquered by the Dutch in 1655, which means this state and New York were the only two original colonies to be founded by non-Anglos. The British conquered in 1664, and Delaware's three counties became socially divided between the Tidewater South and small-farm-centric Pennsylvania. The colony was the first to ratify the Constitution.

Although founded as a slave state, Delaware remained in the Union during the Civil War. Its proximity to cities like Philadelphia – as well as a manufacturing economy underlaid by the resident DuPont family – kept the state within the Northeast economic orbit. Today its main industry is being a corporate tax shelter.

LANDSCAPE

Delaware runs between shaggy fields, groves of Loblolly pine and brackish wetlands. The coast is typically marshy, but widens into a sunny belt of beach in Sussex County. The state's center and north are peppered with small towns, suburban subdivisions and the well-groomed manors of the Brandywine Valley.

NATURAL BEAUTY

Delaware Seashore State Park is a genuinely wild, windy spit of wave-tossed coastline, while the wetlands near Route 9 (including Thousand Acre Marsh) are long, low and lovely. Much of the aesthetic value of the state is wrapped up in its small towns and preserved countryside.

TRADEMARKS

- Vice President Joe Biden
- Tax haven
- Mid-Atlantic beach resorts
- Horseshoe crabs

A FIELD PLANTED IN STYLISH CORNROWS. ⌃

PEOPLE

Little Delaware has a little of everything: tidewater farmers and fisherfolk, pockets of Jews and West Indies immigrants in Wilmington, African Americans (both Southern country and East Coast urban) throughout, a white, black and brown working class tied to cities like Philadelphia, military families near Dover, the old money aristocracy of the Brandywine Valley and subdivided suburban USA everywhere.

CULTURE & TRADITIONS

Delaware is a typical mid-Atlantic soup that's heavily spiced by Philadelphia. Cheesesteaks and pizza are popular, but so is Nascar and swimmin' in the crik. Beach towns like Rehoboth somehow jumble Philly working-class gruff and Dale Earnhardt tees with Confederate flags and an older gay party scene that pulls in DC policy wonks and middle-aged art gallery enthusiasts. The state fair, held in July, showcases the many faces of the Small Wonder.

ECONOMY

Farming (specifically of chickens) was once the state's backbone and is still a bedrock of rural Delawarean identity, but today the Small Wonder is a big tax haven. Because Delaware exempts non-state subsidiaries from income taxes, it houses the 'headquarters' of more than half the USA's corporations (ie they keep a

Delaware address for tax purposes and operate elsewhere). The state makes money via franchise taxes, and supports large chemical and pharmaceutical interests, most famously DuPont. Per capita income is above the national average and is usually close to being in the top 10 states in the country.

CUISINE

Chicken is big – unsurprising, given the importance of the poultry industry. A heavy, Southern-influenced flavor predominates in rural Delaware, and horseshoe crabs are as prized here as they are in nearby Maryland. In the cities ethnic cuisine dominates, and Northeast favorites such as subs, wings, deli and pizza prevail.

DID YOU KNOW?

○ Delaware became the first state to ratify the Constitution, on December 7, 1787.

○ The first steam railroad in the country originated in New Castle in 1831.

URBAN SCENE

Wilmington is the only big city around; it's working-class with a backbone of citizenry whose roots go back multiple generations, plus new immigrants carving out a piece of the American Dream. Delaware's largest city has a

small, loyal arts scene, great dining for a 'burg of its size and the dignity to forego a chip on its shoulder despite – or perhaps, because of – the fact that it is the most ignored major city in the Northeast corridor. Dover, on the other hand, is a typical small state capital: trimmed, provincial and obsessed with the political horse trading that goes on in its back rooms.

REPRESENTATIONS

○ *Dead Poets Society* (1989); although set in Vermont, the quintessential US prep school movie was filmed in St Andrew's School in Middletown, DE

○ *Tales of the Chesapeake* (1880); an excellent collection of poems and stories from Delaware and the Eastern Shore, compiled by Delawarean George Alfred Townsend (one of the most prolific journalists of the 19th century)

○ Wilmington native George Thorogood and the Destroyers (formerly the Delaware Destroyers)

DELAWARE LEGEND

The blue hen, the state bird, was the mascot of the Delaware regiment during the American Revolution. The regiment was commanded by John Caldwell, an avid gamecock fighter who preferred the blue hen breed, which originated in Kent County. The regiment gained a tough fighting reputation during the war, and its avian emblem has been a state icon ever since.

TEXT ADAM KARLIN

MARK NEWMAN // LONELY PLANET IMAGES

⌃ LOOK WHO'S COMING TO DINNER: HORSESHOE CRABS INVADE DELAWARE'S SHORES EACH YEAR.

80/81 | THE USA BOOK

ESSENTIAL EXPERIENCES

○ Attending an art gallery opening, monster truck rally and bachelorette night in one evening in Delaware's beach resorts

○ Getting Jamaican takeaway in one of Wilmington's many Caribbean cafés

○ Driving through the rolling countryside of Sussex County

○ Antique shopping and colonial 'fayre' in New Castle

○ Visiting Winterthur, the grand estate of the DuPont family

○ Catching the Cape May ferry from Lewes

○ Realizing Delaware is actually kind of cool

MAP REF // PAGE 5 W6

FLAG PAINTING CAN BECOME ADDICTIVE. ≫

ODDS ARE THAT'S ONE LIMBER JOCKEY HORSE RACING AT WILMINGTON. ≫

FLORIDA

WELCOME TO FLORIDA: HOME TO SUN, CUBANS, PANTHERS, DISNEY WORLD, NASA, CITRUS, ALLIGATORS, THE SEMINOLES (THE PEOPLE) AND THE SEMINOLES (THE FLORIDA STATE UNIVERSITY TEAM), THE HURRICANES (THE MIAMI UNIVERSITY TEAM) AND THE HURRICANES (THE NATURAL DISASTERS), AND AN EMERALD NECKLACE OF OVER 100 KEYS.

≈ FLORIDA'S SHORES OFFER MANY SPOTS GORGEOUS ENOUGH TO BELONG ON A DESERTED ISLAND.

○ **Etymology of the State Name** From the Spanish *pascal florida* (feast of flowers), a reference to the Easter season when conquistadors landed here

○ **Nickname** Sunshine State

○ **Motto** In God we trust

○ **Capital City** Tallahassee

○ **Population** 18.3 million

○ **Area** 65,758 sq miles

○ **Time Zone** Eastern, Central

○ **State Bird** Mockingbird

○ **State Flower** Orange blossom

○ **Major Industries** Tourism, agriculture, aerospace, phosphate mining

○ **Politics** Swing state (blue in 2008)

○ **Best Time to Go** March to May – get the best weather but avoid the crowds

HISTORY IN A NUTSHELL

Massachusetts, Virginia – pah! Florida is the site of North America's oldest permanent European settlement: St Augustine was founded by Spanish conquistadors in 1565. Settlements of black slaves may even pre-date St Augustine; these refugees generally married into local native communities. From the 16th to 18th centuries Florida was contested between Britain, Spain, France and, later, the new USA, whose settlers found and eventually conquered local Native Americans and escaped slaves. Florida grew into a Southern agricultural state, but by the 20th century the sunny peninsula was turning to tourism. Today Florida is considered a Pan-American mosaic, although this reflects merely a change of perception, rather than identity – this state has always been a melting pot of the Americas.

LANDSCAPE

Florida is flat: Britton Hill (345 feet) is the lowest of all the state 'high points' in the USA. Moving south, the terrain shifts from wiry Southern pineland into a scrubby, sub-tropical plain studded with palm trees, which stretches to the Everglades, a prairie of grass constantly flooded by overflow from the Kissimmee River basin. Golden beaches edge the blue Atlantic and teal Gulf of Mexico, and ringing the bottom of the state are the mangrove-and-sandbar spits of the Florida Keys, which terminate just 90 miles from Havana, Cuba.

NATURAL BEAUTY

A drive down the Overseas Hwy, which overlays the Florida Keys, is the American road trip evolved into tropical, ocean-lined perfection. Florida's beaches are beautiful, but the state reaches natural nirvana in the Everglades, where the entire matrix of nature, from food chain to water cycle, is put on display in a fuzzy grassland cut by black rivers, white cypress, dark alligators and thunderclouds of birdlife. The slow-moving manatee, or sea cow, is something of a state mascot, best spotted in Crystal River National Wildlife Refuge.

HOT WHEELS FOR CRUISING THE WATERFRONT. »

PEOPLE

Florida's population, the fourth biggest in the nation, isn't easily pigeonholed. North Florida is the American South and its associated demographics, but South Florida is a Latin-Caribbean-American festival. And everything mixes; in cities such as Hialeah over 90% of the population speaks Spanish as a first language, but 20 minutes away there'll be Confederate flags flying proudly over the Tamiami Trail.

CULTURE & TRADITIONS

Voodoo botanicas that sell Haitian 'dragon's blood' sit minutes from BBQ shacks and jai alai courts in Florida. But the Disney World state is essentially the great homogenizer. While cities like Miami have their Little Havanas, the sun here seems to bake everyone into a certain mould – more Dixie up north and more yuppie-integrated down south, but distinctly Florida throughout. Coworkers are comfy with rice and plantains but just as happy with the Publix deli; Cuban girls act like US-born mallrats; and blonde Anglos drop Spanish slang with a Matanzas' accent.

CUISINE

North Florida eats Dixie cuisine of the Georgia/Gulf Coast variety: Brunswick stew, vinegar BBQ and fried anything. South Florida has given the world Floribbean food: mango salsa, tilapia with dirty rice, and pork slow cooked in orange juice. This is a culinary expression of the region's demographics, which also includes Jewish deli, Argentine *parilla* and Cuban sandwiches.

TRADEMARKS

○ Disney World

○ Miami art deco

○ The Everglades and the Keys

○ Citrus

○ The 'Fins, the 'Bucs, the 'Canes, the Rays, the 'Noles and the 'Gators

○ Alligators

○ Retirees

○ Manatees

ECONOMY

NASA supports an enormous aerospace industry, the Bone Valley mines a quarter of the world's phosphate, 40% of all Latin America–bound exports pass through the state and Florida harvests 67% of the USA's citrus crop. But it's tourism that is the backbone of the state economy, with some 60 million visitors a year.

URBAN SCENE

Jacksonville is the largest city in the state, but Miami, with half the population, is by far the most interesting. Florida's only global city is the most mixed Latin and Caribbean entrepôt in the USA, and if you stay away from South Beach, it's a surprisingly unpretentious one too. Cities like Fort Lauderdale and Tampa are reminiscent of Southern California overlaid with Old Florida – malls and Botox alongside colonial Spanish villas – while the aforementioned Jacksonville is a mass of sprawling sun-belt development and high-rises.

REPRESENTATIONS

○ *Scarface* (1987); this gangster epic shines a dark light on the immigrant experience in South Florida and Miami's (and the USA's) culture of excess

○ *The Birdcage* (1996); portrays the sunny side of Miami Beach in all its wacky, endearing diversity: Jewish boy with gay parents, cross-dressing Guatemalans, that sort of thing

○ Anything by Carl Hiaasen and Edna Buchanan, authors and journalists who love their state so much they've made careers out of exposing everything insane about it

DID YOU KNOW?

○ Suntan cream was invented in Miami Beach in 1944.

○ Frost has never been reported in the Florida Keys (although it did snow in Miami Beach in 1977).

○ The state has the highest average precipitation in America.

FLORIDA MYTH

Spanish explorer and conquistador Juan Ponce De León was the first European to set foot in Florida, supposedly while searching for the fountain of youth. More likely, De Leon was searching for gold and territory to add to the Spanish empire.

TEXT ADAM KARLIN

⤢ IT'S A LONG WAY DOWN TO THE FLORIDA KEYS AND LAID-BACK ISLANDS LIKE UPPER MATECUMBE.

MAP REF // PAGE 5 V14

ALLIGATORS TAKE A POST-LUNCH NAP IN EVERGLADES NATIONAL PARK. ⩘

MEN IN LITTLE HAVANA, MIAMI, CLACK DOMINOES. ⩘

EVEN THE LIFEGUARD TOWERS ARE FASHIONABLY ART DECO IN MIAMI. ⩘

GEORGIA

WHAT KEEPS GEORGIA ON MY MIND? IT MUST BE THE SWEET SMELL OF PEACHES, THE ARISTOCRATIC AIR OF SAVANNAH MANSIONS, THE BUZZ OF BIG-CITY ATLANTA AND THE WILD AND SANDY DUNES OF THE BARRIER ISLANDS.

⌃ LADIES WEAR HATS IN GENTEEL SAVANNAH (DOUBLE POINTS IF THEY'RE PEACH COLORED).

- **Etymology of the State Name** Named in honor of King George II of England
- **Nickname** Peach State
- **Motto** Wisdom, justice and moderation
- **Capital City** Atlanta

- **Population** 9.5 million
- **Area** 59,441 sq miles
- **Time Zone** Eastern
- **State Bird** Brown thrasher
- **State Flower** Cherokee rose

- **Major Industries** Food and agriculture, textiles, timber
- **Politics** Red state in 2008
- **Best Time to Go** April, May, October – tourism drops off and the weather is mild

HISTORY IN A NUTSHELL

The last of the original 13 colonies, English settlement in this area dates to 1733; Georgia became the fourth state to join the union, in 1788. During the Civil War, Union General Sherman marched to the sea through this Confederate state, burning everything in his path – including Atlanta – but saving Savannah on Christmas Eve. Post-emancipation, racial discrimination became the norm. It wasn't until native son Martin Luther King Jr led marches and rallies in the 1960s that Civil Rights legislation was enacted in Georgia in 1965. Farming and textile production continue today, but at much lower levels than they once did.

LANDSCAPE

The coastal plains are dotted with marshlands and tidal rivers; Okefenokee Swamp, on the Florida border, is the largest freshwater wetland habitat in the USA. Ocean currents and stormy Atlantic seas have contributed to the development of a string of barrier islands filled with sand dunes and sea oats. Inland, to the north, the mountains belong to the Cumberland and Blue Ridge ranges. In general, Georgia's temperate climate averages no more than 88°F (31°C) in July and hovers above freezing in January.

NATURAL BEAUTY

Nearly 80 miles of the Appalachian Trail wind through the rugged north Georgia mountains, past waterfalls and through second growth forests – at elevations between 2500 and 4400 feet. And then there's the 100 miles of Atlantic coastline to explore. In addition to white sand beaches, Cumberland Island National Seashore, on the southernmost of the barrier islands, protects maritime forests, marshlands and a herd of wild horses that numbers around 300.

TRADEMARKS

- Coca-Cola and peaches
- The Georgia Bulldogs and Atlanta Braves
- Jimmy Carter and peanut farming
- Martin Luther King Jr

TRAVERSING GEORGIA'S BEACHES BY BICYCLE ON A SUNNY AFTERNOON.

PEOPLE

Original settlers were of Scots-English decent and the population in the rural inland areas of the state still reflects that heritage, though a 65% white population is spread across the state. On the coast there's a mix, with many of the 30% of residents that are of African American heritage living there or in the cities. Georgia is part of the Southern Bible Belt and a whopping 86% of the population claims Christian affiliation.

CULTURE & TRADITIONS

Genteel Southern manners and football obsession are two of the stereotypes associated with Georgians, and rightly so. Add a passion for God and you have a pretty good overview. Atlanta's big-city, big-business hustle is in stark contrast to Savannah's slow Southern charm. A close association with the land reflects rural roots and is still evident in the popularity of hiking and bicycling in the mountains or on the coast. Come fall, hunting season is in full swing, and fishing goes on all year long.

REPRESENTATIONS

○ *Gone With the Wind* (1939); Rhett Butler (Clark Gable) and Scarlett O'Hara (Vivien Leigh) defined not only Georgia plantation life, but all of the Civil War South for filmgoers

○ *Midnight in the Garden of Good and Evil* (1997); John Berendt's book (and the subsequent movie) exposed Savannah's eccentric wealthy society; based on the true story of a male hustler's shooting death and the trial of an internationally known antiques dealer

○ *The Color Purple* (1982); Alice Walker's best-selling book chronicles the struggle of a poor African American girl in rural Georgia

○ Author Flannery O'Connor's short stories reflect her Catholic background and Georgia upbringing

ECONOMY

Rice and cotton first brought Georgia wealth, but today pecans, peaches and peanuts make up more of the agricultural output. Timber harvests and textile production continue to be major economic players, but technology and business are taking on increasing roles as Atlanta expands. Coca-Cola is probably the most visible of the home state manufacturer headquarters. Georgia's median household income is $42,679.

URBAN SCENE

Atlanta, often called the capital of the South, is a flashy, multicultural city with top-notch restaurants and postmodern buildings such as Michael Grave's 10 Peachtree Place. The colossal Georgia Aquarium, the largest in the world, draws tourists, as does the glitzy World of Coca-Cola entertainment complex–museum. Graceful Savannah is set apart by 21 central squares filled with flowering gardens, fountains, trees and monuments. The antebellum architecture and genteel manors conceal a more sinful side; think of the city as a pint-sized New Orleans.

DID YOU KNOW?

○ Coca-Cola was first sold to the public at Jacob's Pharmacy soda fountain in Atlanta in 1886; and yes, it contained traces of cocaine until the early 1900s.

○ The Washington Oak in St Mary's, GA, is the remaining of four trees planted the day George Washington was buried, in 1799.

CUISINE

Georgian food shares much with the rest of the southeast: fried chicken, hoecakes (pancakelike cornbread), okra and greens, boiled peanuts. Brunswick, GA, prides itself on being the originator of Brunswick stew, a much-enjoyed, hearty concoction of meat (chicken, beef, pork or all three; note that at one time squirrel was used) and vegetables with a large helping of hominy. Crab stew, crab shacks and shrimp-and-crab boils are part of the beach communities of the Lowcountry. And don't forget the peaches – peach pie, peach cobbler, peach tea, peach everything.

GEORGIA MYTH

An enduring, but false, legend has it that the state was founded by convicts. Trustee of the original settlement, James Edward Oglethorpe did plan to populate the colony with the less-advantaged recently released from debtors' prison, plus those fleeing Protestant persecution. Lofty goals were overridden, however, by the need for farmers, merchants and soldiers to be among the first 5500 to arrive.

TEXT LISA DUNFORD

ESSENTIAL EXPERIENCES

○ Wandering historic Savannah streets

○ Sleeping on a platform above the water during a multiday canoe trip on the Okefenokee Swamp

○ Watching in hushed silence during the Masters tournament at Augusta National Golf Course

○ Digging into a succulent peach cobbler made in season (mid-July to early August)

○ Hiking a section of the Appalachian Trail

○ Bellying up to a big pile of shellfish, mallet in hand, at an island crab shack

○ Catching a laser light show at Atlanta's Stone Mountain Park

⌃ AN ANGEL SCULPTURE IN THE GARDEN OF GOOD AND EVIL: BONAVENTURE CEMETERY IN SAVANNAH.

Biedenharn Candy Co.
Vicksburg, Mississippi

Birmingham, Al

PEACHES AWAIT THEIR FATE AS A SWEET PIE FILLING. »

VINTAGE BOTTLES AT ATLANTA'S WORLD OF COCA-COLA MUSEUM. »

CYPRESS TREES REFLECTED IN THE MIRRORED WATERS OF OKEFENOKEE SWAMP. »

HAWAII

OFTEN MYTHOLOGIZED BY FOREIGNERS' EXOTIC TALL TALES, THE POLYNESIAN ISLANDS OF HAWAII ARE UNLIKE ANYWHERE ON THE US MAINLAND: ROOTED DEEPLY IN ANCIENT TRADITIONS AND BELIEFS, THIS MODERN MULTI-ETHNIC SOCIETY IS WHERE EAST AND WEST TRULY SHAKE HANDS.

≫ SHARKS COVE SURF SHOP ON OAHU BLENDS IN WITH ITS BLUE AND GREEN SURROUNDS.

- **Etymology of the State Name** Polynesian, possibly meaning 'homeland'
- **Nickname** Aloha State
- **Motto** *Ua mau ke ea o ka 'āina i ka pono* (The life of the land is perpetuated in righteousness)

- **Capital City** Honolulu
- **Population** 1.3 million
- **Area** 10,932 sq miles
- **Time Zone** Hawaii–Aleutian Standard
- **State Bird** Nēnē (Hawaiian goose)

- **State Flower** Native yellow hibiscus
- **Major Industry** Tourism
- **Politics** Blue state in 2008
- **Best Time to Go** September to October – calmer ocean waters, little rain, fewer tourists

HISTORY IN A NUTSHELL

Before AD 1000, seafaring voyagers from Polynesia arrived in outrigger canoes using only the sun, stars, wind and wave patterns to navigate by. The first European to visit was Captain Cook, christening the islands the Sandwich Isles in 1778. After a bloody 20-year campaign, Kamehameha the Great united the Hawaiian Islands into one kingdom in 1819; his monarchy survived Christian missionaries, whaling ships and rising European and Asian immigration, though Queen Lili'uokalani was deposed by a conglomeration of sugar plantation interests in 1893. The new republic became a US territory in 1900 and, though it played a pivotal role during WWII, was not admitted as the 50th state until 1959.

LANDSCAPE

The world's longest island chain, Hawaii stretches 2200 miles across the Pacific. Its more than 130 islands and eroded atolls were formed by volcanoes, with active lava still flowing on the Big Island of Hawai'i today. The main islands, which make up over 99% of the state's total land mass, are Hawai'i, Maui, O'ahu, Kaua'i, Moloka'i, Lāna'i, Ni'ihau and uninhabited Kaho'olawe. Hawaii's climate is tropically hot and humid, although cooling trade winds blow year-round. Winter brings more rainstorms and bigger ocean waves.

NATURAL BEAUTY

Bountiful beaches call to swimmers and surfers, while snorkelers and scuba divers explore underwater volcanoes and coral reefs. Hikers amble through bamboo forests to waterfalls, traverse beautifully eroded *pali* (cliffs) and scale volcanoes. Hawaii's geographic isolation is responsible for its stunning biodiversity, with 10,000 endemic and unique species of flora and fauna.

TRADEMARKS

- Beaches and surfing
- Flower lei
- Hula dancing
- Luaus
- Mai tais
- Outrigger canoes

WATER FALLS FROM THE REALM OF THE GODS IN IAO VALLEY STATE PARK, MAUI.

PEOPLE

Identity is a complex issue for state residents. The term 'Hawaiian' refers only to those of Native Hawaiian ancestry, which includes one in every 10 people in Hawaii. Regardless of race, anyone who grew up in the islands and lives there is considered 'local.' Caucasians may be called *haole,* while those of mixed ancestry are *hapa.* Almost 40% of residents share at least some Asian heritage. You'll find Buddhist temples, Protestant and Catholic churches, and ancient Hawaiian *heiau* (temples) on each main island.

REPRESENTATIONS

- ○ *Ki'i* carvings made from tropical hardwoods
- ○ *Six Months in the Sandwich Islands* (1875); Isabella Bird's account of traveling in 19th-century Hawaii
- ○ 'Aloha 'Oe' ('Farewell to Thee'); a song composed by Queen Lili'uokalani
- ○ Volcano School of landscape painting
- ○ *From Here to Eternity* (1953), directed by Fred Zinnemann
- ○ 'Hawaii '78' (1978) as recorded by the Makaha Sons of Ni'ihau with Israel 'Bruddah Iz' Kamakawiwo'ole
- ○ *Shark Dialogues* (1995), a novel by Kiana Davenport

CULTURE & TRADITIONS

Many ancient Hawaiian practices were suppressed by 19th-century Christian missionaries. Since the 1970s, the islands have experienced a cultural renaissance, including of traditional arts like hula dancing and long-distance wayfaring (navigation) by outrigger canoe. More people are learning the Hawaiian language, with a growing number of immersion schools. Renewed pride in island identity has also led to a fragmented but influential Hawaiian sovereignty movement. Currently the federal government doesn't recognize Native Hawaiians as an indigenous people.

CUISINE

Traditional Hawaiian food features many of the staples and specialties brought by the first Polynesians, including *poi,* a sticky paste made of pounded *kalo* (taro) root; *niu* (coconut); and pigs, often roasted in an underground oven called an *imu.* Most representative of contemporary island cooking is a 'mixed plate' lunch, featuring 'two-scoop rice,' macaroni salad and a meat or seafood dish, such as teriyaki chicken or *kalbi* short ribs, from one of the islands' many ethnic groups. *Poke* (raw, marinated fish) and *saimin* (noodle soup) are also popular dishes. Hawaii Regional Cuisine is a medley of Eurasian fusion and Pacific Rim tastes featuring island produce. Hawaii is the only US state to grow coffee, most famously in Kona on the Big Island. *'Awa* (kava) is a mildly intoxicating ancient Polynesian brew.

ECONOMY

Despite attempts at diversification, Hawaii's economy remains rooted in tourism. Prior to WWII and the arrival of passenger jets, the islands ran on a plantation economy, exporting sugar cane, pineapples and coffee to the US mainland and abroad. Today agriculture takes second place to the development of tourism infrastructure (resort hotels, golf courses etc). The cost of living averages 30% higher than on the mainland and housing prices are more than double, even though most employment consists of minimum-wage hospitality jobs.

URBAN SCENE

Hawaii's capital, Honolulu, is on the island of O'ahu, aka 'The Gathering Place.' Its vibrant Chinatown is crammed with noodle shops, produce markets, antique stores and art galleries. Dignified 19th-century buildings like missionary churches, sugar-plantation offices and Hawaii's royal palace (the only one in the USA) stand beside modern high-rises downtown. On the Neighbor Islands, the old whaling port of Lahaina on Maui and sugar plantation–era Hilo, on the Big Island, offer more glimpses of Hawaii's past.

DID YOU KNOW?

- ○ Hawaii leads the nation in SPAM (tinned meat) consumption per capita – nearly 7 million cans are sold annually.
- ○ Surfing was invented in Hawaii, where it was the favorite sport of *ali'i* (royalty).
- ○ The Hawaiian archipelago is Earth's most remote and isolated land mass.

HAWAII MYTH

Pele, the Hawaiian goddess of fire and volcanoes, makes her home at Halema'uma'u Crater, inside the Big Island's Kīlauea volcano. According to tradition, she is responsible for the fiery eruptions and lava flows that both create and destroy the Hawaiian Islands.

TEXT SARA BENSON

ESSENTIAL EXPERIENCES

- ○ Paddling a surfboard off Waikiki Beach
- ○ Pondering WWII history at the USS *Arizona* Memorial
- ○ Watching fiery lava hiss and steam as it flows into the ocean on the Big Island
- ○ Driving Maui's serpentine, waterfall-strewn road to Hana
- ○ Trekking along Kaua'i's arrestingly beautiful Nā Pali cliffs
- ○ Maneuvering 4WD Jeep roads to windswept shipwreck beaches on Lāna'i

ANN CECIL // LONELY PLANET IMAGES

⌃ A RAINBOW OF SHAVE ICE OFFERS A SWEET WAY TO BEAT THE HEAT.

KAUA'I
Lihue
NI'IHAU   Hale'iwa   O'AHU
HONOLULU   MOLOKA'I
                 Lahaina MAUI
      LĀNA'I   Hana
KAHO'OLAWE   Kihei
PACIFIC
OCEAN   Mauna Kea
                      (13,796ft) Hilo
                      Mauna Loa
                      (13,677ft)
         HAWAI'I
         (The Big Island)

MAP REF // PAGE 4 H15

A LOCAL SHOWS OFF HIS WARES AT A FARMERS MARKET. ≪

AN IRIDESCENT WAVE BREAKS ON O'AHU'S NORTH SHORE. ≪

LAVA FLOWS FROM KILAUEA VOLCANO, ON HAWAI'I (THE BIG ISLAND). ≪

IDAHO

TIME STANDS FOREVER FROZEN IN A STATE INFUSED WITH A REMARKABLE HISTORY, EVOCATIVE PLAINS AND SUN-KISSED MOUNTAIN RESORTS – AND, OF COURSE, MORE POTATOES THAN YOU'LL SEE IN YOUR LIFETIME.

≈ COWBOYS PREPARE TO KICK BUTT WITH FANCY SPURS.

- **Etymology of the State Name** The origins are shaky at best, but it may be derived from the Shoshone for 'gem of the mountains'
- **Nicknames** Gem State, Spud State
- **Motto** *Esto perpetua* (Let it be forever)
- **Capital City** Boise
- **Population** 1.5 million
- **Area** 83,574 sq miles
- **Time Zones** Pacific, Mountain
- **State Bird** Mountain Bluebird
- **State Flower** Syringa
- **Major Industries** High-tech, farming, manufacturing, mining, tourism
- **Politics** Red state in 2008
- **Best Time to Go** Winter

HISTORY IN A NUTSHELL

Some of North America's oldest artifacts have been found in Idaho, and archaeologists believe this region may have been settled as far back as 14,500 years ago. The major tribes were the Nez Percé (Mimíipuu) and Coeur d'Alene in the north and the Shoshone and Bannock in the south. Gold was discovered here in 1860, which kicked off stampedes of colonists and, of course, wars with the Native Americans, which the latter eventually lost. The territory gained statehood in 1890, the 43rd star on the US flag. In the later part of the 20th century, a sizable group of white supremacists and neo-Nazis moved into Idaho's northern panhandle. They are slowly losing momentum.

LANDSCAPE

This Rocky Mountain state has a rippled and rugged topography, an astounding density of lakes and some of the West's fastest rivers, including the Salmon, Snake, Clearwater and Clark Fork. It also boasts Hells Canyon, the deepest canyon in the USA, and Shoshone Falls, which is actually higher than Niagara Falls. And, after all these dramatic landmarks, there are, of course, miles upon miles of high plains, perfect for growing the state's signature crop, the potato.

NATURAL BEAUTY

While Idaho's mountains are quite beautiful, especially near the central resorts of Sun Valley and Ketchum, it's really that big void of space, wind, earth and horizon that is the state's most evocative feature. And there's a lot of space out there. Idaho has more national forests and wilderness areas than anywhere else in the continental USA (only Alaska has more), areas that are filled with chartreuse river valleys, arching mountain sides and those big vistas that extend till the end of time.

PEOPLE

This starched-white state is about 90% Caucasian. The only sizable minorities are Hispanics and Native Americans, who make up about a combined 10% of the population. A large portion of the population identify themselves as Protestants or Mormons.

FARMING AT THE FOOT OF THE MOUNTAINS BY BELLEVUE. »

A SNOWBOARDER SHREDS THE SLOPES IN SUN VALLEY. »

CULTURE & TRADITIONS

The small towns that make up the Idaho heartland largely embrace 'traditional American values' – family, God and apple pie – and life centers around the plow and pulpit. But in larger cities like Boise and some of the funkier mountain communities, voices of dissent are rising, and you'll still find plenty of liberals in a state that's voted Republican in presidential elections since 1964. Farming traditions mean bake offs, the county fair and square dancing, while resort communities like Sun Valley and Ketchum have a more cosmopolitan feel. Native American traditions continue to this day, with sweat lodges, powwows and large reservations, plus a few casinos.

TRADEMARKS

o Potatoes

o Neo-Nazis in some pockets

o Glitzy Sun Valley part-timers like Demi Moore, Bruce Willis and Ashton Kutcher

o White water

o Bluebird ski days – when a foot of fresh powder is met at dawn by a bright sunny day

URBAN SCENE

Boise is the big boy in town with funked-out coffee shops, and galleries and theaters aplenty, but a few other towns dappled throughout the state are noteworthy. Idaho Falls is the cultural crossroads of the eastern part of the state, and has a couple of theaters and museums. Pocatello is home to Idaho State University and has all the trappings of a small university town. And then there are mountain-town standouts like Ketchum and Sun Valley, where the culture – and glitterati – come for winter amusement.

ECONOMY

Though potato farming and manufacturing are still significant earners, the big mover today is the science and technology field, which accounts for more than 25% of the state's total revenue. It's not a rich state, though; the average income per capita hovers around $26,000.

REPRESENTATIONS

o *Napoleon Dynamite* (2004); set and filmed in eastern Idaho – sweet

o The Ernest Hemingway Festival is held in late September in Ketchum to honor this prodigal American writer, who wrote some of the best US novels before killing himself with a shotgun in his Ketchum home

o *My Own Private Idaho* (1991); sleeper hit film starring Keanu Reeves and River Phoenix, based very loosely on Shakespeare's Henry IV, Part I

o 'Private Idaho' (1980); the B-52s' very fine 'mod-fi' pop song, which inspired the film's title

CUISINE

On the menu are potatoes au gratin and potato salad, baked potatoes and potato skins. But Idaho does think beyond the spud, with traditional ethnic foods like Finnish Lobinmuhennos, a salmon chowder; Welsh *bara brith*, a raisin and currant bread; and Basque lamb and split-pea soup. For dessert there's Idaho's world-famous huckleberry pie.

DID YOU KNOW?

o A Presbyterian missionary, Henry Harmon Spalding, first planted potatoes here in 1836. He'd brought the spuds with him to teach the Nez Percé a bit about agriculture. Today it's the state vegetable, and one-third of US potatoes come from here.

o Nez Percé comes from the French for 'pierced nose,' but most historians agree the name is incorrect – the true Nez Percé were a piercing-bedecked tribe downriver.

IDAHO LEGEND

The Nez Percé were among the last Native American tribes to surrender to United States forces. Under the brilliant leadership of Chief Joseph, this nation, which originally called Idaho, Oregon and Washington home, finally surrendered on October 5, 1877, in northern Montana. Upon surrendering Chief Joseph uttered the famous words: 'Hear me, my chiefs. I am tired. My heart is sick and sad. From where the sun now stands, I will fight no more forever.' Years after the battle cries died out, the Nez Perce National Historic Trail follows the tribe's retreat through Idaho and into Montana.

TEXT GREG BENCHWICK

ESSENTIAL EXPERIENCES

o Heading out into the cold and blue to make some turns at one of North America's preeminent ski resorts, Sun Valley

o Holding your breath as you pass through a wall of white water on the Salmon River

o Discovering your 'own private Idaho' over a steaming cup of coffee in a cozy coffee shop/bookstore in Boise

o Losing yourself in the dark depths of the USA's deepest rift at Hells Canyon

o Stopping to fish, ski or just sky gaze as you travel up through the panhandle, visiting towns like Coeur d'Alene, Kellogg and Sandpoint

CHRISTINA DAMEYER // LONELY PLANET IMAGES

⩘ SHOSHONE-BANNOCK TRIBAL MEMBER IN TRADITIONAL DRESS.

MAP REF // PAGE 4 G5

NOT WET YET – PADDLING DOWN THE SALMON RIVER. ≫

FRESH-FROM-THE-FIELD SPUDS ROLL DOWN THE CONVEYOR BELT. ≫

A SLIPPERY SLOPE AT BRUNEAU DUNES STATE PARK. ≫

ILLINOIS

THE HEART OF THE MIDWEST BEATS IN CLOUD-SCRAPING CHICAGO, BUT VENTURING FURTHER AFIELD REVEALS MUCH MORE, INCLUDING SCATTERED SHRINES TO LOCAL HERO ABE LINCOLN, A CYPRESS SWAMP AND A TRAIL OF CORN DOGS, PIE AND DRIVE-IN MOVIE THEATERS DOWN ROUTE 66.

▲ THE BEAN (FORMALLY CALLED *CLOUD GATE*), BY ANISH KAPOOR, SHINES IN CHICAGO'S MILLENNIUM PARK.

- **Etymology of the State Name** Possibly from the Algonquian for 'tribe of superior men'
- **Nicknames** Prairie State, Land of Lincoln
- **Motto** State sovereignty, national union
- **Capital City** Springfield

- **Population** 12.9 million
- **Area** 57,918 sq miles
- **Time Zone** Central
- **State Bird** Cardinal
- **State Flower** Purple violet

- **Major Industries** Manufacturing, financial services, agriculture
- **Politics** Blue state in 2008
- **Best Time to Go** June to August – Chicago festivals and the state fair

HISTORY IN A NUTSHELL

In AD 1200 Illinois' urban action wasn't in Chicago, but in Cahokia to the south. Illinois became the Union's 21st state in 1818, and by then the only trace that remained of Cahokia, at the time one of North America's largest cities, was mounds built by some of its 20,000 residents. In the meantime Chicago developed as an industrial centre. Workers fought the poor conditions in Chicago factories in the late 1800s, and after violent strikes the world's labor movement was born (so thank Illinois for your lunch break). Al Capone's gang more or less ran things during the 1920s and corrupted the state's political system. State government has had troubles ever since, with several governors going to jail (four of the last eight leaders, so far). But it has nurtured winners too, like Barack Obama, who was a senator before becoming the nation's first African American president.

LANDSCAPE

Just outside Chicago, urbanity falls away fast and the state opens into a wide horizon of corn and soybean fields. Flat farmland covers three-quarters of Illinois, with the only real exceptions coming in the hilly northwest and knobby, bluff-strewn far south. The seasons are distinct: cold and wind blow in for winter, while heat and humidity grip the state in summer.

REPRESENTATIONS

- *Illinoise* (2005); Sufjan Stevens' album covers everything from the Pullman strike to Rahm Emmanuel in this primer on state culture

- *The Untouchables* (1987); Brian DePalma's gangster flick shows how Eliot Ness brought down Al Capone in Jazz Age Chicago

- *A Raisin in the Sun* (1959); in Lorraine Hansberry's play an African American family on Chicago's south side struggles with money and race issues

- *The Adventures of Augie March* (1953), by Saul Bellow; a boy comes of age in Depression-era Chicago in this novel

EARLY-GROWTH CORN RISES FROM FERTILE FIELDS – ILLINOIS IS A TOP-TWO GROWER OF THE GRAIN IN THE USA.

NATURAL BEAUTY

Cottonwood trees, grazing horses and roads that twist over old stagecoach trails fill the northwest pocket around Galena. From there, the Great River Road hugs the Mississippi down Illinois' western boundary, often edged with pretty cliffs and wee, time-warped towns. The 18 canyons and waterfalls of Starved Rock State Park appear miragelike amid the central cornfields. Shawnee National Forest's green hills and rocky outcrops swell over the state's southern tip, which also holds a big surprise: the swampland and croaking bullfrogs of Cypress Creek National Wildlife Refuge.

PEOPLE

Illinois' population mirrors the US population – it's 65% white, 15% Hispanic, 15% African American, 4% Asian and 1% other – which is why companies flock here to test new products before launching them nationally. Two-thirds of state residents live in the Chicago metropolitan area. Nearly 30% are Catholic, a number influenced by the growing Hispanic population.

CULTURE & TRADITIONS

Illinois has a split personality that pits liberal, big-city Chicago against the smaller, more conservative downstate farming and manufacturing towns. It isn't easy for the two sides to get along – except in August, when the state fair in Springfield brokers peace through its pig races, butter cows and corn dogs.

CUISINE

Chicago rocks the USA's culinary scene. In recent years it has stolen 'top restaurant city' honors from the coasts. Big-deal chefs like Charlie Trotter, Rick Bayless and Grant Achatz cook alongside traditionalists serving up the holy trinity of local specialties: deep-dish pizza, hot dogs 'dragged through the garden' and juicy Italian beef sandwiches. Stir in a massive array of ethnic eats – Mexican tacos, Indian samosas, Vietnamese pho, Polish pierogi, to name a few – and you can see why you'll need to loosen the belt. Outside Chicago folks go heavy on meat, potatoes and corn dogs (the cornmeal-battered hot dog on a stick was supposedly invented in Springfield).

TRADEMARKS

- Chicago skyscrapers and deep-dish pizza
- Abe Lincoln sights
- Route 66 starting (or end) point
- Corrupt governors
- Inventiveness (the skyscraper, zipper, Lava Lite and Twinkie)
- Oprah Winfrey

ECONOMY

With cosmopolitan Chicago and its business and financial services at the helm, it's easy to forget how agricultural Illinois is. It raises the most soybeans, second-most corn and fourth-most hogs in the USA. Food and machinery manufacturing spark the industrial economy: McDonald's, Sara Lee, John Deere, Boeing and Caterpillar are all based in Illinois. Transportation is also big business in the state: the Port of Chicago connects the Great Lakes to the Mississippi River (via the Illinois River), and the city is home to railroad and airline hubs. Illinois' household income ranks in the nation's upper third, at $54,120.

URBAN SCENE

Chicago is the USA's third-largest city, and it dominates Illinois with sky-high architecture, lakefront beaches and superlative museums. It's a tremendous cultural stew, where you can puzzle over the burnished Bean and Picasso sculptures and other public art by morning; eat hot dogs, drink Old Style beer and watch the Cubs get clobbered by afternoon; and squash into a sweaty blues, jazz or rock club by night. The capital, Springfield, isn't really urban, but it has bountiful Abe Lincoln shrines (home, tomb, museum with Gettysburg Address) and Route 66 icons.

DID YOU KNOW?

- Illinois has more nuclear plants than any other state.
- Frank Lloyd Wright launched his Prairie School style of architecture in Illinois, designing several dwellings in Chicago and suburban Oak Park, where he lived.
- The University of Illinois used to teach a class called History 298: Oprah Winfrey, the Tycoon.

ILLINOIS LEGEND

The 'lady in red' who betrayed gangster John Dillinger was actually wearing dark orange. Anna Sage, the Romanian landlady of Dillinger's girlfriend, was about to be deported by the FBI for operating brothels. To avoid this fate, Sage agreed to set up Dillinger – the FBI's 'Public Enemy Number One' – at Chicago's Biograph Theater. Her orange skirt (glowing red in the marquee light) was the tip-off to agents, who shot Dillinger dead in the alley. The FBI deported Sage anyway.

TEXT KARLA ZIMMERMAN

ESSENTIAL EXPERIENCES

- Having a Ferris Bueller day (Art Institute, Sears Tower, Cubs game, swanky dinner) in Chicago
- Rubbing Abe Lincoln's nose on the bust by his Springfield tomb
- Pulling up to a Route 66 drive-in and ordering a corn dog and chocolate shake
- Watching stubby-legged pigs chase an Oreo prize at the Illinois State Fair
- Wondering what happened to all the traffic and tall buildings once you're 30 minutes outside Chicagoland

⌃ CHICAGO'S FAMOUS DEEP-DISH PIE AT ITS BIRTHPLACE, PIZZERIA UNO.

MAP REF // PAGE 5 Q7

ILLINOIS' LANDSCAPE LOOKS A WHOLE LOT DIFFERENT AFTER LEAVING THE BIG CITY. ⟰

CONTESTANTS TAKE OFF AT THE ILLINOIS STATE FAIR PIG RACES. ⟰

RICHARD CUMMINS // CORBIS

WRIGLEY FIELD WOWS BASEBALL FANS DESPITE THE CUBS' ⟰
CURSED, 100-YEAR CHAMPIONSHIP DROUGHT.

INDIANA

THE STATE REVS UP AROUND THE INDY 500 RACE – AND DURING HIGH-SCHOOL BASKETBALL GAMES – BUT OTHERWISE CORN-STUBBLED INDIANA IS ABOUT SLOW-PACED PLEASURES: PIE EATING IN AMISH COUNTRY, PADDLING A LANGUID RIVER, SLIDING DOWN SAND DUNES AND MEDITATING IN TIBETAN TEMPLES.

⌃ CARS WHIZ BY AT 200 MILES PER HOUR AT THE INDIANAPOLIS 500 RACE, THE STATE'S PREMIER EVENT.

- **Etymology of the State Name** Latin for 'land of Indians'
- **Nickname** Hoosier State
- **Motto** Crossroads of America
- **Capital City** Indianapolis
- **Population** 6.3 million
- **Area** 36,420 sq miles
- **Time Zone** Eastern (some western counties are Central)
- **State Bird** Cardinal
- **State Flower** Peony
- **Major Industries** Manufacturing, agriculture
- **Politics** Swing state (blue in 2008)
- **Best Time to Go** May – Indy 500; September and October – fall colors and farm harvest bounty

HISTORY IN A NUTSHELL

Farmers from Kentucky (including Abraham Lincoln's family) were the first Europeans to settle Indiana. Expansion created conflict with the local Native Americans, who fought their final battle in 1811 at Tippecanoe. Five years later, Indiana became the 19th state. Many early carmakers (such as Studebaker) opened shop in Indiana but were eclipsed by the Detroit giants. The carmakers did leave a lasting legacy, though – a 2.5-mile rectangular test track, which became the site for the first Indianapolis 500 race in 1911.

LANDSCAPE

Endless flat fields of corn and soybeans dominate Indiana. The wooded dunes in the northwest corner provide a brief, bird-filled respite, as do the 200,000 acres of oak, hickory and birch in south-central Hoosier National Forest. Undulating green hills, limestone caves and lazy rivers make a nice change of pace in the far south. Indiana's climate is typical Midwestern, with hot summers and icy winters.

NATURAL BEAUTY

The Indiana Dunes stretch along 21 miles of Lake Michigan shoreline. Holidaymakers flock here for the beaches, towering sand hills and woodlands striped with hiking trails. Hikers and horseback riders descend on Brown County State Park near Nashville, especially in fall when the trees flame orange and gold. Amish Country's serene beauty and slow-moving buggies let visitors drift back in time in places like Shipshewana.

PEOPLE

A vast majority (84%) of Hoosiers are white, with African Americans (9%), Hispanics (5%) and Asians (1%) comprising the remainder of residents. Catholics and Baptists fill the most churches, but there are pockets of Buddhism in Fort Wayne (home to the nation's largest Burmese community) and in Bloomington (where a large Tibetan community lives). Indiana also has the third-largest Amish population in the USA.

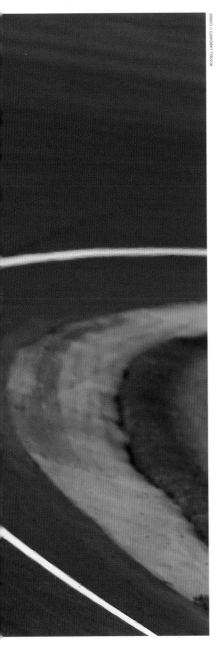

TEAM COLORS FILL THE STANDS AT AN INDIANA UNIVERSITY FOOTBALL GAME IN BLOOMINGTON. »

CULTURE & TRADITIONS

Small towns and farming communities make up most of the state. Chicago writer Mike Royko described the local culture rather ungraciously: 'In Indiana, a real good time consists of putting on bib overalls and a cap bearing the name of a farm equipment company and sauntering to a gas station to sit around and gossip about how Elmer couldn't get his pickup truck started.' Hoosiers laughed that off though (particularly after Royko said he meant Iowa, in deference to the angry letters he received from Indiana), and point out the state's agricultural identity led to its basketball dominance. Winter is off-season for farmers, and how better to spend one's time than by playing hoops? The sport is crazily huge here, and we mean it literally: nine of the nation's 10 largest high-school gyms are in Indiana.

REPRESENTATIONS

- *Hoosiers* (1986); in David Anspaugh's classic film, a small-town basketball team wins the state championship against all odds (last-minute buzzer shot and all)
- *Breaking Away* (1979); Peter Yates' film pits four poor town kids in a bike race against rich college kids in Bloomington
- 'Small Town' (1985); local John Mellencamp wrote this hit tune about growing up in Seymour, Indiana (not far from Bloomington)

TRADEMARKS

- Indianapolis 500
- Basketball fanaticism
- Hoosiers (the movie and the puzzling state nickname)

- Flat farmland
- Pork tenderloin sandwiches
- David Letterman
- John Mellencamp

CUISINE

Wonder Bread was invented in Indiana, and that pretty much sums up the local culinary story of uncomplicated comfort foods. The pork tenderloin sandwich is the state's most eminent offering, a deep-fried breaded pork loin (akin to wiener schnitzel) encased in a bun. Fried biscuits with apple butter accompany meals in the state's south but whether they're a side dish or dessert no one can say for sure. In the northern Amish areas you'll gorge on baked steak, fried ham and chicken and noodles. Sugar cream pie follows for dessert.

ECONOMY

Hoosiers love cars, and not just because of Indy 500 tourism dollars – the state also produces a whopping amount of auto parts, truck bodies and motor homes. Two-thirds of the nation's RVs came off the line here (before the industry nosedived in 2008), most in the north around Elkhart County. Gritty steel plants cluster in the northwest along Lake Michigan, and limestone quarrying takes place in the south. The rock has quite a reputation and forms the walls of many a state capitol as well as the Empire State Building. All those fields of corn, soybeans and chubby pigs (of which Indiana is a top-five producer) plump up the economy too, though Hoosiers' household income ranks just 31st in the nation, at $47,450.

URBAN SCENE

Clean-cut Indianapolis (aka Indy) won't win any excitement contests but it does have a nice mix of museums and sports venues, all watched over by the silent dome of the state capitol. A trio of intriguing small towns lie in south-central Indiana: breezy Bloomington holds Indiana University and Tibetan temples; Columbus is big on architecture, with buildings by IM Pei and Eero Saarinen; and Nashville has artists, antiques and country music.

DID YOU KNOW?

- Indiana is called 'the mother of vice presidents' for the five veeps it has spawned. The national VP Museum is in Huntington.
- There have been 67 deaths at the Indy 500, including seven unfortunate spectators.

INDIANA LEGEND

Folks have called Indianans 'Hoosiers' since the 1830s, but the word's origin is unknown. One theory is that early settlers knocking on a door were met with 'Who's here?' which soon became 'Hoosier.' Another notion is that pioneers walking into a tavern on a fight-filled Saturday night would find a displaced body part and say 'Whose ear?' Scholars suggest it derives from 'hoozer' (from an early English dialect), which people used in the 19th-century South to describe hillbillies. Whatever the source, the word has only honorable attributes today within Indiana.

TEXT KARLA ZIMMERMAN

ESSENTIAL EXPERIENCES

- Pulling up a chair in a small-town diner for a pork tenderloin sandwich and slice of sugar cream pie
- Spinning around the Indy 500 track (albeit on a bus tour at 37 miles per hour)
- Slowing down for clip-clopping horses and buggies on Amish Country roads
- Watching hoops at Indiana University and reminiscing about coach Bobby Knight
- Leaving a lipstick kiss on James Dean's grave in Fairmount
- Hearing the low hum of Indiana Dunes' singing sands (made when zillions of grains strike each other in the wind)

⌃ INDIANA DUNES' TALLEST SANDPILE, MOUNT BALDY, LOOKS OVER LAKE MICHIGAN.

ELLEN SKYE // PHOTOLIBRARY

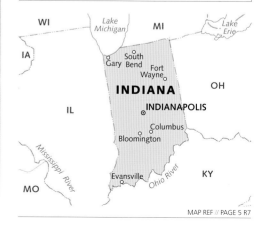

MAP REF // PAGE 5 R7

RURAL ROADS, LAZY RIVERS AND THE ODD COVERED BRIDGE ARE PART OF THE STATE'S SLOW-PACED CHARM. »

HOOSIERS NEVER MISS A SHOT TO WATCH HOOP-BALL. »

SHUCKING SWEET CORN ON A FAMILY FARM. »

IOWA

HOME TO SOME OF THE COUNTRY'S GREAT RURAL ADVENTURES, IOWA'S SCENIC TAN-AND-GREEN STRIPED FIELDS OF CORN AND SOYBEAN MAY SOUND LIKE A BORE, BUT THE CASCADING WAVES OF ROLLING PRAIRIE OFFER FURTHER VISTAS THAN IN ILLINOIS, JUST EAST.

- **Etymology of the State Name** From the French pronunciation of the Dakotan name for the Iowa tribe
- **Nicknames** Hawkeye State, Tall Corn State
- **Motto** Our liberties we prize and our rights we will maintain

- **Capital City** Des Moines
- **Population** 3 million
- **Area** 56,276 sq miles
- **Time Zone** Central
- **State Bird** Eastern goldfinch

- **State Flower** Wild prairie rose
- **Major Industries** Agriculture, manufacturing
- **Politics** Swing state (blue in 2008)
- **Best Time to Go** August – Iowa State Fair

HISTORY IN A NUTSHELL

Long after French settlers roamed by, the 1832 Black Hawk War pushed local Native Americans westward and storms of immigrants hit the (very fertile) ground farming. Eventually Iowa attained its current status as 'Food Capital of the World' and US leader in hogs and corn. Iowa – which became the 29th state, in 1846 – has produced one president (Herbert Hoover was from West Branch) and has made many others; since the early 1970s, the Iowa Caucus has opened the national election battle.

LANDSCAPE

Often considered part of the Great Plains, Iowa is – scientifically speaking – just a neighbor. But the fields of tallgrass prairie (and crops) *are* flat. The state's biggest topographical bumps occur at its east and west borders – with the Loess Hills along the Missouri River to the west, and steeper hills along the Mississippi River to the east. Iowa's continental climate brings in winter lows of -10°F (-23°C) and humid summer highs in the 80°F to 90°F (27°C to 32°C) range.

NATURAL BEAUTY

Iowa's Mississippi River shoreline is stunning, with winding two-lane drives weaving up hills to roadside diner towns and lookouts over the big river. There is also a network of scenic drives and hiking trails through the green Loess Hills, which are made from wind-blown silt.

PEOPLE

After a dip in the 1980s, the Iowa population, which is about 94% white, has been rising over the past decade and a half. This is largely because of a steady increase in Latino immigrants, which now make up about 3% of the total population. Many are Mexicans, hired to harvest the corn and soybean fields. African Americans make up less than 2% of the population, while about half of the state's Asian American population (1%) is Chinese American. Most Iowans are Christian: European immigrants from England, Germany and Scandinavia resulted in many Catholic and Lutheran communities, as well as traditional groups like the Amana Colonies and Quakers' Society of Friends.

TRADEMARKS

- Corn!
- Iowa State Fair
- The *Field of Dreams* baseball diamond
- John Deere tractors
- Locals faithfully adhering to speed-limit laws

CULTURE & TRADITIONS

Many Iowan events focus on farming. The biggest – going strong since 1854 – is Des Moines' Iowa State Fair, a national classic. The 400-acre setting of livestock and country music shows (plus butter sculptures and nearly three dozen 'on a stick' foods) draws 1 million visitors each August. Iowans get their kids thinking farming early, too, with farm toys. Dyersville's quirky National Farm Toy Museum toy show every November draws 20,000 people.

CUISINE

Iowa leads the nation in the production of corn, eggs and hogs, so visitors can expect to eat plenty of all of these. Corn's been grown there for over 2000 years, leading to many a corn casserole in the oven, or jars of the distinctively Iowan corncob jelly. If you like pork, come in early June for the World Pork Expo in Des Moines. Meanwhile, the Amanda Colonies, a network of traditional German villages, serve hearty pork chops and sauerkraut dishes that beat a McDonald's stop. The Iowa Wine Trail – in the upper Mississippi River Valley – is home to more than a dozen wineries.

ECONOMY

Iowa's gross product is about $125 billion annually, with about 40% coming from its hogs, corn, soybeans, oats and eggs, and another 40% from various manufacturing (including much farm equipment, plus the Amana Colonies' refrigerator industry). Iowans' average household economy is $47,300 annually. In recent years, rural flight has attracted more Latin American workers to the state – particularly from Mexico – who come as paid *campesinos* (farmers).

A FACE YOU'LL SEE A LOT OF – PIGS OUTNUMBER PEOPLE FIVE TO ONE IN IOWA. »

DID YOU KNOW?

○ Ozzy Osbourne's famed biting the head off a bat happened in Des Moines in 1982.

○ USSR premier Nikita Khrushchev happened through Coon Rapids in 1959, and befriended Iowan farmer Roswell Garst, who described the unlikely encounter as the 'funniest damn thing you ever saw.'

○ Iowa's famed John Deere tractors are all green. Why? 'Well, they can't be red,' a John Deere factory worker told us. 'Barns are red.'

URBAN SCENE

The capital, Des Moines, has a few moments – particularly the arty East Village, with many galleries, eateries and gay bars just east of the Des Moines River. Otherwise, tiny Dubuque on the Mississippi (the state's oldest town) has a surprisingly urban downtown with 19th-century Victorian homes, a few attractions and cafés (including the clanky 4th Street Elevator rising the steep hill overlooking the waterfront).

REPRESENTATIONS

○ American Gothic (1930); Iowan Grant Wood's iconic painting of two farmers in Eldon – with a pitchfork and grumpy faces

○ Bridges of Madison County (1995); a Clint Eastwood film of the Robert James Waller book, set in south Iowa

○ State Fair (1945); this Rodgers and Hammerstein musical, a hit of Broadway and Hollywood, takes in Iowa's greatest event

○ What's Eating Gilbert Grape? (1993); an early Johnny Depp film that unravels Iowan countryside ennui

IOWA LEGEND

For years, mystery surrounded the 1959 plane crash at Clear Lake that claimed the lives of Buddy Holly, JP 'The Big Bopper' Richardson and Ritchie Valens. Some say Holly's gun was found at the site, and that a firing spree led to the crash (Richardson's body was exhumed in 2007 to prove he hadn't been shot). Some believe the plane's name was 'American Pie,' confusing it with the overplayed Don McLean anthem, which describes the crash as 'the day the music died.' The plane's real name was a less snappy 'N3794N.'

TEXT ROBERT REID

ESSENTIAL EXPERIENCES

○ Bridge-hopping around the scenic, half-dozen bridges of Madison Country

○ Feasting on traditional German dishes at the traditional Amana Colonies community, northwest of Iowa City

○ Driving up the stunning Mississippi River bluffs along Iowa's east border

○ Meditating at the Maharishi University – yes, named after the same yogi who drew the Beatles to India – in a surreal locale amidst Iowan cornfields

○ Cycling across the state in the annual RAGBRAI ride in July

MAP REF // PAGE 5 O6

⌃ CYCLISTS PEDAL FROM COUNCIL BLUFFS TO BURLINGTON FOR THE ANNUAL RAGBRAI RIDE.

IOWA REAPS 40% OF ITS GROSS PRODUCT FROM FARMS LIKE THIS ONE NEAR DES MOINES. ⌃

AGSTOCK IMAGES // CORBIS

A GOSLING SITS ON GRANDPA'S LAP. ⌃

FIELD OF DREAMS FOR CORNCOB JELLY MAKERS. ⌃

KANSAS

THANKS TO A CERTAIN PIGTAILED DOROTHY, KANSAS WILL FOREVER BE SEEN AS THE TEMPLATE FOR 'MIDDLE OF NOWHERE' – THE CENTRAL STATE WITH NO HILLS AND, SOME LIKE TO THINK, NO CULTURE. BUT REALITY DIFFERS, PARTICULARLY IN PROGRESSIVE LAWRENCE OR COUNTRY DRIVES THROUGH THE FLINT HILLS.

⌃ DON'T WORRY, DOROTHY, IT'S NOT A TORNADO (YET), JUST A SUPERCELL THUNDERSTORM.

- **Etymology of the State Name** Sioux for 'south wind people,' as the Kansa tribe were called
- **Nickname** Sunflower State
- **Motto** *Ad astra per aspera* (To the stars with difficulty)

- **Capital City** Topeka
- **Population** 2.8 million
- **Area** 82,282 sq miles
- **Time Zone** Central
- **State Bird** Western meadowlark

- **State Flower** Sunflower
- **Major Industries** Agriculture, aviation
- **Politics** Red state in 2008
- **Best Time to Go** June to August – for most festivals (and to avoid those icy winter winds)

HISTORY IN A NUTSHELL

Kansas has always had something to say about the country's hottest debates. Following the Kansas–Nebraska Act of 1854, settlers rushed in on both sides of the slavery-or-no question; shortly after the state went 'free' when it became the 34th state (in 1861) the Civil War erupted. One of the war's worst scenes happened in Lawrence, where 183 men and boys were killed when William Quantrill led Confederate guerrillas in a surprise attack. Prohibition got a head start here, with temperance advocate Carrie Nation hacking up bars with her tomahawk. Segregation in elementary schools in Topeka led to the 1954 Supreme Court decision in Brown vs the Board of Education of Topeka.

LANDSCAPE

Kansas looks flat from the interstate, but the eyes deceive (it actually slopes from 400 feet in the southeast to about 4000 feet in the west). Look for nearby horizons, which often sit above sweeping plains that tower over the rolling contours of prehistoric seafloors. The east has some hills (notably the Flint Hills) and western mounds include Mount Sunflower (4039 feet), the state's highest point. A couple of major rivers pass through, too – including the Missouri and the Arkansas (called the ar-KAN-sas here, kiddo).

NATURAL BEAUTY

The 48-mile Flint Hills National Scenic Byway, cutting across Hwy 177 northwest of Wichita, is Kansas' nicest drive, passing ranches, tallgrass, wildflowers and 19th-century towns such as Cottonwood Falls.

PEOPLE

The ethnic mix of Kansas is slowly changing. Though the state's population is still overwhelmingly white (86%), and includes many German and Swedish communities, in recent years the number of Latin Americans has steadily been increasing, and they now make up nearly 8% of the state population. Kansas' African American population accounts for 6%. Another trend is that more and more youth are moving to the cities and some towns are being abandoned altogether.

A FARMER WONDERS WHAT WEATHER IS COMING HIS WAY. »

CULTURE & TRADITIONS

Some interesting towns reflect the different pioneers that settled Kansas in the 19th century (some pushing out the namesake Kansa tribe to present-day Oklahoma). Lindsborg, for example, is a Swedish-American town that pulls out the traditional garb (and blue-and-gold flags) for Midsummer's Day Festival (June) and the Svensk Hyllningsfest (October of odd-numbered years). Kansas drew thousands of African Americans from the South during the Black Exodus of 1879. The last remaining town founded during the exodus, wee Nicodemus (population 25), welcomes past residents in late July for the Annual Homecoming Celebration.

TRADEMARKS

○ Kansas Jayhawk basketball

○ *The Wizard of Oz* (1939)

○ Tornadoes

○ Wyatt Earp (and others, like *Gunsmoke's* Matt Dillon) telling bad guys to 'get out of Dodge'

URBAN SCENE

No offense, but Kansas City's better half is across the border in Missouri, leaving smaller towns to vie for the role of Kansas' great urban center. Most agree Lawrence's sizzling bar/restaurant life and antique shops on Massachusetts Street (near the campus of Kansas University, and the last home of beat writer William S Burroughs) is of more interest than the bigger aviation-hub Wichita (with a few museums and a nicely spruced up river-walk downtown).

CUISINE

The destination of so many Texan cows headed to steakhouses, Kansas has plenty of meat on the menu. Many immigrants put their own touch on the food, too. You can find Polish sausages across the state, Czech bologna in Lucas, Mennonite meats in Yoder, or Croatian *povitica* (cake bread) in Lenexa. And let's not forget Pizza Hut – the franchise was born in Wichita.

ECONOMY

Despite the endless sea of wheat, soybean and corn (more crop acres than any state but Texas and Montana), agriculture isn't Kansas' chief economic player – manufacturing and services have taken over, with a particularly strong aviation sector in Wichita (the so-called 'Air Capital of the World'). Countryside Kansans' average salary is about $28,500; for city dwellers it's $38,500.

REPRESENTATIONS

○ 'Home on the Range'; the state song, written by Kansan Brewster M Higley in the 1870s

○ Many movie settings blaze a path through Kansas, including *National Lampoon's Vacation* (1983), *Bonnie & Clyde* (1967), *The Only Good Indian* (2009) and, of course, *The Wizard of Oz*

○ *In Cold Blood* (1966); Truman Capote documents the brutal slaying of a wealthy family in Holcomb

○ Kansas winds are known to occasionally knock over 18-wheelers, or inspire ballads like 'Dust in the Wind' by Topeka-based band Kansas

DID YOU KNOW?

○ A fairly absurd 2003 study (using a cross-section photo of a real pancake) determined that Kansas was actually 'flatter than a pancake' – but it neglected to mention that the state isn't as flat as Florida or Delaware.

○ Before it was a flyover state, it was a pass-through one; famous 19th-century dirt trails crossing Kansas include the Santa Fe trail, watched over by Ft Larned, west of Wichita, and the Chisholm, which linked Texas cattle to the train station in Abilene.

○ Liberal, a town in the southwest corner, fashions itself as the home of the world's most famous Dorothy, with a cheesy yellow-brick center and a replica of her house.

KANSAS MYTH

You're as likely to spot a centaur attacking an orc round here as a real-live Kansas 'jayhawk.' The fictional merger of a blue jay (loud jerk of a bird) and sparrow hawk (excellent hunter), the 'jayhawk' lore began in the mid 1800s, when quarrelling settlers battled over Kansas' status as a free or slavery state. The word was co-opted later for the 7th Kansas Cavalry 'Jayhawker' Regiment, and is now the name for all sports teams from University of Kansas. Why their logo wears shoes, however, remains clouded in strongly debated mystery.

TEXT ROBERT REID

ESSENTIAL EXPERIENCES

○ Taking a stroll on Lawrence's busy Massachussetts Street

○ Detouring for a spooky lunch at the Monument Rocks (like the Jawa hangout in *Star Wars*), south on US-83 from I-70

○ Seeing the little house of Laura Ingalls' classic pioneer-days series, *Little House on the Prairie,* in Independence

○ Expanding the mind at chess camp; world-champ Russian chess master Anatoly Karpov opened a chess school in tiny Lindsborg

○ Stopping by a grain elevator – the skyscrapers of the plains – and asking for a DIY tour of where all that wheat goes

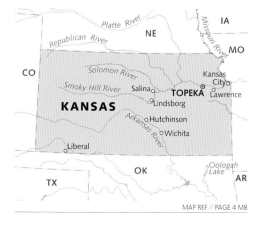

⌃ GREYHOUND RACING IS POPULAR STATEWIDE, WITH ABILENE HOSTING THE SPORT'S HALL OF FAME.

MAP REF // PAGE 4 M8

MUSHROOM ROCK POPS UP AT THE EPONYMOUS STATE PARK NEAR SALINA. «

SHY SUNFLOWERS TURN THEIR BACKS TO THE CAMERA. «

NOTHING LIKE AN ANTIQUE TRACTOR PULL TO ROUSE THE CROWD AT THRESHING DAYS. «

KENTUCKY

HORSES THUNDER AROUND RACETRACKS, BOURBON POURS FROM DISTILLERIES AND BANJOS TWANG IN KENTUCKY, A GEOGRAPHICAL AND CULTURAL CROSSROADS THAT'S PART NORTH, PART SOUTH, PART GENTEEL AND PART APPALACHIAN-RURAL.

≫ IT'S NOT ALL BLUE GRASS IN KENTUCKY.

- **Etymology of the State Name** Native American for 'land of tomorrow' or, possibly, 'meadowland'
- **Nickname** Bluegrass State
- **Motto** United we stand, divided we fall
- **Capital City** Frankfort
- **Population** 4.2 million
- **Area** 40,411 sq miles
- **Time Zones** Eastern, Central
- **State Bird** Cardinal
- **State Flower** Goldenrod
- **Major Industries** Coal, cars, tobacco, horses
- **Politics** Red state in 2008
- **Best Time to Go** April, May and October – horse racing seasons

HISTORY IN A NUTSHELL

Legendary frontiersman Daniel Boone blazed a trail through the Cumberland Gap in 1775, and pioneers began pouring over the Appalachian Mountains soon thereafter. Kentucky joined the Union in 1792; it was the 15th state and first member west of the Appalachians. Though a slave state, Kentucky was bitterly divided during the Civil War, with 30,000 soldiers fighting for the Confederacy and 64,000 for the Union. Both Union President Abraham Lincoln and Confederacy President Jefferson Davis were Kentucky-born, complicating the matter further. After the war, Kentucky focused on tobacco growing, horse breeding and coal mining, pursuits it continues today.

REPRESENTATIONS

- Bluegrass music: Kentucky's own genre, created by Bill Monroe in the 1940s. The country-meets-blues style is typically fuelled by finger-pickin' guitars, banjos, mandolins and fiddles. Everyone from Elvis to McCartney has covered Monroe's 'Blue Moon of Kentucky.'

- 'My Old Kentucky Home' (1853); before the big race, Kentucky Derby–goers croon Stephen Foster's plantation-life tune, the state's official song.

- *Coal Miner's Daughter* (1980); the biographical film of country singer Loretta Lynn shows her early life in an impoverished Kentucky coal-mining town.

LANDSCAPE

The Appalachian Mountains rise in the state's east. The range features towering cliffs and sharp forested ridges, and is dented by narrow valleys, which are called 'hollows,' or 'hollers' in local parlance. Removal of some mountaintops for coal mining in the 19th and 20th centuries has scarred many parts of the area's environment, and coalfields dominate the hilly west of the state. The floodplains in the southwestern area provide a pit stop for migrating birds, and rolling horse-farm land, also known as the Bluegrass Region, unfurls through north-central Kentucky. The overall climate is temperate and wet.

TEAMS HEAD TO THE DERBY STARTING GATE FOR A RACE THAT'LL LAST ALL OF TWO MINUTES. ⌃

NATURAL BEAUTY

Deep ravines and high sandstone cliffs fill vast Daniel Boone National Forest in the Appalachian foothills. Cumberland Falls is one of the few places in the world one can see a moonbow, a rainbow that forms in the water's mist at night. On the Virginia border, Breaks Interstate Park claims to be 'the Grand Canyon of the South,' and indeed it holds the deepest gorge east of the Mississippi River. Mammoth Cave's otherworldly beauty lies beneath the ground. Scenic byways thread through the Bluegrass Region, where long-legged horses, poplar trees and estate houses dot blue-green hills.

PEOPLE

Kentucky is less diverse than its neighbors to the south, with more Caucasians (88%) and fewer African Americans (8%). Hispanics (2%) and Asians (1%) round out the tally. Kentucky does stack up to its southern brethren in terms of religion: one in three residents worships in a Baptist church. Sizeable Muslim and Jewish populations exist around Louisville.

CULTURE & TRADITIONS

While the days of moonshine and jug bands are pretty much gone, eastern Kentucky embraces its backwoods reputation with events such as April's cheeky Hillbilly Days, in Pikeville. Settled by Scots and the Irish, the region retains strong folk-music traditions (banjos, dulcimers, fiddles), and even has its own dialect called Appalachian English (in which a long 'o' is pronounced 'er,' so 'hollow' becomes 'holler'). The folksy vibe dissipates towards the west, in Lexington or Louisville, where more of a 'Southern belle' culture prevails.

CUISINE

In the early days, Kentucky burgoo, aka 'varmint stew,' mixed squirrel, rabbit and whatever other game settlers could shoot and stuff in a pot with veggies. Today there's more likely to be beef, lamb and chicken simmering in burgoo's meaty broth. Many restaurants serve the 'hot brown,' an open-faced turkey and bacon sandwich smothered under cheesy sauce, followed by chocolate-nut Derby Pie for dessert. Colonel Harland Sanders whipped up the super-secret recipe for Kentucky Fried Chicken in 1930. Perhaps the only local delicacy more famous is bourbon – Kentucky produces 95% of the knee-buckling nectar, at its best when swirled amid crushed ice, sugar and mint in a julep.

TRADEMARKS

- Thoroughbred horses and the Kentucky Derby
- Bourbon
- Bluegrass music
- Kentucky Fried Chicken
- Daniel Boone
- Feuding Hatfields and McCoys
- Fort Knox and piles of gold

ECONOMY

On the industrial side, Kentucky is the nation's third-largest coal producer and fourth-largest auto manufacturer. Any Corvette you see zipping down the road was made here. Tobacco lights up the economy on the agricultural side, with Kentucky growing more smokers' delight than any state besides North Carolina. Thoroughbred horse breeding adds billions to the state's coffers, and bourbon and baseball bats also contribute. Still, Kentucky's median household income remains one of the country's lowest, at $40,300.

URBAN SCENE

Kentucky's two main cities jockey for supremacy. Genteel Lexington has the million-dollar homes and multimillion-dollar horses (whose stables are known to sport polished oak walls and chandeliers). Riverfront Louisville is far larger and more blue-collar, though it also has its share of aristocrats, plus the Kentucky Derby. Wee Frankfort, the postcard-pretty capital, lies between the two, all red brick and gingerbread trim.

DID YOU KNOW?

- There *is* something in the water: the Bluegrass Region's limestone-rich streams give bourbon its unique flavor and horses their strength (the limestone produces extra calcium in the soil, for extra-nutritious grass).
- Trappist monk and well-known spiritual writer Thomas Merton is buried at Gethsemani Abbey near Bardstown, where he lived and pondered for a quarter century.
- Mammoth Cave stretches more than 300 miles underground, making it the world's longest cavern.

KENTUCKY LEGEND

A pig caused the infamous feud between the Hatfields and McCoys, or so the story goes. West Virginian Floyd Hatfield had the hog. Kentuckian Randolph McCoy said it was his. They glared at each other from their homes across the Tug Fork River, and ignited years of property disputes and family murders. The two states eventually called in their militias to restore order, and the clans agreed to stop fighting in 1891.

TEXT KARLA ZIMMERMAN

ESSENTIAL EXPERIENCES

- Donning your finest hat and threads to attend the Kentucky Derby
- Studying the odds and betting the daily double on a horse race at Keeneland or Churchill Downs
- Swirling, sniffing and sipping fresh-from-the-barrel bourbon at a distillery
- Spelunking through bizarre, undulating rock formations in Mammoth Cave
- Swinging a Louisville Slugger at the factory's batting cages
- Paying your Civil War respects at Abe Lincoln's and Jefferson Davis' birthplaces
- Floating in a houseboat on Lake Cumberland

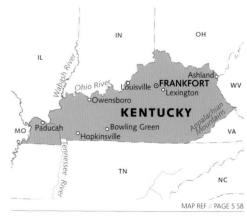

⌃ BASEBALL BATS LINE UP FOR ASSEMBLY AT THE LOUISVILLE SLUGGER FACTORY.

MAP REF // PAGE 5 S8

KENTUCKIANS SWING THEIR PARTNERS 'ROUND AND 'ROUND IN APPALACHIAN-ROOTED SQUARE DANCING. ⌃

CALUMET FARM IN LEXINGTON BREEDS THOROUGHBREDS, A MULTI-BILLION-DOLLAR STATE INDUSTRY. ⌃

LOUISIANA

DESPITE SINKING SWAMPS AND REPEATED GULF COAST STORM ASSAULTS, YOU CAN'T KEEP THE FREE-WHEELING, JAZZY, CAJUN SPIRIT OF THIS SOUTHERN STATE DOWN – *LAISSEZ LES BON TEMPS ROULER!*

≫ JAZZ BAND MEMBERS TUNE UP FOR NEW ORLEANS' MARDI GRAS.

- **Etymology of the State Name** From the French ruler Louis XIV of France
- **Nickname** Bayou State
- **Motto** Union, justice and confidence
- **Capital City** Baton Rouge

- **Population** 4.3 million
- **Area** 51,843 sq miles
- **Time Zone** Central
- **State Bird** Brown Pelican
- **State Flower** Magnolia

- **Major Industries** Oil, gas and petrochemical industries, agriculture, timber
- **Politics** Red state in 2008
- **Best Time to Go** March to April – a temperate time when gardens are in bloom

HISTORY IN A NUTSHELL

Several Native American tribes resided on the land that includes modern Louisiana when the first Western explorer arrived in the 1700s. The territory then passed from Spanish to French to British to French control before being purchased by the USA and, in 1812, becoming the 18th state. Mississippi steamboats helped make New Orleans a major port before Union armies occupied the Confederate state during the Civil War. Tourism and agriculture prospered in the 20th century and early 21st until Katrina (August 2005) and subsequent hurricanes struck. The state was devastated and race relations strained in the flooding of New Orleans. The process of rebuilding will continue for years to come.

LANDSCAPE

From a high of 535 feet above sea level, Louisiana slopes to the coast (parts of New Orleans are actually below sea level). A complicated series of canals and levees attempts to control the Mississippi's perpetual floods and to direct the flow toward the commercial ship channel and away from the Atchafalaya River. Swamplands, marshes and slow-moving bayous make up the southwestern parts of the state, but without alluvial sediment being restored, wetlands are returning to the sea inch by inch. A warm, semi-tropical climate means lots of rain and humidity; hurricanes and tropical storms sporadically pound the coast from June through October.

NATURAL BEAUTY

The beauties of Louisiana are subtle: Spanish moss hanging from a cypress tree, a stately line of 100-year-old oaks on a plantation road, a riot of pink and white azaleas. The protection of the American alligator has been so successful that the state reinstated a legal cull of the reptile.

TRADEMARKS

- Creole cooking
- Hurricane Katrina
- Mardi Gras
- Tabasco
- Jazz

THE 24-MILE LAKE PONTCHARTRAIN CAUSEWAY LEADS INTO THE BIG EASY. ⌃

PEOPLE

According to the census bureau, the population of Louisiana is roughly 35% African American and 63% white. This doesn't accurately reflect age-old interracial mixing. And though 'white' sounds homogeneous, it's the offspring of English Anglo-Saxon Protestants in the north and of French and Spanish Catholics in the south that populate the state. About 17% of the residents claim Catholic affiliation. No one's certain exactly how many believe in the talismans of voodoo – a religion that's the amalgamation of Afro-Caribbean traditional worship, Catholic saints and Christian beliefs.

CULTURE & TRADITIONS

An obscure population of French Canadians, banished by the British and transported to New Orleans in 1765, had a profound effect. Some Acadians, or Cajuns, as they have come to be called, still speak a distinct French dialect, and Cajun food and music are ubiquitous. The latter has a fiddle- and accordion-based rhythm, similar to a quick country two-step. Zydeco music, on the other hand, comes out of the French-speaking African American, or Creole, community. Rub boards, fashioned after old washboards, are the key instrument in helping create the pounding, Afro-Caribbean–inspired beat.

CUISINE

Cajun cooking mixes French country techniques with locally available ingredients like crawfish, shrimp, rice and cayenne pepper. Put them together and you get spicy étoufée (a roux-based spicy seafood stew), gumbo (the soup version of the same dish) and jambalaya (a Cajun take on paella, with rice, seafood, sausage and chicken). Creole cooking tends to be more refined, using more expensive meats and less pepper. Come spring it's crawfish season, when big pots of 'mudbugs' are boiled up with spicy seasoning salts. Locals pinch the tails of these minilobster-like creatures, eat the extracted tail meat, then suck the heads.

ECONOMY

Louisiana's economy is largely dependent on its natural resources – timber farming and food-based agriculture make up a large sector, but the state's fortunes rise and fall with that of the oil and gas (and related) industries. The state's median household income is a relatively low $35,216.

URBAN SCENE

New Orleans is synonymous with Mardi Gras, the raucous pre-Lenten festival when the town celebrates with outrageous costumes, parades, beads and alcohol. But, despite a sizable loss of population post–Hurricane Katrina, revelry goes on pretty much every day in the beguiling French Quarter and the French Quarter Festival is the locals favorite fete. Since the big storm, boutique shopping along Magazine Street (in the lower Garden District) has re-emerged more eclectic and vibrant than ever.

REPRESENTATIONS

- *The Big Easy* (1989); Dennis Quaid laid on a sultry N'awlins accent in this film about Crescent City corruption

- *Interview with the Vampire* (1976); Anne Rice's New Orleans–set novels inspired a movie (1994), a city tour and an obsession

- *A Streetcar Named Desire* (1954); playwright Tennessee Williams lived in New Orleans, as did Blanche and Stanley in this landmark play

- Born in Louisiana, Truman Capote set several of his short stories there

DID YOU KNOW?

- Under Louisiana law, biting someone is assault, but biting them with false teeth is aggravated assault.

- The Lake Pontchartrain Causeway is the world's longest bridge over water (24 miles).

LOUISIANA LEGEND

'Down in Louisiana where the black trees grow lives a voodoo lady named Marie Laveau…' Voodoo queen Marie Laveau led a multiracial following with her New Orleans rituals until her death in 1881. She reportedly rests in St Louis Cemetery No 1, where, despite discouragement, devotees scratch Xs in the side of the purported family tomb to commune with the queen.

TEXT LISA DUNFORD

ESSENTIAL EXPERIENCES

- Paddling among reeds and past alligators on a swamp tour

- Getting powdered sugar all over yourself from the beignets (doughnutlike pastries) at New Orleans' Cafe du Monde

- Tapping your toes to live Cajun music at a Saturday night dance in a small town

- Wrapping your hands around a huge, round muffaletta sandwich piled high with Italian meats and olive salad

- Carrying a lethal hurricane (the tropical drink) down the street as you hop from one French Quarter bar to the next

- Listening to the Neville Brothers croon at the Big Easy's annual Jazz Fest

ALAN SCHEIN // CORBIS

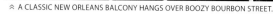
⌃ A CLASSIC NEW ORLEANS BALCONY HANGS OVER BOOZY BOURBON STREET.

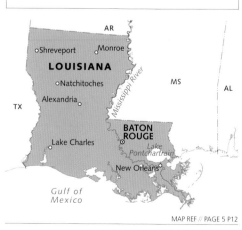

AR

Shreveport   Monroe

LOUISIANA

Natchitoches   MS

AL

Alexandria

TX

BATON ROUGE

Lake Charles

Lake Pontchartrain

New Orleans

Gulf of Mexico

MAP REF // PAGE 5 P12

OAKS PAVE THE WAY TO ROSEDOWN, AN 1835 COTTON PLANTATION IN ST FRANCISVILLE. ⌃

RAY LASKOWITZ//LONELY PLANET IMAGES

SUMMONING SOULS AT THE VOODOO SPIRITUAL TEMPLE, NEW ORLEANS. ⌃

LAURA'S CANDIES PROFFERS MORE SIN IN THE FRENCH QUARTER. ⌃

MAINE

SEQUESTERED IN THE NATION'S NORTHEASTERNMOST CORNER, MAINE EXUDES A FEELING OF WILD ISOLATION UNPARALLELED EAST OF THE MISSISSIPPI; ITS RUGGED COASTLINE, OFFSHORE ISLANDS AND GREAT NORTH WOODS LURE EVERYONE FROM ARTISTS TO HUNTERS, SNOWMOBILERS TO LOBSTER FIENDS.

⌃ A KAYAKER GLIDES THROUGH ISLAND-SPECKLED PENOBSCOT BAY.

- **Etymology of the State Name** From a nautical reference to 'mainland'
- **Nicknames** Pine Tree State, Vacationland
- **Motto** *Dirigo* (I lead)
- **Capital City** Augusta

- **Population** 1.3 million
- **Area** 35,385 sq miles
- **Time Zone** Eastern
- **State Bird** Chickadee
- **State Flower** White pine cone

- **Major Industries** Tourism, forestry, fishing
- **Politics** Blue state in 2008
- **Best Time to Go** May to October – but beware coastal traffic jams in midsummer

HISTORY IN A NUTSHELL

A Native American presence in Maine had already spanned 10,000 years by the time the British established a toehold on these shores in 1607. Maine's Popham colony, predating the Pilgrims' arrival in Massachusetts by over a decade, only survived one year, but subsequent 17th-century coastal settlements fared better, including Falmouth (modern-day Portland). Incorporated into Massachusetts Bay Colony by the late 1600s, Maine remained sparsely settled and contested by the French and British until well after the American Revolution. The USA's claim was finally cemented after the War of 1812, and in 1820 Maine joined the Union as the 23rd state.

LANDSCAPE

Maine is nearly as big as the other five New England states put together. Its tidal shoreline; threaded with deep inlets and dotted with countless islands, measures 3478 miles (making it the fourth longest in the country). North and inland, a vast mosaic of evergreens, lakes and bogs unfolds, rising in the west to the flanks of the Appalachian Mountains. Maine is the most forested state in the nation – roughly 89% of its area is covered with trees – and its interior is the most sparsely populated place east of the Great Plains. Summers are pleasant, but the winters are harsh, with heavy snows smothering the terrain inland and bracing wind chills along the coast.

NATURAL BEAUTY

The picturesque coastline of Maine is characterized by rocky bluffs, pebble-strewn beaches and boats bobbing in sheltered harbors. These elements achieve their finest expression in Acadia National Park, one of the nation's oldest protected areas. Inland, Maine's highest point, Mount Katahdin (5267 feet) presides over the exquisite isolation of Baxter State Park and the Allagash Wilderness Waterway, luring canoeists, kayakers, hikers and campers. Here in Maine's Great North Woods, moose easily outnumber people, private logging roads outnumber state highways, and the loon's eerie call echoes across lonely waters.

EYE-POPPING SCENERY ATOP BUBBLE MOUNTAIN IN ACADIA NATIONAL PARK. »

LOBSTER IS THE MAINE DISH. »

PEOPLE

Maine is noteworthy for its large contingent of 'summer people,' who flock to the coast during the warm months, then overwinter in primary residences elsewhere. Maine is one of the nation's whitest states (96.7%), with more than a third of residents claiming English or Irish extraction. It also boasts the USA's third highest population of French Americans (22.8%) and the highest percentage of people speaking French at home (5.28% versus 4.68% in Louisiana). Roman Catholics and Baptists are the two largest religious denominations.

CULTURE & TRADITIONS

Native year-round Mainers are a hardy lot and proudly distinguish themselves from the 'from aways' – a term applied across the board to non-natives, even if they've lived here for decades. Many Mainers are outdoors enthusiasts, hunting in the Great North Woods and fishing or boating in any body of water. Maine's Aroostook County is also the Northeast's snowmobile capital.

TRADEMARKS

- Lobsters
- Blueberries
- Moose
- Rocky shores
- Lighthouses
- Mosquitoes

CUISINE

Lobster forms the backbone (exoskeleton?) of Maine cuisine; roadside signs hawk lobster rolls, lobster stew and whole red beasts pulled steaming from the pot. Maine's famous potatoes get put to good use in seafood chowders, while pancakes and muffins feature the state's wild blueberries. Visitors to Acadia National Park shouldn't miss the popovers with strawberry jam served on the lawn at Jordan Pond teahouse – a Maine tradition. Also watch for Moxie, a 19th-century patent medicine reincarnated as Maine's official soft drink; creative bartenders occasionally use it as an ingredient in mixed drinks.

REPRESENTATIONS

- *One Man's Meat* (1942); EB White's collection of essays about life in Down East Maine
- *Blueberries for Sal* (1948) and *One Morning in Maine* (1952); illustrated children's books by Robert McCloskey
- *Christina's World* (1948); painter Andrew Wyeth's Maine-based masterpiece
- *Empire Falls* (2001); Pulitzer Prize–winning novel by Richard Russo
- Stephen King's novels

ECONOMY

Maine is the least affluent New England state; it's 36th nationally in both income per capita ($33,962) and median household ($45,888). Tourism accounts for 15% of the economy, creating an annual boom and bust cycle, especially along the coast. Fishing, aquaculture and logging are important – Maine supplies most of the nation's lobster, a sizable percentage of its salmon and 90% of the USA's toothpicks. It also leads the world in wild blueberry production. Bath Iron Works, one of the nation's most active shipyards, carries on the state's proud shipbuilding tradition.

URBAN SCENE

Portland is Maine's largest and most dynamic city. Its recently restored redbrick Old Port bustles with pubs and galleries as well as container vessels, cruise ships and passenger ferries to Canada. The nearby West End is one of the city's most attractive residential neighborhoods, perched atop a hill with long views of the harbor.

DID YOU KNOW?

- Maine has its own desert, north of Freeport, with dunes of glacial silt.
- Over 40% of Mainers own guns, but Maine has the lowest violent-crime rate in the nation.
- Maine is unlike any other state in the Union in two ways: it has a one-syllable name and it only borders one other state.

MAINE LEGEND

The Maine Coon cat is one of the USA's oldest breeds, although its lineage is shrouded in mystery. One legend holds that Maine Coons are descended from Marie Antoinette's pets. Allegedly the French queen planned to escape the guillotine by sailing for America, but only managed to get her cats on board. Abandoned by their soon-to-be-beheaded owner, the kitties had no choice but to endure the lonely journey to Maine... and start breeding.

TEXT GREGOR CLARK

ESSENTIAL EXPERIENCES

- Clambering up rocky faces on steel ladders, lounging on Sand Beach or bicycling early-20th-century carriage roads in Acadia National Park
- Paddling the Northern Forest Canoe Trail or hiking the Appalachian Trail to its terminus in Baxter State Park
- Donning a bib in preparation for your date with Maine's favorite crustacean
- Antiquing in Wiscasset or surveying the windjammers in picturesque Camden harbor
- Posing by the giant hiking boot and shopping for outdoor gear past midnight at LL Bean's 24-hour emporium
- Getting up close and personal with moose and mosquitoes on remote Moosehead Lake

TRAVEL INK // GETTY

≪ NUBBLE LIGHTHOUSE GUARDS THE WATERS AT CAPE NEDDICK ON MAINE'S SOUTHERN TIP.

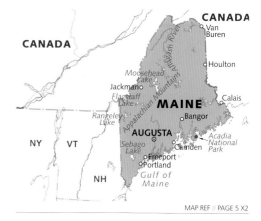

MAP REF // PAGE 5 X2

SCHOONERS SAIL THE BLUFF-STREWN COAST. ⌃

NOT A SURPRISE, REALLY, TO SEE ONE OF THESE GUYS NIBBLING TWIGS NEAR MOOSEHEAD LAKE. ⌃

MARYLAND

IN MANY WAYS MARYLAND IS A MINIATURE APPROXIMATION OF THE USA, CONTAINING ITS WEALTHIEST, MOST DIVERSE HIGHS AND POOREST, NEGLECTED LOWS. THERE ARE ROLLING HILLS, AN URBAN PULSE, SLOW WETLANDS AND GOLDEN BEACHES TO BE DISCOVERED, ALL INTERLACED WITH THE 'MOTHER OF WATERS': THE CHESAPEAKE BAY.

≫ JAPANESE MAPLE TREES SWIRL THROUGH THE VARIED LANDSCAPE IN CYLBURN ARBORETUM, BALTIMORE.

- **Etymology of the State Name** Named for Henrietta Maria, consort of England's Charles I
- **Nicknames** Free State, Old Line State
- **Motto** *Fatti maschii, parole femine* (Manly deeds, womanly words)
- **Capital City** Annapolis
- **Population** 5.6 million
- **Area** 12,407 sq miles
- **Time Zone** Eastern
- **State Bird** Baltimore oriole
- **State Flower** Black-eyed Susan
- **Major Industries** Federal government, services, shipping
- **Politics** Blue state in 2008
- **Best Time to Go** Year-round – fall foliage, winter wonderland, spring blossoms, golden summer haze

HISTORY IN A NUTSHELL

The Piscataway and Susquehanna's tidewater empires were destroyed by the arrival of Catholic refugees from the English Civil War, who founded the first community to legalize freedom of (Christian) worship in North America. These ideals didn't prevent Maryland becoming a slave state, although Baltimore's port kept it within the immigrant- and industry-influenced Northeast Corridor and, thus, not entirely Southern in character. The British siege of Fort McHenry during the War of 1812 inspired Maryland local Francis Scott Key to pen 'The Star-Spangled Banner.' During the Civil War Maryland was only kept in the Union via martial law, but by the 20th century the state had become the major service and staffing sector of the nation's capital.

NATURAL BEAUTY

The mountains and fields of western and central Maryland are fine, but it's the Chesapeake's moon-and-tide carved coast, a waterscape of low sedge and long sky flown over by great blue herons and fish hawks, that is the state's aesthetic exemplar. Preserved historical sites have saved swathes of natural beauty such as the forested, bucolic Chesapeake and Ohio Canal and the rolling hill-and-cornfield-scape of Antietam National Battlefield.

LANDSCAPE

The Catoctin and Allegheny Mountains push the state's western panhandle up into Appalachian ridge-and-valley country before rolling into the lumpy hills and horse farms of the Piedmont Plateau. At the fall line Maryland flattens out into a crosshatch of cornfields, pine and oak forest, and fresh and saltwater marshland. Thousands of miles of squiggled shoreline mark the Chesapeake Bay, the largest freshwater estuary in the world and far and away the defining geographic feature of this state. Maryland has a temperate climate, with only the western mountains becoming very cold in winter.

NOON FORMATION OUTSIDE BANCROFT HALL AT THE US NAVAL ACADEMY, ANNAPOLIS. ⌃

PEOPLE

The state's Washington, DC–Baltimore corridor is populated by a highly educated, multihued palette of Jews, white Americans of all stripes, Native Americans, East Asians, Central Americans and African Americans (Prince George's County is home to DC's outer ghettoes and is also the most affluent majority-black county in the nation). The rest of the state is rural, linked to small-plot agriculture, large-scale chicken farming and harvesting the Chesapeake. Maryland was the first state to be founded by Catholics (refugees fleeing religious persecution); today it remains a bit of a multifaith cauldron representing almost every faith (plus secularism!) under the sun.

CULTURE & TRADITIONS

Culturewise, southern Maryland and the Eastern Shore resemble the tidewater upper South, while the western panhandle is indistinguishable from Appalachia. The rest of Maryland has made a tradition of not holding anyone to traditions – this is a come-as-you-are kind of state, and the main social tensions (besides the income gap) are between Redskins and Ravens (NFL) fans.

TRADEMARKS

- Crabs – catch 'em, pick 'em, eat 'em
- Chesapeake Bay and the Eastern Shore
- Lacrosse – the state has traditionally dominated the sport
- Edgar Allan Poe
- Billie Holiday
- Frank Zappa

CUISINE

Eating in a crab house is an essential Maryland experience. Most self-respecting natives can identify the sex of a blue crab by looking at its apron (belly), and pride themselves on their ability to pick and clean a 'Jimmy' (male crab). Crabs are eaten with sweet corn, spiced with Old Bay seasoning and washed down with beer. The state's huge immigrant population has also created a tasty belt of ethnic eateries all around the DC–Baltimore passage.

ECONOMY

Although Baltimore and the outer stretches of Washington, DC, have some of the poorest ghettos in the country, Maryland consistently has one of the country's highest incomes per capita. The state's workforce is primarily employed as staff and service to the federal government in DC, or in various white-collar roles in Baltimore and surrounding 'burbs. Blue collar shipping, some varied agriculture and the risky business of living off the water – local 'watermen' are some of the last small-scale fishing folk in the country – round out the state's economic edges.

REPRESENTATIONS

- *The Wire* (2002–08); HBO 'TV novel' on the state of the US city, set in and loved by Baltimore
- Anything by singer-songwriter Tom Wisner, troubadour of the Chesapeake and one of the USA's great folk-environmentalists
- Pretty much the entire oeuvre of film directors John Waters and Barry Levinson
- Novelist John Barth, author of the astounding postmodern novels *The Sot-Weed Factor* (1960) and *Giles Goat Boy* (1966)

URBAN SCENE

It's unfair to call Baltimore Maryland's only major city, because Washington, DC, or at least its residential neighborhoods away from the federal government, is essentially a Maryland town, indistinguishable in parts from Baltimore and the wealthy suburbs of Bethesda and Silver Spring. Baltimore itself has sprung from relative obscurity into a weird and wonderful playground for painters, musicians and other creative types lured by the city's blue collar credibility and cheap rent. It's got a culture all of its own, where working class eccentricity is overlaid by out-there artistry, although it's also still – in ways good and bad – something of a small town.

DID YOU KNOW?

- The Chesapeake Bay Skipjacks are the USA's only commercial sailing fleet.
- The first telegraph line in the country was strung between Baltimore and Washington, DC.
- Greenbelt was the first planned community in the USA.

MARYLAND MYTHS

The Blair Witch Project (1999) is based on the legend of Moll Dyer, a 17th-century 'witch' (or persecuted old woman) who was driven out of Leonardtown during a hard winter and froze to death in a forest she still allegedly haunts. And nearby Point Lookout State Park housed thousands of Confederate POWs during the Civil War, many of whom died in captivity; the dead rebels can supposedly be heard whispering in the marshes at night.

TEXT ADAM KARLIN

⌃ MUSLIMS PRAY TOGETHER IN MULTICULTURAL BALTIMORE.

ESSENTIAL EXPERIENCES

- Sucking down crabs and beer on the Chesapeake Bay
- Taking in an Orioles game followed by a night out in Baltimore
- Small-town hopping down the Eastern Shore
- Getting nostalgic on Ocean City's boardwalk
- Crossing the Bay Bridge; avoiding traffic is a big plus

MAP REF // PAGE 5 W7

THE BALTIMORE ORIOLES HIT AND RUN AT RETRO CAMDEN YARDS. «

A YOUNGSTER MULLS OVER WHETHER TO BRING OUT THE OLD BAY SEASONING FOR HIS PINT-SIZED CRAB. «

MASSACHUSETTS

CRADLE OF THE AMERICAN REVOLUTION, MASSACHUSETTS IS NEW ENGLAND'S MOST POPULOUS AND CULTURALLY VIBRANT STATE, WHOSE COLLEGES, MUSEUMS AND ARTS ORGANIZATIONS VIE FOR ATTENTION WITH SCENIC ATTRACTIONS RANGING FROM CAPE COD'S WINDSWEPT DUNES TO THE BERKSHIRES' PASTORAL MOUNTAIN BEAUTY.

≫ CONTEMPLATING THE LOBSTER BUOY SELECTION IN PROVINCETOWN, CAPE COD.

- **Etymology of the State Name** Algonquian for 'at the great hill'
- **Nickname** Bay State
- **Motto** *Ense petit placidam sub libertate quietem* (By the sword we seek peace, but peace only under liberty)

- **Capital City** Boston
- **Population** 6.5 million
- **Area** 10,555 sq miles
- **Time Zone** Eastern
- **State Bird** Black-capped chickadee

- **State Flower** Mayflower
- **Major Industries** Technology, services, commercial fishing
- **Politics** Blue state in 2008
- **Best Time to Go** June to October – sun, sand, summer arts festivals and fall foliage

HISTORY IN A NUTSHELL

Massachusetts' history reads like a who's who of the American colonies. The Wampanoag people, who famously shared the first Thanksgiving, were one of many Native American tribes in the area when the Pilgrims landed. Next came the Puritans, who set up shop in Salem and Boston. In the 17th and 18th centuries Massachusetts held center stage in the colonial Northeast, becoming a hotbed for fraying relations between the British and the colonists. The Boston Massacre, the Boston Tea Party, Lexington, Concord and Bunker Hill were all pivotal moments in the move towards independence. The Commonwealth of Massachusetts joined the Union as the sixth state on February 6, 1788.

LANDSCAPE

Extending from the Atlantic to the Appalachians, and bordering almost every New England state, Massachusetts is the region's geographical linchpin. East of the Connecticut River the terrain is gently rolling, while to the west the Berkshire Mountains rise to 3491 feet at Mount Greylock. Cape Cod, protruding hooklike into the Atlantic, is Massachusetts' most prominent landform, and Martha's Vineyard New England's largest island. Massachusetts' climate has typical New England snowy winters and warm, humid summers.

REPRESENTATIONS

- *The Scarlet Letter* (1850), by Nathaniel Hawthorne
- *Little Women* (1868), by Louisa May Alcott
- *Ethan Frome* (1911), by Edith Wharton
- *The Crucible* (1953); Arthur Miller's play drawing parallels between the Salem Witch Trials and McCarthyism
- *The Perfect Storm* (1997); Sebastian Junger's book about a disaster off the Massachusetts coast
- *Cheers* (1982–93); TV series
- 'Dirty Water' (1966), by The Standells; the hit song immortalizing Boston's Charles River is played after every major Boston sports victory
- 'Massachusetts,' by Arlo Guthrie (1976); official folk song of Massachusetts

A LANGUID ESTUARY CARVES INTO THE COAST BY PLYMOUTH. ⌃

NATURAL BEAUTY

Cape Cod National Seashore, with its dunes, wild cranberry bogs and long sandy beaches, is the state's largest protected area. It's also a key tourist destination. Massachusetts' other scenic draws include the cliffs and coves of Martha's Vineyard and Nantucket in the southeast, and the lush maple-draped slopes of the inland Berkshire Mountains. Bird watching opportunities abound at Mass Audubon's Wellfleet Bay Wildlife Sanctuary, while Stellwagen Bank National Marine Sanctuary, between Cape Cod and Cape Anne, has been recognized by the World Wildlife Fund as one of the world's top 10 whale watching sites.

CULTURE & TRADITIONS

Massachusetts residents are crazy about their sports teams. The Red Sox' run to the World Series in 2004 (after an 86-year drought) achieved mythic proportions and allowed many an old Bostonian to die happy. Higher education and the arts also occupy an important place in Massachusetts' culture. North America's first college, Harvard, heads an all-star list that includes MIT, the Berklee College of Music, Woods Hole Oceanographic Institution and the Five Colleges (Amherst, Hampshire, Mount Holyoke, Smith and the University of Massachusetts Amherst). Visual arts venues include the Gardner Museum and the Museum of Fine Arts in Boston, the Peabody Essex Museum in Salem, the Clark Art Institute in Williamstown and Mass MoCA in North Adams.

ECONOMY

An economic powerhouse, Massachusetts ranks third in the nation in income per capita ($49,142) and seventh in median household income ($62,365). Communications, computer and high-tech industries figure prominently, as do education, health care, biotech, insurance and financial services. Commercial fishing has declined but, measured by value of catch, Massachusetts still ranks third in the country, and New Bedford is the nation's leading port.

Southeastern Massachusetts produces one quarter of the nation's cranberries.

TRADEMARKS

- Kennedy family
- Cape Cod
- Clam chowder
- Boston accents
- Pilgrims and Puritans
- Click and Clack (of NPR's *Car Talk*)
- Boston Tea Party
- Gay marriage

CUISINE

Massachusetts' food ranges from the traditional (cranberry sauce) to the zany (lobster ice cream). Boston offers a galaxy of multi-ethnic cuisine alongside classics such as Boston cream pie (invented at Boston's Parker House Hotel) and Boston baked beans, slow cooked in molasses. Along the coast, clam shacks and larger venues like Legal Sea Foods dish up chowder, fried clams, scallops and scrod (young whitefish). Sausage-kale soup is an old Portuguese favorite.

PEOPLE

Massachusetts boasts the USA's largest Irish American population (24%) and, by New England standards, has high percentages of Hispanics (7.9%), African Americans (6.9%) and Asian Americans (4.9%). New Bedford is home to the country's largest Portuguese American community and Boston has become a prime destination for Brazilians, Cambodians and other international immigrants.

URBAN SCENE

New England's biggest city, Boston is Massachusetts' historical hub and its center of culture and higher learning. Big tourist draws include the city's fine museums, the Freedom Trail and Black Heritage Trail, Faneuil Hall (a giant waterfront market), Fenway Park (America's oldest major league baseball stadium), and the Boston Common and Public Garden (leafy downtown parks). Student life focuses on Cambridge, home to both Harvard and MIT.

DID YOU KNOW?

- Despite its famous chowder, Fenway Franks and Boston cream pie, Massachusetts has the lowest obesity rate in the nation.
- Massachusetts hosted the world's first basketball and volleyball games, and began construction of America's first subway system, all in the 1890s.
- Famous (and infamous) Massachusetts residents have included Dr Seuss and Lizzie Borden.

MASSACHUSETTS LEGEND

Massachusetts' most resonant legend is undoubtedly Paul Revere's midnight ride. On April 18, 1775, Revere, charged with alerting colonists west of Boston of the movements of British troops, arranged to have warning lanterns hung in Boston's Old North Church, then raced through the night to Lexington on horseback to announce the impending British arrival. His efforts permitted a strong colonial response in what was to become the American Revolution's first battle.

TEXT **GREGOR CLARK**

ESSENTIAL EXPERIENCES

- Admiring the whaling mansions of Nantucket, or discovering your own Moby Dick off Cape Cod
- Cruising through the sand dunes along the bike paths outside Provincetown
- Joining the chorus of 'Sweet Caroline' (an eighth-inning tradition) at a Red Sox game in Fenway Park
- Picnicking amid fireflies during an open-air performance by the Boston Symphony Orchestra at Tanglewood
- Attending a mock witch trial at Salem or a Revolutionary War reenactment at Lexington, Concord or Boston

⌃ FANS WAIT FOR MORE AUTOGRAPHS AT FENWAY PARK, PRO BASEBALL'S OLDEST PLAYING FIELD.

TODD GIPSTEIN // CORBIS

MAP REF // PAGE 5 X4

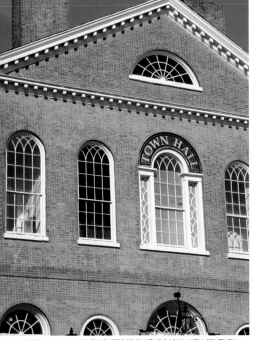

HE OLD TOWN HALL IN SALEM DATES FROM THE EARLY 19TH CENTURY. ≫

LOU JONES // LONELY PLANET IMAGES

IF THE BRITISH RETURN, THIS MINUTEMAN ACTOR ON BOSTON'S COPLEY SQUARE IS READY. ≫

THE LIKELY AFTERMATH OF A NOR'EASTER ON COMMONWEALTH AVENUE, BOSTON. ≫

MICHIGAN

SURROUNDED BY FOUR OF THE FIVE GREAT LAKES, MICHIGAN IS SO MUCH MORE THAN CARS AND MOTOWN – IT'S THE LAND OF TOWERING SAND DUNES, ENDLESS VINEYARDS, FOUR RUGGED NATIONAL FORESTS AND THE FINEST TROUT STREAMS EAST OF THE MISSISSIPPI RIVER.

⌃ PARTS OF LAKE MICHIGAN FREEZE SOLID.

- **Etymology of the State Name** From the Native American word *michigama* (large lake)
- **Nickname** Great Lakes State
- **Motto** *Si quaeris peninsulam amoenam, circumspice* (If you seek a pleasant peninsula, look about you)

- **Capital City** Lansing
- **Population** 10.1 million
- **Area** 96,810 sq miles
- **Time Zone** Eastern
- **State Bird** Robin

- **State Flower** Apple blossom
- **Major Industry** Automobile manufacturing
- **Politics** Blue state in 2008
- **Best Time to Go** August – warm nights and 40,000 cool cars at the Woodward Dream Cruise

HISTORY IN A NUTSHELL

Seeking furs, the French reached Lake Superior by the 1620s, and in 1668 Father Jacques Marquette established Sault Ste Marie, making it the oldest settlement in the Midwest. Detroit was founded 33 years later. Great Britain's victory in the French and Indian War (1758) saw them gain control of the fur trade and of Michigan, but they ceded the territory to the Americans after the Revolutionary War. After settling a land dispute with Ohio known as the Toledo War, Michigan was admitted to the Union in 1837 as the 26th state. It was in 1913 that Henry Ford introduced the world's first moving assembly line, securing Detroit's reputation as Motor City.

LANDSCAPE

Split by the 45th parallel and surrounded by the Great Lakes, Michigan is a pair of peninsulas with a temperate four-season climate. Falls are cool with spectacular colors; winters are cold with an abundance of snow. In summer everyone heads to the beach because the state's most notable feature is its 3288 miles of Great Lakes shoreline.

NATURAL BEAUTY

Michigan doesn't have mountains – it has sand dunes. Lots of them. Along its Lake Michigan shoreline is the most extensive collection of freshwater dunes in the country. These mountains of sand, which can tower more than 450 feet, border the sweetest lakes you'll ever dip your toes into. Cross the Mackinac Bridge and you'll discover Michigan's Upper Peninsula, a rugged region that features vast forests, more than 200 waterfalls and the Pictured Rocks, colorful sandstone cliffs that border Lake Superior.

PEOPLE

Michigan is overwhelmingly white (81%) and Christian in faith. African Americans make up 14% of the state's population but in Detroit they represent more than 80%, the highest percentage in any major US city and the reason many consider the city to be the center of African American culture in the Midwest.

RUGGED FOREST MEETS GREAT LAKES: 14 MILE POINT LIGHTHOUSE ON LAKE SUPERIOR. »

CULTURE & TRADITIONS

The birth of the auto industry in Michigan not only spurred the state boasting the first paved roads and traffic lights in the USA, it also gave rise to car camping. The Michigan State Park system dates to 1919 and has the third highest number of campsites (14,500) of any such system in the country. With 11,000 inland lakes, the state is also a sailor's dream and has more than 800,000 registered boats – the country's fourth highest rate. And only Texas and Pennsylvania sell more fishing licenses. Michigan residents also love their sports, even when their professional football team, the winless Lions, sets an NFL record for futility.

CUISINE

The Great Lakes give Michigan an ideal climate to grow fruit that is turned into strawberry jam, blueberry muffins, peaches-and-cream pies and sweet apple cider. But a lot of it also ends up bottled and corked: Michigan has 56 commercial wineries, with a combined 14,600 acres of vineyards, making it the fourth largest grape-growing state.

TRADEMARKS

o Classic cars – great American autos are on display in museums across the state

o Giant sand dunes – the first mountain every Michigan kid conquers

o Cherries – there's a lot of fruit in Michigan but none sweeter than its cherries

o Michael Moore – the Academy Award–winning filmmaker of the highest-grossing documentaries in Hollywood history, including *Bowling for Columbine*

o Motown – The Supremes, Stevie Wonder et al

ECONOMY

Already struggling from a 'one-state recession' since 2002, Michigan was dealt a crippling blow with the near collapse of the US auto industry in 2008. The result was the highest unemployment rate of any state and an economy lagging behind the rest of the country as Michigan's auto manufacturing sector was restructured. Though Michigan has made gains in diversifying into other fields like information technology, life sciences and advanced manufacturing, and though agriculture and tourism remain important industries, the hard times are reflected in the fact that Michigan has slipped to 27th in median household income ($47,950).

URBAN SCENE

Gritty, edgy and blue collar, Detroit's nickname, Motown, is more about music than cars. Jazz and blues musicians were already well established when Motown swept the nation in the 1960s, with such singers as Stevie Wonder, Marvin Gaye and the Supremes. Today the city's clubs are a breeding ground for techno, rock, rap and hip-hop, giving rise to Kid Rock, Eminem and the White Stripes. Ann Arbor, to the west, is home to the Harvard of the Midwest, University of Michigan (a top-notch university with the country's largest football stadium).

REPRESENTATIONS

o *8 Mile* (2002); Academy Award–winning film starring Eminem and set against Detroit's hip-hop scene

o 'Old Time Rock and Roll' (1978); this song by Detroit native Bob Seger helped launch Tom Cruise's career in *Risky Business*

o Elmore 'Dutch' Leonard, the Detroit author of crime fiction, Westerns and *Get Shorty*

o 'Big Two-Hearted River' (1925); Ernest Hemingway's classic short story about trout fishing in Michigan's Upper Peninsula

o *Middlesex* (2003); Jeffrey Eugenides' beautiful Pulitzer Prize–winning novel is set in Motor City

DID YOU KNOW?

o Michigan has the most lighthouses in the country.

o The Woodward Dream Cruise is the world's largest one-day automotive event, drawing 1.5 million spectators.

o Detroit's Ambassador Bridge is North America's busiest international border crossing.

o Battle Creek is home to Tony the Tiger and Kellogg's Corn Flakes.

MICHIGAN MYTH

During Prohibition, bootleggers would boat across the Detroit River to purchase liquor in Canada, where it was legal, and return to Michigan dragging the booze through the water on a line. If a police vessel approached, they would merely have to cut the rope. This has led to speculation that the bottom of Detroit River is covered with bottles of fine whiskey and scotch.

TEXT JIM DUFRESNE

ESSENTIAL EXPERIENCES

o Running or rolling down the Dune Climb in Sleeping Bear Dunes National Lakeshore

o Entering the International Cherry Pit Spitting Championship in Eau Claire (record: 93 feet)

o Renting a horse and buggy at Mackinac Island

o Heading to the Big House in Ann Arbor for a University of Michigan football game

o Feeling the mist and hearing the roar of Tahquamenon Falls, third largest cascade east of the Mississippi River

o Walking across the 5-mile Mackinac Bridge with 70,000 people on Labor Day

o Taking in a flick at Ford-Wyoming Drive-in near Detroit; its eight screens make it the largest drive-in movie theater in the Midwest.

DETROIT'S MOTOWN MUSEUM MOVES TO THE GROOVE OF STEVIE WONDER, MARVIN GAYE AND MORE. ☁

MAP REF // PAGE 5 Q4

FANS GO WILD AT UNIVERSITY OF MICHIGAN FOOTBALL GAMES IN ANN ARBOR. »

MACDUFF EVERTON // CORBIS

TAHQUAMENON FALLS LET LOOSE A MIGHTY CASCADE IN THE UPPER PENINSULA. »

MICHIGAN REIGNS AS THE NATION'S TOP CHERRY GROWER. »

MINNESOTA

ROCK BANDS AND DOGSLEDDERS, THEATER MAVENS AND ICE FISHERS ALL FIND COMMON GROUND IN MINNESOTA, A WIDE-OPEN STATE THAT SPANS MINNEAPOLIS' CAFÉ COOLNESS, THE BOUNDARY WATERS' WOLF-HOWLING WILDERNESS AND WEE TOWNS DOTTING THE PROVERBIAL 10,000 LAKES.

⌃ LAKE ITASCA AND 10,000 LIKE IT MAKE MINNESOTA A PADDLER'S PARADISE.

- **Etymology of the State Name** Dakota word for 'sky-tinted water'
- **Nicknames** Land of 10,000 Lakes, North Star State
- **Motto** *L'etoile du nord* (Star of the north)
- **Capital City** St Paul

- **Population** 5.2 million
- **Area** 86,943 sq miles
- **Time Zone** Central
- **State Bird** Common loon
- **State Flower** Showy lady's slipper

- **Major Industries** Agribusiness, manufacturing
- **Politics** Blue state in 2008
- **Best Time to Go** June to August – warmer weather

HISTORY IN A NUTSHELL

The Eastern Sioux and Ojibwa had Minnesota pretty much to themselves before French trappers arrived in the 17th and 18th centuries. Timber was the territory's first boom industry, and water-powered sawmills rose along the Mississippi River at Minneapolis, St Paul and Stillwater in the mid-1800s. Wheat from the prairies also needed to be processed, so flour mills churned into the next big business. Shortly after entering the Union in 1858 (state number 32), Minnesota was the first to send volunteers to fight in the Civil War. The population boomed in the late 19th century with mass immigration (especially from Scandinavia) and the development of the northern iron mines.

LANDSCAPE

Gentle plains roll through much of Minnesota and are prized as rich farmland. The piney North Woods are a different story, pocked by rocky ridges and deep lakes. In winter this area is called the 'frozen tundra' and 'icebox of the nation' thanks to snowy, 40°F-below-zero temperatures (-40°C). The scrubby, red-tinged mountains of the Iron Range slice the northeast of the state, tallgrass prairies coat the west, and valleys and bluffs hug the Mississippi River in the southeast. As for the state's most dominant feature: yes, this really is the land of 10,000 lakes, and then some. A burst of cool summer follows the long, blustery winter.

REPRESENTATIONS

- *Fargo* (1996); don't be fooled by the North Dakota title, this Coen brothers film takes place mostly in snowbound Minnesota, with unforgettable renditions of the local accent
- *Prairie Home Companion* (1974–present); Garrison Keillor's radio program tells the tongue-in-cheek tales of Lake Wobegon, a fictional small Minnesota town
- *Mary Tyler Moore Show* (1970–77); independent career gal Mary Richards worked in a wacky Minneapolis newsroom in this TV comedy series – a statue downtown marks where she threw her hat in the air during the opening theme song

THE PINES IN CHIPPEWA NATIONAL FOREST WOULD PLEASE PAUL BUNYON. ≫

NATURAL BEAUTY

The northeast's Boundary Waters Canoe Area Wilderness has more than 1000 lakes and streams in which to dip a paddle. Wolves, moose and black bears patrol the unspoiled forests, and the aurora borealis' green-draped lights fill the night sky. Next door and more remote is Voyageurs National Park, where roads disappear, and access to the pristine backcountry is by boat only. Scenic byways crisscross the bluff-strewn southeast.

PEOPLE

Minnesota's population is 86% white, 5% African American, 4% Hispanic, 4% Asian and 1% Native American. About half its residents are either Catholic or Lutheran; Minnesota, like the states that surround it, is a stronghold for the latter. The nation's largest enclaves of Somali and Hmong immigrants live in the Twin Cities (Minneapolis and St Paul), so mosques and Buddhist temples are also here.

TRADEMARKS

- Minnesota (long 'o') accent
- 10,000 lakes
- Paul Bunyan and axe-swinging lumberjacks
- Snow
- Walleye fish
- Minneapolis skyways

CULTURE & TRADITIONS

Residents are so hospitable there's a term for it: Minnesota nice. It even appears in dictionaries, though sometimes in a less positive context as 'non-confrontational' or 'passive aggressive.' Taken literally the niceness plays out in high rates of volunteerism – Twin Cities denizens rank first in the nation for helping others, and the state has a long tradition of resettling refugees, particularly from Africa and Southeast Asia. Two-thirds of Minnesotans claim German, Norwegian or Swedish ancestry, and the Scandinavian cultures have influenced the local accent and language. Phrases like 'yah, you betcha,' 'doncha know' and 'uff da' (meaning 'oops') give conversations here a distinct sound.

CUISINE

Walleye is the state fish, reeled in from the myriad lakes. The fried walleye sandwich – a breadcrumb-battered, deep-fried fillet cushioned on a hoagie roll – appears on most pub menus. Native American–grown wild rice is a Minnesota specialty and often turns up in breads and soups. So many coffee shops percolate in the Twin Cities it's one of the nation's top 10 most caffeinated places. Ethnic eats also spice up the cities, with an emphasis on Vietnamese and other Asian cuisines. Otherwise, open wide for meat and potatoes outside the metro areas.

ECONOMY

Minnesota is the number-three hog producer in the USA. Farmers also grow corn, soybeans, sugar beets and wheat. True to its milling history, Minnesota remains the leading producer of flour, which is processed into cereals and mixes (Lucky Charms and Pillsbury rolls are made here). Iron-ore mining and paper processing remain big businesses in the north, while wind turbines power the southwest's economy. Minnesota's median household income sits in the nation's top 10, at $55,800.

URBAN SCENE

Minneapolis is the artiest (and biggest) town on the prairie, with all the trimmings of progressive prosperity – swanky art museums, cool rock clubs, organic and ethnic eateries, and enough theaters to be nicknamed Mini-Apple (second only to the Big Apple, New York City). Nearby 'twin city' St Paul is smaller, quieter and more historic; it's home to F Scott Fitzgerald, Garrison Keillor and the impressive capitol building. The freighter-filled port of Duluth is a big city/North Woods mix, combining funky arts and music scenes with skiing and outdoorsy pursuits.

DID YOU KNOW?

- Bloomington's Mall of America covers the length of 88 football fields and is the nation's largest shopping center.
- SPAM, the beloved blue tin of pork, was born in Austin, Minnesota in 1937. Not only has it fed armies, it has inspired poets: more than 20,000 haiku praise its meaty goodness online and in books.

MINNESOTA MYTH

A giant with a 7-foot stride, Paul Bunyan was Minnesota's most famous lumberjack. He was so strong he dug the hole for Lake Superior with his bare hands. So great was his booming voice that limbs fell from trees when he spoke. The town of Kelliher claims to hold Bunyan's gravesite, though other states maintain they're the giant's final resting place.

TEXT KARLA ZIMMERMAN

ESSENTIAL EXPERIENCES

- Nursing coffee in a Minneapolis café while pondering last night's play or rock band
- Paddling to a remote Boundary Waters campsite and sleeping under a blanket of stars
- Driving through Bob Dylan's childhood town of Hibbing while listening to *Highway 61 Revisited*
- Fishing for walleye in a North Woods lake
- Bundling up for ice sculpting and cocoa drinking at January's St Paul Winter Carnival
- Learning to dogsled, build a boat or brew beer in artsy Grand Marais

⌃ CLAES OLDENBURG'S *SPOONBRIDGE & CHERRY* HEADLINES AT THE MINNEAPOLIS SCULPTURE GARDEN.

JOHN ELK III // LONELY PLANET IMAGES

MAP REF // PAGE 5 N3

AN ICE FISHER REELS 'EM IN. ⌃

THE LANDMARK SIGN OVER MINNEAPOLIS' ST ANTHONY MAIN AREA HAS TEMPTED WORKERS SINCE THE 1940S. ⌃

SHOVEL POINT IN TETTEGOUCHE STATE PARK ⌃
LEADS HIKERS TO SUPERIOR VIEWS.

MISSISSIPPI

IT MAY BE POOR AND FOREVER BURDENED BY ITS RACIST HISTORY, BUT MISSISSIPPI DISTINGUISHES ITSELF WITH RUSTIC SMALL TOWNS, SLEEPY BACK ROADS, JUKE JOINTS, ANTEBELLUM MANSIONS, SOUTHERN MEALS PILED HIGH ON LARGE PLATTERS, AND AN IMPRESSIVE LITERARY LEGACY.

≫ BBQ JOINTS SUCH AS THE PIG OUT INN PERFUME THE AIR FROM TUPELO TO BILOXI.

- **Etymology of the State Name** From the Chippewa *mici zibi* (great river)
- **Nickname** Magnolia State
- **Motto** *Virtute et armis* (By valor and arms)
- **Capital City** Jackson

- **Population** 2.9 million
- **Area** 48,434 sq miles
- **Time Zone** Central
- **State Bird** Mockingbird
- **State Flower** Magnolia

- **Major Industry** Agriculture
- **Politics** Red state in 2008
- **Best Time to Go** April, May, June and August – for blues festivals

HISTORY IN A NUTSHELL
The USA claimed Mississippi in 1798, and in 1817 it became the 20th state. The era of cotton, steamboats and slavery followed. Mississippi was quick to join the Confederacy in 1861, but a crippling siege at Vicksburg was key to the Union's victory. After slavery was abolished Mississippi resisted social change all the way through to the Civil Rights era of the 1960s. From 1920 to 1950, many African Americans departed for the industrial North. Hurricane Katrina walloped the Mississippi coast in 2005.

LANDSCAPE
The flattest part of the state is the Delta, which is the Mississippi River's alluvial plane rather than a true delta. Lush greenery covers the gentle, rolling hills of the midlands and north. The southern border is beachfront property on the Gulf of Mexico.

NATURAL BEAUTY
Mississippi's most pristine wilderness, the Gulf Islands National Seashore, is accessible only by private boat. The Mississippi River, while awesome, isn't necessarily pretty, and the Piney Woods are mostly denuded. But the state is blessed with a balmy climate that ensures long, hazy sunsets and a beguiling atmosphere. Spanish moss droops from sturdy oak trees and invasive kudzu vines swallow old barns. Along the Natchez Trace, a centuries-old trading path (now paved for cars) that diagonally traverses the state, all is quiet but for the chirp of birds and the hum of cicadas.

TRADEMARKS
- Delta blues (Muddy Waters, BB King, Robert Johnson, Howlin' Wolf)
- Civil Rights struggles
- William Faulkner
- 'Ole Miss' (University of Mississippi)
- Old Man River (Mississippi River)
- Elvis' birthplace in Tupelo
- Cotton gins

A PINK MIST AT SUNRISE NEAR THE MISSISSIPPI RIVER. »

PEOPLE

Mississippi is 60% white and 37% African American. The remainder is primarily Hispanic, Asian and Native American. More than 360,000 African Americans left the state in the 1940s, but the Delta remains predominantly black, with figures exceeding 75% in several counties. Two-thirds of the state's population lives in rural communities. Mississippians are generally conservative and a traveler is guaranteed to meet a Bible-thumper or two.

CULTURE & TRADITIONS

Mississippi's greatest contribution to world culture is blues music. Electric guitars, harmonicas and plaintive singing can still be heard in the Delta, which may seem sleepy during the day but often comes alive at night, when juke joints and blues clubs get cooking. Catching, cleaning, frying and eating catfish are all favorite pastimes in Mississippi, and Belzoni locals celebrate this custom with the World Catfish Festival in April.

CUISINE

Cylindrical grills are parked in front of rib joints all over the state – the sweet smell of barbecued meat may well explain why vegetables get short shrift. Pork comes in many forms (pulled pork, chops and rinds) and greens (collard greens, mustard greens, green beans) are typically stewed with ham. If meat's not your thing, there's always catfish. Perhaps unexpectedly the Delta is known for its distinctive tamales – cigar-shaped variations on the Mexican delicacy.

ECONOMY

This is not Mississippi's favorite subject. In every major US economic indicator, Mississippi ranks at or near the bottom. With an income per capita of below $16,000, high unemployment, and around 20% of the state's citizens living below the poverty level, Mississippi could be described as a 'developing' state. Agriculture (poultry and eggs, forestry, soy beans, corn, cotton) is the state's largest industry. It also produces most of the USA's farm-raised catfish. Taxes generated by casino gaming contributed nearly $35 million to the state coffers in 2007.

URBAN SCENE

Mississippi is a rural state. Jackson (population 176,000) is by far the largest city. Its historic downtown is an odd mix of state government buildings and boarded-up shop fronts. Most modern development is happening in Jackson's surrounding suburbs, which are bland expanses of tract homes and Walmart stores. Mississippi's next largest metropolitan area, Gulfport-Biloxi, was devastated by Hurricane Katrina's 30-foot storm surge. Both towns, once thriving with casinos and resorts, are still recovering.

REPRESENTATIONS

○ *O, Brother, Where Art Thou?* (2000); the Coen brothers' farcical odyssey poked fun at Mississippi's backwardness while reviving interest in 'old timey' folk songs

○ *Mississippi Burning* (1988); gripping portrayal of the Civil Rights struggle as a latter-day Civil War battle; set in 1964 and filmed on location

○ The novels of William Faulkner, set in the fictional Yoknapatawpha County

○ 'Mississippi Goddam' (1963); Nina Simone's Civil Rights lament begins: 'The name of this song is Mississippi Goddam/And I mean every word of it'

DID YOU KNOW?

○ Mississippi is among the most literary states. Faulkner, Larry Brown, Richard Ford, Ellen Gilchrist, John Grisham, Barry Hannah, Richard Wright, Tennessee Williams, Eudora Welty and Shelby Foote – all are/were Mississippians.

○ Root beer was invented in Biloxi by Edward Adolf Barq in 1898.

MISSISSIPPI MYTH

Robert Johnson (1911–38) is often touted as the greatest of the Delta blues guitarists. According to some, he could only have acquired such a prodigious talent by selling his soul to the devil. Johnson eagerly promoted the idea, claiming he'd struck a deal at a Delta crossroads. Clarksdale residents will tell you this happened at the intersection of Hwys 61 and 49 (within the town limits) but darker, lonelier crossroads can be found throughout the Delta, all suitable spots to swap your soul for nimble fingers. If Johnson really did make such a bargain, the devil was quick to exact his price. Johnson died under mysterious circumstances at the age of 27.

TEXT TOM DOWNS

PATRICK FRILET // CORBIS

⌃ CRAWFISH SLIDE INTO THE POT AT A VICKSBURG FESTIVAL.

ESSENTIAL EXPERIENCES

○ Getting your mojo working in the Delta

○ Eating rib tips from a Styrofoam tray

○ Inspecting William Faulkner's notes, scrawled on the wall of his study, in Oxford

○ Making a pilgrimage to Elvis' birthplace, in Tupelo

○ Boning up on Civil War history in Vicksburg

○ Following an ancient footpath, the Natchez Trace, by car

MAP REF // PAGE 5 Q11

DELTA FARMERS HAVE HARVESTED 'KING COTTON' SINCE THE EARLY 1800S. »

THE *DELTA QUEEN* STEAMBOAT CHUGS DOWN OLD MAN RIVER. »

A GUITARIST IN CLARKSDALE, WHERE BLUES MUSICIANS HAVE BEEN KNOWN TO MAKE DEALS WITH THE DEVIL. »

MISSOURI

LINKED WITH THE GREAT PLAINS, MIDWEST AND THE SOUTH, MISSOURI HAS FRENCH ROOTS, RIVAL CITIES, GORGEOUS OZARK HILLS, FORESTS, STREAMS AND A FONDNESS, IN SOME PARTS, FOR BANJO-PICKERS AND SQUARE DANCING.

⌃ RESIDENTS IN RURAL MISSOURI PERSONALIZE THEIR FENCE POSTS TO HELP VISITORS FIND THE RIGHT ADDRESS.

- **Etymology of the State Name** From a Sioux word for 'those with dugout canoes'
- **Nickname** Show-Me State
- **Motto** *Salus populi suprema lex esto* (Let the welfare of the people be the supreme law)
- **Capital City** Jefferson City
- **Population** 5.9 million
- **Area** 69,709 sq miles
- **Time Zone** Central
- **State Bird** Native bluebird
- **State Flower** White hawthorn blossom
- **Major Industries** Aerospace machinery, mining, tourism
- **Politics** Swing state (red in 2008)
- **Best Time to Go** May, June, September, October – miss the big summer crowds

HISTORY IN A NUTSHELL

Home to Mississippi Native American groups who farmed the land at the time France claimed the area in 1682, Missouri passed to US hands with the Louisiana Purchase in 1803. In 1821 it became the nation's 24th state, admitted as a slave state per the Missouri Compromise. The issue didn't go away, and the Missouri–Kansas border was full of tension between slaveholders and abolitionists through the Civil War. At the turn of the 20th century, St Louis – a major hub on railway and river routes – hosted both the Olympic Games and World's Fair in 1904. The next 100 years weren't as good, with the decline of railroads cutting many jobs.

LANDSCAPE

Missouri's southern half is crossed by winding roads through glaciated hills of the Ozark Mountains, which spread to the Arkansas border. Further north, plains stretch towards the Iowa and Nebraska borders, with many hills and river bluffs along the Missouri River, as well as the Mississippi, which makes up the eastern border. Missouri's continental climate brings humid hot summers (reaching 90°F/32°C most days of July), while in January high temperatures hover just above freezing.

NATURAL BEAUTY

Missouri is the Great Plains' most consistently scenic state, particularly in the southern third of rolling Ozarks and streams cutting through the dense Mark Twain National Forest. A worthy detour from I-70 between St Louis and Kansas City follows Hwy 100 along the Missouri River through the German–US wine town Hermann.

PEOPLE

Missouri's population is 87% white (many with German, French, Irish or English surnames), while the two urban centers have large African American populations (12% of the state population). In recent years, St Louis has become a 'Little Bosnia,' with some 50,000 refugees. Nearly four in five Missourians are Christians.

THE GATEWAY ARCH DENOTES ST LOUIS' HISTORIC ROLE AS 'GATEWAY TO THE WEST.'

CULTURE & TRADITIONS

Branson's country-music scene is legendary, but the state has further musical contributions. The fiddle is the state instrument, celebrating a long fiddler tradition that began with French and Scot settlers and morphed into Ozark square dances. A state championship is held in the State Fair, in Sedalia, in August. Other sorts of Missouri-bred tunes take over during the Scott Joplin Ragtime Festival, held in June in Sedalia.

ECONOMY

Missouri hauls in about $225 billion annually, from sources including tourism, limestone and aerospace machinery. St Louis is a major aviation and metal manufacturer, and houses Budweiser's headquarters. Kansas City, meanwhile, is big on livestock and grains. Missouri's mines bring in about 90% of the USA's principal lead. Agriculture is less important than in some Great Plains states, though African American innovator George Washington Carver researched peanut and sweet potato as better alternative crops to cotton. Missourians' average household income is about $45,000 annually.

DID YOU KNOW?

o So few legislators wanted to move to the capital in Jefferson City that a law was passed requiring they live there.

o Missouri's southeastern 980-square-mile 'boot heel' isn't part of Arkansas because in 1820 a wealthy farmer there petitioned to become part of Missouri when it joined the Union.

TRADEMARKS

o Branson's country music shows and cornball hillbilly spoofs

o Ozark Mountains

o St Louis' Gateway Arch

o Headwaters of the Missouri River

o Mark Twain

o Dueling banjos

CUISINE

Kansas City's sweet BBQ sauce justifies a trip for many, while St Louis' square-cut 'St Louis pizza' comes wafer-thin (try it at Imo's or Serra's). St Louis' famed World's Fair in 1904 saw the debut of the ice-cream cone (some say it was an accident; waffle was used only when cups ran out), and the Soulard Market here is the oldest west of the Mississippi. The local Norton/Cynthiana grape – the state's official grape since 2003 – is used in Missourian wines. Out in the country you'll find Ozark pudding served with fresh apples and pecans.

URBAN SCENE

St Louis looks east, Kansas City looks west. Both are fun places, with a lot of changing urban character depending on the neighborhood. Beyond the Arch, St Louis's Soulard is a red-brick French-era neighborhood that's home to Budweiser and wild Bastille Day parties. Student-filled Delmar Loop is all clubs, such as Chuck Berry's Blueberry Hill. In Kansas City, 18th and Vine is a historic African American neighborhood, with good jazz (Robert Altman's *Kansas City* was filmed here) and BBQ, while the ritzy Westport is another dining scene.

REPRESENTATIONS

o *Meet Me in St Louis* (1944); the classic musical starring Judy Garland, set around the 1904 St Louis World's Fair

o *Adventures of Huckleberry Finn* (1884); Mark Twain's follow-up to 1876's *The Adventures of Tom Sawyer* follows Huck's adventures on the Mississippi

o *The Twenty-Seventh City* (1988); Jonathan Franzen's surreal version of a St Louis run by a corrupt police chief from India

o *The Assassination of Jesse James by the Coward Robert Ford* (1983); Ron Hansen's account of the Missouri outlaw's famous demise became a film in 2008

MISSOURI LEGEND

Over the years 'Show Me' has taken on a new meaning for this central swing state that professes to be more skeptical than its neighbors. Many attribute the slogan to Missouri congressman Willard Duncan Vandiver, who voiced his discomfort with all the 'frothy eloquence' at a fancy East Coast dinner in 1899, and said 'I am from Missouri. You have got to show me.' It's less likely due to a 1974 mass streak (naked running) across Missouri University that kick-started a streaking phenomenon across the USA.

TEXT ROBERT REID

ESSENTIAL EXPERIENCES

o Driving backcountry on hilly roads through the Ozarks

o Taking a space-capsule–like ride up the Gateway Arch in St Louis

o Getting your fingers dirty with some Kansas City BBQ (either Gates or Arthur Bryant's)

o Foot-tapping to country tunes at a cheesy Branson show

o Seeing Tom Sawyer's fence (from the Mark Twain book) in Hannibal

⌃ TOES TAP AND HANDS CLAP WHEN BRANSON'S BANJO-PICKERS GET GOING.

MAP REF // PAGE 5 P9

PRISTINE WATERS FLOW THROUGH THE OZARKS AT ALLEY SPRING, IN THE JACKS FORK RIVER. ≫

PLAYING SOCCER IS ONE WAY TO WORK OFF THAT KANSAS CITY BBQ DINNER. ≫

MONTANA

THIS FREE-THINKING, INDEPENDENT STATE HAS SKIES SO BIG YOU'D THINK THE HORIZON HAD RUN FOR COVER. IT'S ALSO HOME TO GLACIER AND YELLOWSTONE NATIONAL PARKS, TOWERING PEAKS, GRIZZLY BEARS AND MOOSE.

- **Etymology** Derived from the Spanish word *montaña* (mountain)
- **Nicknames** Treasure State, Big Sky Country, Land of Shining Mountains, The Last Best Place
- **Motto** *Oro y plata* (Gold and silver)

- **Capital City** Helena
- **Population** 957,861
- **Area** 147,046 sq miles
- **Time Zone** Mountain
- **State Bird** Western meadowlark

- **State Flower** Bitterroot
- **Major Industries** Farming, ranching, logging, mining, tourism
- **Politics** Red state in 2008
- **Best Time to Go** June to August – Fourth of July rodeos and hiking in the national parks

HISTORY IN A NUTSHELL

Before the trappers and the traders, the gold rush of 1863 and the 'white gold' rush of the 1980s (when developers stampeded the state to develop ski areas, national parks and resorts), this territory was home to the Crow, Cheyenne, Blackfeet, Assiniboine, Gros Ventres, Kootenai, Salish, Pend d'Oreille and Kalispel peoples. These native tribes fought fiercely for their lands, and many historic battles took place here, including the Battles of Big Hole, Big Horn (Custer's Last Stand) and Rosebud. In 1889 Montana became the 41st state of the Union. Since then, it's maintained its frontier personality.

LANDSCAPE

There's plenty of land up in Big Sky Country and not many folks to share it with – Montana is the fourth largest state in the nation but ranks 44th in population. Of course, there are the Rocky Mountains – and the hodgepodge of 'smaller' ranges like the Bitterroot and Lewis that collide to form this massive American spine – but nearly 60% of the state is actually high prairie. Glaciers and rivers have also played their roles in the formation of the state's dramatic topography.

NATURAL BEAUTY

Montana is home to glaciers and brawny, snow-choked mountains, iceberg lakes, icy mountain rivers and the big-time fauna of Glacier and Yellowstone National Parks. It's a place of hard-won existence, and from the stark, stoic landscape comes the roughest and toughest of creatures. Here buffalo still charge across velvety prairie grasslands, while America's big cats (lynx, bobcat and mountain lion) patrol the night. Hovering above it all is the arching blue sky.

PEOPLE

This fast-growing state is home to a primarily white population of mainly German, Scandinavian and Irish descent. There's also a fairly sizable Native American population (about 6.4%). Most folks are Protestant, though Catholics make up about 24% of the population and 18% declare no religious affiliation.

CULTURE & TRADITIONS

With so much big sky up here, as well as a few good universities, there's a mix of mountain hippie types and conspiracy-theory-riddled gun nuts. But these small subcultures are far outweighed by the starched-shirt ranchers and farmers that'd sooner shoot a coyote than save one. While 'family values' are big here, so is personal freedom, and what you do on your own land is up to you.

CUISINE

There's more for dinner than just beef. How about buffalo burgers and ethnic specialties such as Russian beet soup, Scandinavian porridge and Scottish scones? Also on the menu are native ingredients like white honey and huckleberry bread, and maybe even a pepper-crusted trout fresh caught this afternoon.

DID YOU KNOW?

- Livestock outnumber people in Montana by 12 to one!
- Montana has the largest grizzly bear population in the continental USA.
- Both actor Gary Cooper (1901–61) and motorcycle daredevil Evel Knievel (1938–2007) were born in Montana.

ECONOMY

This is a poor state. Income per capita is around $25,000; the nation's fourth lowest. But raising your own cattle and your own crops on your own terms doesn't require that much money. While the growing season is relatively short, agriculture remains one of the state's biggest producers, with folks growing wheat, barley, sugar, beets, oats and more. Cattle and sheep ranching are also big, as are logging and mining for gold, coal, silver and talc. Millions of visitors come to the state each year to see Glacier National Park, portions of Yellowstone National Park, Flathead Lake and the battle sites of several Indian Wars, including Little Bighorn.

SO MUCH ROOM TO ROAM HAS LEFT THIS CRITTER DOG-TIRED BY DAY'S END. »

URBAN SCENE

Helena is the capital city, but with only 28,000 residents, it still feels like a small town. Billings is the largest city in the state, but there's less to do there than in the cultural hotspots of Missoula and Bozeman. The latter are both university towns, where 'culture' tends away from the theater and gallery beat to the 'let's go out and play in the mountains' scene.

TRADEMARKS

○ Glaciers

○ Custer's Last Stand

○ Fluffy 'Big Sky' clouds that look like bunnies and spaceships

○ Freedom – some Montana highways didn't even have a speed limit until the 1990s

○ Fly fishing

○ Dinosaur fossils

○ Lewis and Clark sites

○ Rodeos and powwows

○ Bison

REPRESENTATIONS

○ Portions of many classic movies were filmed here, including *The River Wild* (1994), *The Horse Whisperer* (1998), *Hidalgo* (2004) and *Under Siege 2* (1995)

○ *A River Runs Through It* (1992); probably the most famous Montana movie, starring Brad Pitt and based on a story by Montana author Norman Fitzroy Maclean

○ Cowboy poetry events are held throughout the summer, as are Native American powwows

MONTANA MYTH

There's not just gold in them thar hills. There are ghosts aplenty. Two of Montana's most famous haunting stories come from the old mining boomtown of Bannack, where the 'senior ghost in residence' is Henry Plummer. Plummer started out in Bannack as a lawman, but he soon changed sides and joined a group of roughriders known as the 'Innocents,' who terrorized the people of the region. In 1863, the local miners had had enough of Plummer's Innocents, and they brought them in, hanging 24 gang members and Plummer himself. His ghost is said to still haunt the town, as is the ghost of a teenage girl, who drowned in a nearby dredge and now haunts the Hotel Meade.

TEXT GREG BENCHWICK

JOHN ELK III // LONELY PLANET IMAGES

ESSENTIAL EXPERIENCES

○ Pretending you look as good as Brad Pitt as you cast your rod along some of the best creek fishing in the West

○ Getting lost on the more than 700 miles of trails in Glacier National Park, only to find yourself again

○ Sipping on a glass of chardonnay as you chat with an artist in residence during Missoula's First Friday Art Walks

○ Taking the quick way down as you test those mountain-bike shocks on summer downhill runs like War Dance and Wounded Knee at Big Sky Resort

○ Visiting Little Bighorn Battlefield Monument, where General George Custer made his last stand and Native Americans, including Crazy Horse of the Lakota Sioux, got some final licks in

○ Attending a cowboy-poetry event or Native American powwow

MAP REF // PAGE 4 I4

⌃ ATTENDING A NATIVE AMERICAN POWWOW IS A MONTANA MUST.

A FLY FISHER MAKES HER WAY TO A RUBY RIVER CASTING CALL. «

MONTANA'S FAMOUS BIG SKY DWARFS THE RURAL LANDSCAPE. «

CRACKER LAKE'S TURQUOISE WATER GLEAMS IN GLACIER NATIONAL PARK. «

NEBRASKA

FAMED FOR CORN AND WIDE-OPEN SPACES, NEBRASKA HAS PLAINS THAT ROLL A LITTLE MORE TO THE SOUTH THAN THOSE IN KANSAS – AS WELL AS A COUPLE OF SURPRISING CITIES (HISTORIC OMAHA AND THE CAPITAL, LINCOLN) AND SOME EYE-POPPING ROCK FORMATIONS IN THE PANHANDLE.

≈ SPECTATORS WAIT UNTIL THE COWS COME HOME AT A CATTLE DRIVE IN OGALLALA.

○ **Etymology of the State Name** Omaha-Ponca name for 'flat water,' the original name of the Platte River

○ **Nickname** Cornhusker State

○ **Motto** Equality before the law

○ **Capital City** Lincoln

○ **Population** 1.8 million

○ **Area** 77,358 sq miles

○ **Time Zones** Central, Mountain

○ **State Bird** Western meadowlark

○ **State Flower** Goldenrod

○ **Major Industry** Agriculture

○ **Politics** Red state in 2008

○ **Best Time to Go** March – to see cranes; June to August – canoeing; September to November – football

HISTORY IN A NUTSHELL

Nebraska was home to many nomadic tribes at the dawn of the USA's independence, including some 10,000 Pawnee. Lewis and Clark tiptoed through the northeast corner in 1804 and a smattering of trappers followed, the trickle turning to a flood by the 1840s, as pioneers crossed on the Oregon Trail. Railroads had replaced covered wagons by the time the 1862 Homestead Act opened up 160-acre allotments of the rich soil. In 1867 Nebraska became the 37th state and during WWII was home to prison camps.

LANDSCAPE

Nebraska consists of plains: the Loess Plains, near the Missouri River valley on the Iowa border to the east turn into the Dissected Till Plains and Great Plains to the west. The state's main river, the 310-mile Platte, follows I-70 on an east–west path. Nebraska's steppelike climate averages roughly 75°F (24°C) in July and 21°F (-6°C) in January. Rainfall is heaviest in the east (about 30 inches annually, and half that in the panhandle).

NATURAL BEAUTY

Off I-70, western Nebraska offers some surprises. The nicest natural attractions are clustered in the panhandle – including eroded rock formations like Chimney Rock and Scotts Bluff, and spooky hikes around Toadstool Geological Park, outside Crawford. Further east, following US-20, you can paddle the Niobrara River or detour south into the dune- and pond-filled Sand Hills, a broad 20,000 square mile area in north-central Nebraska, reached by US-83.

PEOPLE

Ancestors of 19th-century German, Irish, English, Czech and Swedish settlers make up some 85% of Nebraska's population. Only about 5% of Nebraskans are African American, overtaken in numbers recently by Hispanic Americans (now about 7.5%). Thurston County is almost fully Native American, as it's home to Omaha and Winnebago reservations. Recent migration to Lincoln or Omaha has resulted in some areas of western Nebraska reverting to 'wilderness' (as determined by person-per-acre ratio!).

PIVOT IRRIGATION WETS ONE OF THE STATE'S UBIQUITOUS CORNFIELDS. ≫

CULTURE & TRADITIONS

Nebraskans can take, or give, a joke. Every June, little Norfolk – the hometown of Johnny Carson – stages the Great American Comedy Festival. Meanwhile, state fairs have gone retro, bringing back a long-dead event – a ribbon for biggest pig. A recent winner was Broken Bow's Teddy Bear, breaking the 800-pound mark before his second birthday. Nebraska football fans are considered the nation's best sports, often cheering opponents' good plays.

TRADEMARKS

o Corn!

o University of Nebraska's 'big red' Cornhusker football

o Millionaires – Omaha has more per capita than any other US city (yes, Warren Buffet lives here)

o Steakhouses

CUISINE

Despite all that corn, Nebraska often bills itself as the 'Beef State,' as one in five US steaks and burgers have Nebraskan birth certificates. Omaha has the most famous steakhouses, including Johnny's, a 1940s supper club near the old stockyards. Meanwhile, a couple of notable creations include Kool-Aid powdered drink (from Hastings, 1927), the Russian *pirozhki*-influenced Runza sandwich, and (though debated) the Reuben sandwich, supposedly invented in Omaha in 1925.

ECONOMY

Nebraska's ultra-comfy tax laws (low to no tax) have helped spawn a giant insurance industry. Otherwise, it takes corn, soybeans, cattle, hogs and wheat to get Nebraska ticking. Crops are bringing in increasing sums this decade, up to $9 billion in 2008. Nebraskans earn about $38,000 on average in the cities, $29,000 in rural areas.

URBAN SCENE

Nebraska's two main cities cluster at the east end of the state. The bigger of the two, Omaha – set on the Missouri River banks – has a big art scene (including the lovely Joslyn Art Museum and cutting-edge Bemis Center), plus the bohemian-chic gallery and restaurant scene of the restored Old Market district, along with a rising music scene of indie-cred Saddle Back Records (home to Bright Eyes). Lincoln ('Star City') is compact by comparison, with a busy pedestrian-friendly center, Nebraska University, the Haymarket dining/drinking area and the lovely capitol, all within short walks of each other.

REPRESENTATIONS

o Jack Nicholson's *About Schmidt* (2002) and Matthew Broderick's *Election* (1999) were filmed in Nebraska

o *Pioneers!* (1913); Willa Cather wrote many books inspired by her Nebraskan childhood – this one became a 1992 film with Jessica Lange

o Omaha is frequently sung about, but no one seems to know where it is: the Counting Crows say it's 'somewhere in middle America' ('Omaha,' 1993), while Groucho Marx put it in the 'foothills of Tennessee' in the 1940 song 'Omaha, Nebraska'

o *Nebraska* (1982); Bruce Springsteen's classic album was based on the true story of teenage murderer Charles Starkweather

DID YOU KNOW?

o Nebraska has more miles of river than any other state.

o On fall Saturdays Lincoln's Memorial Stadium is the third most-populous 'city' in the state; all 85,000 seats have sold out since 1962.

o Lincoln's tall capitol – sometimes called 'the penis of the prairies' – was deemed one of the world's 50 most beautiful buildings when opened in 1932.

NEBRASKA LEGEND

The little town of Max, in the southwestern corner, had UFOs before Roswell, NM, was even founded. In 1884, as one yarn goes, a cowboy roundup near Max was interrupted by a crashing flyer saucer that burned a guy and tore up the land. Local publications the *Nebraska Nugget* and *Nebraska State Journal* reported the story, but no evidence remains. Anyone wonder why UFOs don't land in big cities?

TEXT ROBERT REID

≫ SCOTTS BLUFF AND OTHER GEOLOGICAL ODDITIES RISE IN THE PANHANDLE.

RICHARD CUMMINS // LONELY PLANET IMAGES

ESSENTIAL EXPERIENCES

o Exploring the panhandle – one of the nation's great cross-country secrets, home to natural monuments and the campy Carhenge collection of cars replicating Stonehenge (in Alliance)

o Watching some of the half-million sandhill cranes stopping to roost in February and March along the North Platte River area

o Canoeing the Niobrara River, just east of cowboy town Valentine

o Dining and gallery-hopping in Omaha's downtown and restored Old Market district

MAP REF // PAGE 4 L7

ALLIANCE'S CARHENGE – IS THE RESEMBLANCE CLOSE ENOUGH TO FOOL A DRUID? ≫

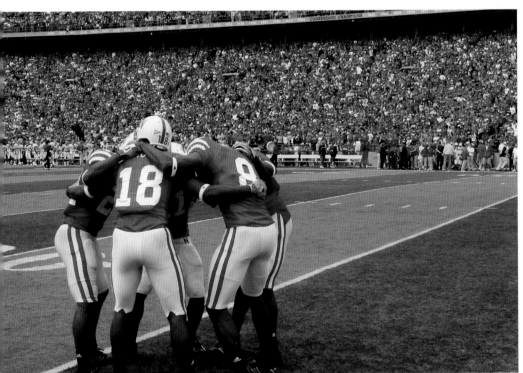

UNIVERSITY OF NEBRASKA'S BELOVED CORNHUSKERS FOOTBALL TEAM HAS SOLD OUT ALL GAMES SINCE 1962. ≫

HISTORIC WAGON – THAT'S HOW PIONEERS ROLLED. ≫

NEVADA

INFAMOUS FOR ITS NEON-LIT CASINOS AND THE HURLY-BURLY LAS VEGAS STRIP, NEVADA HAS MORE RURAL HEARTLAND THAN YOU'D EXPECT – COWBOY RANCHES, OLD WEST MINING TOWNS AND A WILD OUTBACK MADE FOR HIGH-OCTANE ADVENTURES, STRETCHING FROM THE MOJAVE DESERT NORTH TO THE RUBY MOUNTAINS.

- **Etymology of the State Name** Spanish for 'snow-capped'
- **Nickname** Silver State
- **Motto** All for our country
- **Capital City** Carson City
- **Population** 2.6 million
- **Area** 110,567 sq miles
- **Time Zone** Pacific
- **State Bird** Mountain bluebird
- **State Flower** Sagebrush
- **Major Industry** Tourism
- **Politics** Swing state (blue in 2008)
- **Best Time to Go** March to May – desert wildflowers and milder temperatures in the south; mostly snow-free highways in the north

HISTORY IN A NUTSHELL

In the mid-19th century, trappers and traders on the Spanish Trail blazed through the final area of the USA to be explored by Anglos. After Mexico's defeat in 1848, this area became US territory. Not long afterwards, in 1859, the Comstock Lode, the richest vein of silver ever discovered in the USA, was struck at Virginia City. Pro-Unionist Nevada was ratified by President Lincoln as the 36th US state during the Civil War in 1864. The state was carried through the Great Depression by legalized gambling and the construction of the Hoover Dam. In Nevada's remote deserts, nuclear bomb testing took place between WWII and 1992.

LANDSCAPE

Much of southern Nevada is a desert plateau that receives very little rainfall. Desert flash floods are likely in spring though, and in summer the mercury soars above 100°F (38°C). The Great Basin, in northern Nevada, is an arid region with large tracts of desert, which is dominated by north–south mountain ranges and valleys. Nevada's highest mountains peak above 13,000 feet and are covered with snow in winter. Today the federal government owns more than 85% of Nevada's land, a state of affairs that was fiercely contested during the 'Sagebrush Rebellion' of the late 1970s.

NATURAL BEAUTY

Not far from Las Vegas, the psychedelic sandstone formations of Valley of Fire are among the most fantastically eroded in the Southwest, while climbers head to Red Rock Canyon, a rugged escarpment formed by dramatic tectonic-plate collisions. Lake Tahoe straddles the California state line in the north, where the Black Rock Desert calls to adventurers. East near Utah, Great Basin National Park protects an incredible range of geologic zones, from underground limestone caves and the desert floor to ancient bristlecone pine forests, ice fields and the summit of Wheeler Peak (13,063 feet).

PEOPLE

Nevada's majority population is white. But one out of four state residents has some Latino ancestry, with Spanish spoken in approximately 15% of homes. Native American tribal bands are scattered across the state. Roughly half of Nevadans are Christians, with over 100,000 Mormons as well.

CULTURE & TRADITIONS

Despite the free-wheelin' reputation of Las Vegas (famously known as 'Sin City'), as well as the fact that prostitution (in brothels) is still legal in many rural counties, Nevadans are generally conservative when it comes to social mores. More acceptable pursuits than gambling are attending professional rodeos, which happen year-round across the state, most famously at Reno in June and Las Vegas in December. The National Cowboy Poetry Gathering takes place at Elko's Western Folklife Center in January.

REPRESENTATIONS

- *The Cooler* (2003), directed by Wayne Kramer; independent film about an old-school Las Vegas casino
- *Live from Las Vegas* (2005); swingin' 1960s lounge sounds as recorded by Rat Packer Dean Martin
- *CSI: Crime Scene Investigation;* this hit TV series shows off real-life Las Vegas locations
- 'Viva Las Vegas' (1964); the city's unofficial theme song, as recorded by Elvis Presley
- *Fear and Loathing in Las Vegas* (1972), by Hunter S Thompson; drug-addled adventures with the gonzo journalist
- *Casino* (1995), directed by Martin Scorsese; a mafia epic set in Las Vegas
- *Brothel: Mustang Ranch and Its Women* (2001), by Alexa Albert; a narrative of life at Nevada's once-most-famous brothel
- *Bugsy* (1991), directed by Barry Levinson; Hollywood's fairy-tale version of the start of the Las Vegas Strip

IT PAYS TO HAVE A GPS DEVICE IN THE BLACK ROCK DESERT. »

CUISINE

Because much of Nevada is open range for cattle, this is an unbeatable place for steaks. The influence of 19th-century Basque immigrants, who came to work as shepherds, ranch hands and hoteliers, can still be tasted at traditional Basque dinner houses, where hearty meals are served family-style. Tourists gorge themselves at all-you-can-eat buffets in casino hotels too. Since the invasion of US and international star chefs, restaurants in Las Vegas now compete with LA, San Francisco and NYC.

ECONOMY

Historically speaking, what made Nevada's economy grow was its ranch lands and vast underground mineral deposits, especially silver, gold and copper. The Transcontinental Railroad arrived in the early 20th century, and the Hoover Dam was built during the Great Depression to generate hydroelectric power. WWII brought military bases, munitions factories and atomic-bomb testing projects. Today Nevada runs on tourism, dominated by the casino gaming industry. Henderson, a suburb of Las Vegas, is one of the fastest-growing metropolitan areas in the USA. However, most Nevadans would have to work three full-time minimum-wage jobs just to afford their own house there.

TRADEMARKS

o Casinos and gambling

o Las Vegas Strip

o Showgirls

o Brothels

o Silver mines

o Pony Express Trail

o Atomic bombs

URBAN SCENE

Las Vegas has been an infamous haven for dirty weekend getaways since mobsters, the Rat Pack and Hollywood starlets partied here. Vegas' biggest attractions these days aren't just casinos – there's an edgy cuisine scene, as well as over-the-top spas and shopping arcades, and an eclectic visual-arts community. Las Vegas' northern counterpart is Reno, nicknamed the 'Biggest Little City in the World,' which has casinos aplenty. It's also an outdoor-sports mecca, offering quick access to Lake Tahoe. The cowboy communities of Elko and Winnemucca line the I-80 corridor, while more rural interior towns like Ely and Austin preserve tales of Nevada's hardscrabble pioneer mining days.

DID YOU KNOW?

o Nevada's nickname is the 'Silver State,' but its biggest mining industry is gold.

o Boulder City is the only town in Nevada where gambling is illegal.

o The Stratosphere Tower on the Las Vegas Strip is the tallest building west of the Mississippi River (1149 feet).

NEVADA LEGEND

According to Hollywood myth, there was little more than tumbleweeds and cacti the day gangster Benjamin 'Bugsy' Siegel rolled into Las Vegas and finished building a glamorous casino resort under the searing desert sun. But in fact Bugsy's Flamingo wasn't the first casino on the Las Vegas Strip – the El Rancho opened in 1941. Even more hoary gambling halls with sawdust-covered floors started dealing cards in downtown Las Vegas in 1905.

TEXT SARA BENSON

⌃ FLY GEYSER SPEWS A WETTER VIEW OF BLACK ROCK'S WILDERNESS.

ESSENTIAL EXPERIENCES

o Playing Texas hold 'em poker at 2am on the Las Vegas Strip

o Walking across art-deco Hoover Dam, once the world's largest

o Getting naked at the Burning Man 'experiment' in the Black Rock Desert

o Driving US-50, aka 'The Loneliest Road in America'

o Cheering on the camel races in the 19th-century mining boomtown of Virginia City

o Keeping watch for UFOs along the Extraterrestrial Hwy outside Area 51

MAP REF // PAGE 4 E7

LAKE TAHOE SENDS OUT ITS SIREN SONG TO KAYAKERS COME SUMMERTIME. ≫

RYAN FOX // LONELY PLANET IMAGES

TAKING A BREAK FROM BLACKJACK AT VEGAS' TREASURE ISLAND HOTEL. ≫

A COWGIRL GETS THE NEON TREATMENT. ≫

NEW HAMPSHIRE

CROWNED BY THE GRANITE GRANDEUR OF THE WHITE MOUNTAINS, INDEPENDENT-MINDED NEW HAMPSHIRE HAS A SPLIT PERSONALITY: PART BOSTON SUBURB, PART WOODSY WILDERNESS, WITH A TAD OF SEACOAST THROWN IN FOR GOOD MEASURE.

⌃ FALL PAINTS A SHELBURNE FOREST IN IMPRESSIONIST BRUSH STROKES.

- **Etymology of the State Name** Named after the English county of Hampshire
- **Nickname** The Granite State
- **Motto** Live free or die
- **Capital City** Concord
- **Population** 1.3 million
- **Area** 9350 sq miles
- **Time Zone** Eastern
- **State Bird** Purple finch
- **State Flower** Purple lilac
- **Major Industries** High-tech and service industries
- **Politics** Blue state in 2008
- **Best Time to Go** May to October – camping, hiking, sailing and leaf-peeping

HISTORY IN A NUTSHELL

New Hampshire lured settlers with the calm waters and vast forests that had long supported the native Abenaki people. Straight evergreens perfect for ship masts helped the British establish a thriving shipbuilding and timber trade, with permanent settlements concentrated along the coastal strip near Portsmouth. New Hampshire declared independence in January 1776, half a year before the signing of the Declaration of Independence, and joined the Union on June 21, 1788, as the ninth state.

LANDSCAPE

Southern New Hampshire is relatively flat. Heading north, rolling hill and lake country builds dramatically to the granite peaks of the White Mountains before easing back down into the Great North Woods at the state's northern tip. The climate is cold and snowy in winter and warm and humid in summer, but rarely scorching thanks to the tempering influences of altitude, latitude and ocean breezes.

DID YOU KNOW?

- The highest sustained wind speed ever recorded on earth was 231 miles per hour at the top of Mount Washington.
- New Hampshire has more roller coasters per capita than any other state.
- It has the USA's lowest poverty rate (8%).

NATURAL BEAUTY

New Hampshire is most famous for the White Mountains. Hiking trails, a road and cog railway climb to the exposed granite of Mount Washington (6288 feet), the state's loftiest peak. For hikers, the Appalachian Trail runs through the heart of White Mountain National Forest, and the Kancamagus Hwy is one of New England's most scenic drives. The central, mountain-backed Lake Winnipesaukee is the largest of several lakes popular for boating, while sandy beaches line the state's short southeast seacoast. Northern New Hampshire shelters prime moose habitat amid the lakes at the Connecticut River's headwaters; look for the highway sign: 'Brake for Moose: It Could Save Your Life – Hundreds of Collisions!'

CANOEISTS HAVE THE ANDROSCOGGIN RIVER TO THEMSELVES. ⌃

TRADEMARKS

o Granite

o Midnight voting

o Presidential primaries

o Low taxes

o Rugged individualism

PEOPLE

New Hampshire is predominantly white (96%). The state has more people of French and French Canadian ancestry (roughly 25%) than any other state in the Union. Population density is heaviest in southern New Hampshire, where cross-border commuters have congregated, seeking lower taxes and rural living within driving distance of Boston. More than half of New Hampshire's residents are émigrés from other states (nearly 56%); New Hampshire ranks sixth in the nation in this category. Catholics and Protestants each constitute roughly one third of the population.

CUISINE

New Hampshire's French Canadian roots show through at Christmas, when some families still make the traditional spiced meat pie, known as *tourtière*. In the fall, abundant crops of pumpkins, apples and corn make their way into pies, cider donuts and chowder. A popular winter tradition is 'sugar-on-snow' – boiling maple syrup poured over snow, sometimes accompanied by sour pickles to cut the sweetness.

CULTURE & TRADITIONS

New Hampshirites' libertarian streak is manifest everywhere: from the tax code (no sales or income taxes) to the state motto (Live free or die); from loose firearms restrictions to a devil-may-care attitude towards seatbelts, motorcycle helmets and car insurance (none required). Early voting is another long-standing tradition – midnight ballots in Dixville Notch and Hart's Location are routinely the first cast in every US presidential election; and New Hampshire's first-in-the-nation presidential primary dates back to 1920. More than a third of voters are registered Independents. Residents love the great outdoors (boating, fishing, hiking and hunting). As elsewhere in New England, harvest festivals are popular, but nothing measures up to the annual Keene Pumpkin Festival, where more than 20,000 jack-o'-lanterns are lit on 40-foot scaffolds around the village green.

ECONOMY

Computers and electronics are a driving force in southern New Hampshire, as are finance, insurance and real estate. Statewide, tourism and retail trade round out the service economy. New Hampshire's manufacturing sector produces machinery and metal products, while agricultural specialties include Christmas trees, dairy products, apples and maple syrup. New Hampshire's income per capita ($41,440) and median household income ($62,370) both rank within the national top 10.

URBAN SCENE

New Hampshire's urban centers cluster near the state's southeastern corner. Manchester is the largest city and Concord – its cousin upstream on the Merrimack River – is the capital, but for charm, nothing beats the historic city of Portsmouth on the Atlantic seacoast. Portsmouth has an appealing collection of old redbrick buildings, a prominent white-steepled church and a picturesque waterfront featuring 17th-century gravestones, leafy parks and a collection of historic homes converted into the Strawbery Banke Museum.

NEW HAMPSHIRE LEGEND

Nature has an ironic sense of humor. New Hampshire's iconic image, a rock formation called The Old Man of the Mountain for its appearance in profile, has long been emblazoned on state license plates and highway signs, and is represented prominently on New Hampshire's state quarter. Sadly for residents, The Old Man was smashed to smithereens in a rock slide on May 3, 2003. Many still mourn his loss and plans are underway for a monument to keep his memory alive.

TEXT GREGOR CLARK

ESSENTIAL EXPERIENCES

o Climbing New England's tallest mountain, Mount Washington, by foot, car or cog railway

o Cruising down the Kancamagus Hwy through the heart of the White Mountains

o Strolling the colonial streets of Portsmouth or sunbathing along New Hampshire's 18-mile Atlantic seashore

o Boating or swimming in Lake Winnipesaukee, New Hampshire's largest lake

o Moose-spotting along state Route 3 in New Hampshire's northern tip, locally known as 'Moose Alley'

o Picking heirloom apples at one of New Hampshire's many orchards

≫ A WOMAN GOES OFF-ROAD IN NEW HAMPSHIRE'S WOODS.

MICHAEL DEFREITAS // GETTY

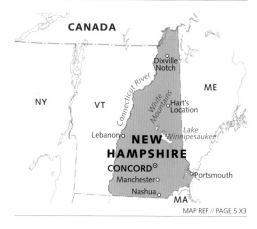

MAP REF // PAGE 5 X3

A WINTRY WONDERLAND AWAITS HIKERS WHO SUMMIT MOUNT WASHINGTON. ≫

THE COG RAILWAY OFFERS AN EASIER WAY TO TOP THE STATE'S LOFTIEST PEAK. ≫

NEW JERSEY

THE STATE GETS A BAD RAP FOR ITS TANGLED WEB OF TARMAC, TOLLS AND SUBURBAN SPRAWL, AND *THE SOPRANOS* PAINTED ITS OWN GRITTY PICTURE, BUT FOR THOSE WILLING TO LOOK BEYOND THE TURNPIKE, NEW JERSEY HAS MANY SURPRISES, LIKE PASTORAL FARMS, WOODSY BACKROADS AND 127 MILES OF SHORELINE.

- **Etymology of the State Name** Named after the Isle of Jersey, England
- **Nickname** Garden State
- **Motto** Liberty and prosperity
- **Capital City** Trenton
- **Population** 8.7 million
- **Area** 8722 sq miles
- **Time Zone** Eastern
- **State Bird** Eastern goldfinch
- **State Flower** Violet
- **Major Industries** Electronics, transport, agriculture
- **Politics** Blue state in 2008
- **Best Time to Go** June, September – just before and after the busy July to August peak season

HISTORY IN A NUTSHELL

The New Jersey area had been home to the Delaware people for 10,000 years (according to some) when Giovanni de Verrazzano rowed ashore in 1524. In 1609 Henry Hudson explored the area to be known as 'New Netherlands' – including the river that was to bear his name – before it passed to the British in 1664. New Jersey played a big role during the Revolutionary War due to its strategic location between Philadelphia and New York City. After becoming the third state, in 1787, New Jersey diversified in the 1800s and early 1900s, with many immigrants coming for manufacturing and (later) electronics jobs. The advent of highways – the Garden State Parkway and New Jersey Turnpike – set up its famous suburbia.

LANDSCAPE

New Jersey's highly populated north features spillovers from the Appalachian Mountains and, closer to New York City, the marshy Meadowlands. Central New Jersey succumbs to lowlands (home to most of the state's farms). Coastal plains extend southward along the shore towards the south tip – where the Delaware Bay and the Atlantic meet – at the woodsy Pine Barrens region. Daily highs during New Jersey's humid summers reach 88°F (31°C), while January highs span only 30°F to 40°F (-1°C to 4°C).

NATURAL BEAUTY

The Palisades Interstate Park's riverside hiking trails have knock-out views over the Hudson, while the shoreline welcomes (many) beach-goers in summer. The popular Jersey Shore, often quite developed and filled with local bodies of various sizes, is a pretty stretch of sand.

REPRESENTATIONS

- 'Born to Run' (1975); Bruce Springsteen's epic refers to an unnamed Jersey town as a 'murder trap,' yet stands as the unofficial state anthem
- *Clerks* (1994); Kevin Smith's $27,500 film taps into strip-mall ennui and boredom, so often linked with the state
- *Harold & Kumar Go to White Castle* (2004); this film depicts a night of mayhem in weed-toking Jersey suburbia
- *Looking for America on the New Jersey Turnpike* (1993), by Angus Gillespie and Michael Rockland; two Rutgers professors add polish and intriguing background to the state's most famous byway
- *Goodbye, Columbus* (1959); Philip Roth's classic novella follows Old World–New World clashes in a Newark Jewish community

ECONOMY

Jersey cashes in on its proximity – with ports, rail links, highway tolls and shipping providing a huge boost to the local economy. Factories have long been a draw card for new immigrants, the focus switching from machinery to things like electronics and food manufacturing over the years. The nickname 'Garden State' isn't a lie – nearly one in five acres in New Jersey is devoted to farmlands (the state makes the nation's top five in production of blueberries, bell peppers, peaches and spinach). New Jerseyans enjoy the nation's second-highest median household income, of $67,035.

URBAN SCENE

Newark's battered image is starting to right itself. A downtown renaissance has been anchored by the $375 million Prudential Center (aka 'the Rock'), which hosts concerts and Devils hockey games. Nearby the Portuguese–Spanish neighborhood of Ironbound is good for an evening drink or a Brazilian-style *cafezhino* coffee. Many Jersey commuters prefer to live in the more intimate towns clutching to the Hudson River, such as Jersey City or Sinatra's home town Hoboken, which has good alt-rock shows at Maxwell's.

JUMPING IN TO THE BEACH SCENE ON THE JERSEY SHORE. »

CUISINE

Jersey-based manufacturing plants are responsible for everything from M&Ms to Campbell's Soup, and Atlantic City's boardwalk is still lined with salt-water taffy vendors (the snack was invented here in the late 1800s). New Jersey is proud of its blueberries, too – the first in the USA were farmed here, and they now find their way into local pie and pizza recipes.

TRADEMARKS

- Atlantic City casinos
- Bruce Springsteen
- *The Sopranos*
- 'Jersey girls'
- Jersey Shore beaches and boardwalks

CULTURE & TRADITIONS

New Jersey's legendary music scene has a list of local stars longer than the New Jersey Turnpike (Sinatra, Whitney Houston, Bon Jovi, Yo La Tengo…). A key music hub, popularized by Jersey's favorite icon, Bruce Springsteen, is beachside Asbury Park, with legendary rock bars like Stone Pony (and a rising gay and lesbian scene these days). Another tradition – since wooed away to Las Vegas – is the Miss America Pageant, held in Atlantic City from 1921 to 2004.

DID YOU KNOW?

- The first passenger flight in the USA flew from New York to Atlantic City, in 1919.
- A colonial geographers' error – the '12-Mile Circle' – gave a piece of New Jersey (on the Delaware River) to Delaware. It's now wild brush, with a few joggers and empty beer bottles.
- You pay to pass through. The state's three major tolls charge, on average, $1 per 18 miles.

PEOPLE

The nation's fifth-smallest state has the 11th-greatest number of residents. The first Europeans were mostly Dutch and Swedish settlers in the 17th century; that soon changed. Today it remains one of the country's most diverse states, with the third-highest number of Italian Americans (18%) and Asian Americans (nearly 8%). About 73% of locals are white. The state also has the second-highest populations of Jews (about 2%) and Muslims (1%).

NEW JERSEY MYTH

No one knows why – some credit it as an unlucky 13th child – but in 1735 'Mother Leeds' gave birth to a devil. The mythical New Jersey Devil supposedly had hooves, a horse head, bat's wings, skinny legs, red eyes and a tendency to screech. One local said, after spotting it in 1909: 'It will bite your head off.'

TEXT **ROBERT REID**

ROBERT SCARBRINO / CORBIS

≫ THIS DEFINITELY ISN'T NEWARK, BUT IT IS THE MOODNA VIADUCT LANDSCAPE.

ESSENTIAL EXPERIENCES

- Finding an empty patch of the Jersey Shore, from Sandy Hook to the Victorian town of Cape May
- Canoeing the Delaware Water Gap on the New Jersey/Pennsylvania border
- Watching for great blue herons or taking a moonlit kayak ride at the Wetlands in south New Jersey
- Hiking the Shore Trail on the Hudson at the Palisades Interstate Park, just across from the Big Apple
- Handing out a few bucks to one of the many New Jersey toll takers

MAP REF // PAGE 5 W5

JERSEY BOYS AND GIRLS MUNCH SLICES IN THE RESORT TOWN OF WILDWOOD. ≫

THE HOLLAND TUNNEL BURROWS BENEATH THE HUDSON RIVER TO MANHATTAN. ≫

BARRY WINIKER // PHOTOLIBRARY

JERSEY FARMS BURST WITH BEEFY TOMATOES. ≫

NEW MEXICO

FLECKED WITH EARTH-TONED ADOBE AND SMELLING OF SAGE, PIÑON NUTS AND ROASTED CHILES, NEW MEXICO IS A LAND WHERE THE FRONTIER PAST STILL FEELS ALIVE, AND CENTURIES-OLD NATIVE AMERICAN TRADITIONS HOLD STRONG.

≫ NATIVE AMERICAN KIDS TAKE PART IN A POWWOW AT THE STATE FAIR.

- **Etymology of the State Name** New territory won after the US–Mexico war
- **Nickname** Land of Enchantment
- **Motto** *Crescit eundo* (It grows as it goes)
- **Capital City** Santa Fe
- **Population** 2 million
- **Area** 121,598 sq miles
- **Time Zone** Mountain
- **State Bird** Roadrunner
- **State Flower** Yucca
- **Major Industry** Energy
- **Politics** Blue state in 2008
- **Best Time to Go** April to May – warm, breezy weather; Native American pueblo dances and powwows

HISTORY IN A NUTSHELL

Native American pueblo culture had flowered by the time Spanish conquistador Francisco Vasquez de Coronado turned up in the region in 1540, searching for the fabled gold of the Seven Cities of Cibola. Spanish colonists founded Santa Fe as their capital in 1610, but were kicked out of that area by Native Americans during the Pueblo Revolt of 1680. The Spaniards later returned, only to be ousted by a newly independent Mexico in 1821. New Mexico became a US territory in 1850 and, afterwards, trade along the Santa Fe Trail transformed the region, as did the arrival of the railroad in 1878. Apache chief Geronimo's surrender signaled the end of armed resistance by Native Americans in 1886. New Mexico became the 47th US state in 1912 and, during WWII, played a key role in nuclear weapons development and testing. During the war, local Navajo 'code talkers' further aided the US military.

LANDSCAPE

New Mexico abounds with thickly forested wilderness, snowy mountains, flat-topped mesas and sprawling desert. Its southern border adjoins Mexico, while the 'Four Corners' region in the northwest borders Utah, Arizona and Colorado. The mighty Rio Grande runs roughly north–south through the middle of the state, and nearly every part of New Mexico averages 300 sunny days every year. Winters can be bitterly cold, especially in the northern mountains around Taos.

NATURAL BEAUTY

Sunsets are phenomenal in this land of seemingly boundless horizons. White-water rafting on the Rio Colorado, Rio Grande and Rio Chama is thrilling, and skiing is popular around Taos. Hikers, spelunkers and birders flock to southern New Mexico, which is studded with spectacular recreational areas including White Sands National Monument, Carlsbad Caverns National Park, Bosque del Apache National Wildlife Refuge and Gila National Forest.

ALMOST A GEORGIA O'KEEFFE PAINTING. »

'IF THE CHILE AIN'T HOT ENOUGH, THE COOK'S NOT MAD ENOUGH,' AS THE OLD ADAGE GOES. »

PEOPLE

Nearly half of New Mexicans have Latino ancestry, while 10% share Native American heritage. A third speak a language other than English at home (primarily Spanish). About two-thirds are Christian, equal amounts Catholic and Protestant.

CULTURE & TRADITIONS

Backcountry roads lead to ancient Native American dwellings like those at Chaco Culture National Historic Park, and contemporary pueblos such as those of the Acoma and Zuni peoples. Tribal powwows and ceremonial dances are sometimes open to outsiders, but remain sacred traditions, not entertainment. Some of New Mexico's most famous ceremonial dances are held at pueblos scattered near Albuquerque and Santa Fe. Hulking casinos were built on some of the same Native American tribal lands.

TRADEMARKS

○ Chile peppers

○ Pueblos and adobe houses

○ Santa Fe Trail

○ Uranium and UFOs

CUISINE

New Mexican food riffs on many of the traditions of northern Mexican cooking, with tostadas, tamales and salsas aplenty. Nothing is more essential than chile peppers; residents often hang *ristras* (dried chile bunches) outside their homes. New Mexico's ubiquitous blue-corn-tortilla wrapped enchiladas are doused in a simmered sauce made from red or green chiles (or both, called 'Christmas' style). Sopaipillas (puffed, deep-fried pillows of dough) are dipped in honey and often served with green chile and pork stew or posole (corn stew). On Native American lands, those stews are usually served with flat fry bread, also used to make Indian (or Navajo) tacos, topped with beans, beef, cheese and lettuce.

ECONOMY

New Mexico has vast ranch lands but much of its wealth comes from natural gas reserves and underground minerals, such as uranium and copper. Renewable energy projects, including solar and wind, provide an increasing number of jobs. About 25% of residents are now employed by the federal government, which maintains huge military bases and scientific installations across the state, as well as public outdoor recreational areas and Native American reservations. Incomes don't measure up to the national average, with one out of every seven state residents living below the poverty line.

DID YOU KNOW?

○ Only 25% of New Mexico's roads are paved.

○ Santa Fe has the highest elevation of any state capital in the USA.

○ New Mexico is the only US state with an official question: 'Red or Green?' (referring to chile sauces).

URBAN SCENE

The state capital of Santa Fe is an arty, affluent, adobe-built town, full of museums, art galleries and creative restaurants. The northern new-age hangout of Taos has long attracted artists, including Georgia O'Keeffe and Ansel Adams, with its jaw-dropping natural beauty. Historic Route 66 runs through the Old Town neighborhood of Albuquerque, the state's biggest city. Gallup is the self-proclaimed Indian capital of the Southwest, a hub for the Navajo and Hopi nations and Zuni Pueblo. Quirky towns include Roswell, allegedly the site of a 1947 UFO crash, and Truth or Consequences, named after a radio game show.

REPRESENTATIONS

○ Turquoise and silver jewelry; pueblo pottery

○ *Death Comes for the Archbishop* (1927), by Willa Cather; haunting novel about a historical Native American revolt

○ *Bless Me, Ultima* (1972), by Rudolfo Anaya; native mysticism struggles with the Catholic Church in WWII-era New Mexico

○ *The Spell of New Mexico* (1984), edited by Tony Hillerman; a reflective collection of essays by famous 20th-century writers

○ *The Milagro Beanfield War* (1988), directed by Robert Redford; based on the political novel about small-town farmers versus big business

○ *Women's Tales from the New Mexico WPA* (2000), edited by María Teresa Márquez; folktales and oral history gathered from Hispanic families during the Great Depression

NEW MEXICO LEGENDS

The tiny town of Las Vegas, NM, once harbored more outlaws and desperadoes than anywhere else in the Wild West. After the railway arrived in 1879, infamous larger-than-life personalities who took up residence here included Doc Holliday, Jesse James, Billy the Kid and Wyatt Earp.

TEXT SARA BENSON

ESSENTIAL EXPERIENCES

○ Shopping for Native American art and crafts outside the Palace of the Governors in Santa Fe, or visiting millennium-old Taos Pueblo and being invited to watch a traditional corn dance

○ Getting your own kicks on old Route 66

○ Gazing skyward during the Albuquerque International Balloon Fiesta

○ Spelunking the colossal depths of Carlsbad Caverns

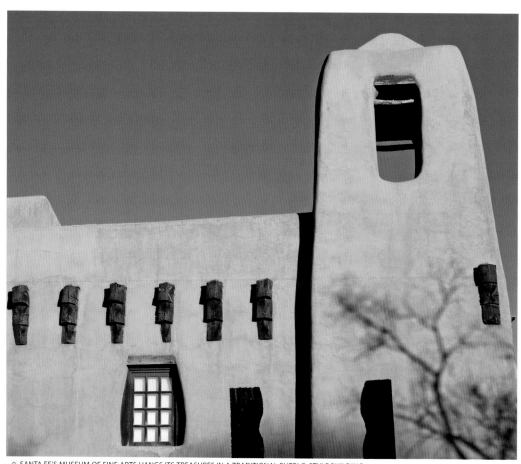

≪ SANTA FE'S MUSEUM OF FINE ARTS HANGS ITS TREASURES IN A TRADITIONAL PUEBLO-STYLE BUILDING.

MAP REF // PAGE 4 J11

GYPSUM DUNES RIPPLE THROUGH WHITE SANDS NATIONAL MONUMENT. «

ARTISTS HAVE LONG BROUGHT OUT EASELS FOR CHIMNEY ROCK AT GHOST RANCH. «

DANCING AT ALBUQUERQUE'S NATIONAL HISPANIC CULTURAL CENTER. «

ROBERT FRIED / ALAMY

NEW YORK

DOMINATED BY ITS SOUTHERN TIP – WHERE THE COUNTRY'S LARGEST CITY REINVENTS ITSELF EVERY YEAR – NEW YORK STATE IS SURPRISINGLY GREEN AND GORGEOUS, WITH SKI RUNS, ROADSIDE FARMERS MARKETS AND A FAR MORE DOWN-HOME PACE THAN YOU'D EXPECT AS YOU TRY TO HAIL A MANHATTAN CAB.

≪ THE ICONIC BROOKLYN BRIDGE CONNECTS THE NAMESAKE BOROUGH TO MANHATTAN.

- **Etymology of the State Name** Named for the Duke of York (later King James II) in 1664
- **Nicknames** Empire State, Knickerbocker State
- **Capital City** Albany
- **Population** 19.3 million
- **Area** 54,556 sq miles
- **Time Zone** Eastern
- **State Bird** Bluebird
- **State Flower** Rose
- **Major Industries** Finance, communications, agriculture
- **Politics** Blue state in 2008
- **Best Time to Go** March to May, September to November – beat the crowds

HISTORY IN A NUTSHELL

The area was home to the Algonquians and Iroquois before 1609, when Henry Hudson claimed the land for the Dutch. When the British took over, the area became the New York colony, then in 1788 the 11th state of the Union. By the 1840s railways linked its major cities and waves of immigration poured in (beginning with the Irish, then African Americans, Chinese and over 12 million Europeans coming through Ellis Island after 1892), helping transform New York into a powerhouse of industry and commerce.

LANDSCAPE

New York is filled with mountains and forests lined with rivers or lakes (Erie and Ontario on the Canadian border). For Manhattanites, 'upstate' begins about 10 miles up the Hudson, in the foothills of the Catskills, but the technical distinction actually begins further towards the Adirondack Mountains or 'Finger Lakes' to the west. The state's humid continental climate brings far colder winters upstate (January hovers around freezing versus 38°F/3°C in New York City), while summer is more consistent (humid and hot), averaging 80°F (27°C) highs in August.

NATURAL BEAUTY

North of the lovely Hudson River Valley, the leafy Catskills have fun towns to explore, including New Paltz, Kingston and Woodstock. Heading west toward Buffalo, Hwy 20 (the east end of the Oregon Trail) tiptoes through the Finger Lakes, while the lovely northern wilderness of the Adirondacks have more hiking and river miles than roads (though Route 73 to Lake Placid is a superb drive).

PEOPLE

The third most-populated state (after California and Texas), New York is one of the USA's most diverse, made up of 17% African Americans, 16% Latin Americans and 7% Asian Americans. White New Yorkers include many Italian Americans (about 14% of the population) and Irish Americans (13%). About one in five state residents were born abroad. About 70% of New Yorkers are Christians, about 8% are Jewish.

FARM → STAND 1000 FEET
OPEN ALL YEAR
BROWN EGGS
BEETS
LETTUCE
RASPBERRIES
BLUE·BERRIES
CUCUMBERS
SQUASH

WE'RE NOT IN NEW YORK CITY ANYMORE, TOTO. »

CULTURE & TRADITIONS

There are two New Yorks: the city (where one in 2.3 of the state's people live on 0.06% of the land) and the state. The city is defined by the drive to be the best – the 'New York minute' can't wait for indecision or second-rate options. Things are more subdued, even laid-back, in most of the other 99.94% of New York, where you'll find let-it-roll towns like New Paltz or Woodstock, with local crops on the menus (and a host of food festivals) and noodly guitar jams extending the songs.

TRADEMARKS

- New York City skyscrapers, taxis and fast-talkers
- Hudson River town's antique scene
- Niagara Falls
- Hampton yuppies on high-end Long Island beach towns
- Adirondack hiking trails

CUISINE

New York has been the gateway to the USA for a world of cuisines, and the birth of many more. Italian Americans introduced the USA to pizza, sold thin and greasy in take-out shops, while other city delis brought in Yiddish specialties such as braided egg bread *(challah),* stuffed pastry shell *(knish)* and the bagel. Upstate, summer roadside stands sell local produce, while fall harvest brings apple- or pumpkin-picking sidetrips. Buffalo's contributions to bad diets include Buffalo wings and the German-influenced beef on weck (or 'kummelweck', with beef stuffed in a salted roll with horseradish).

URBAN SCENE

Bottle-shaped Manhattan – a Native American word for 'inebriation,' funnily enough – is best explored on foot: Uptown's posh streets and boutiques, the latest Harlem renaissance further north, Midtown surprises amidst skyscrapers (like Bryant Park, east of Times Square) and down-town villages with rock clubs and vegan stews. Meanwhile Brooklyn draws its own fans with hipster haven Williamsburg or the more adultlike eating scenes of Boerum Hill and Park Slope's Fifth Avenue. Though New York's second city is a distant runner up, working-class Buffalo has spirit with its revitalized Erie Canal terminus, indie-rock clubs and, of course, the spicy Buffalo wings.

REPRESENTATIONS

- *Buffalo 66* (1998); Vincent Gallo's priceless cinematic exhibit on family dysfunction and Super Bowl tragedies
- *Manhattan* (1979); Woody Allen's classic, Gershwin-backed film of loves lost
- *The New Yorker* (1925–present); covered with illustrations, this weekly runs as a who's-who in American literary and political thought
- 'New York, New York' (1977); the rah-rah anthem to New York City, by John Kander and Fred Ebb, immortalized by Frank Sinatra

ECONOMY

Much of the state's annual gross product – about $1 trillion – is owed to New York City (a financial, media and shipping center), out-earning many countries. Upstate, about two-thirds of the agricultural industry comes from livestock, while New York leads the east in fruit and vegetable production (including apples, grapes, cucumbers, squash, cabbage). The state's median household economy is $53,510.

DID YOU KNOW?

- The first daredevil to go down Niagara Falls in a barrel was a 63-year-old woman, Annie Edson Taylor – she survived her 1901 plunge.
- Woodstock – the 1969 rock festival – took place in Bethel, 45 miles from Woodstock town.
- For years the New York license plate (and now its state quarter) has featured the Statue of Liberty, but technically the statue's in New Jersey.

NEW YORK MYTH

New York author Washington Irving's 1820 short story *The Legend of Sleepy Hollow* followed a long-told local tale of a murderous ghost of a headless Hessian soldier. Though no pumpkin-related deaths have been seen in years, in 1997 North Tarrtytown, the historical location of the story, changed its name to Sleepy Hollow.

TEXT ROBERT REID

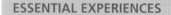
SPENCER PLATT // GETTY

ESSENTIAL EXPERIENCES

- Taking a big bite of the Big Apple – Broadway, indie rock, Central Park picnics, Staten Island Ferry rides
- Dining vegan and buying beads in Woodstock
- Marveling at the 40 million gallons of water gushing over the Niagara Falls every minute
- Dunking a crispy Buffalo wing into spicy chili sauce at their generally attributed birthplace: the Anchor Bar in Buffalo
- Climbing waterfalls at Clark's Gully – believed by the Seneca to be the world's birthplace – in the underrated Finger Lakes region

⌃ BICYCLES, BUSINESSPEOPLE AND GRAFFITI-SCRAWLED TRUCKS SHARE MANHATTAN'S FINANCIAL DISTRICT.

MAP REF // PAGE 5 V4

THE PONCE FAMILY FLYERS SUIT UP WHEN THE CIRCUS COMES TO CONEY ISLAND. ≫

DAN HERRICK // LONELY PLANET IMAGES

NIAGARA FALLS BY BOAT SURE BEATS NIAGARA FALLS BY BARREL. ≫

NATHAN'S HAS BEEN CONEY ISLAND'S TOP DOG SINCE 1916. ≫

NORTH CAROLINA

UNDENIABLY SOUTHERN IN ITS HOSPITALITY, GENTEELNESS AND CUISINE, NORTH CAROLINA HAS RECENTLY SEEN BIOTECH, UNIVERSITIES AND BANKING TRANSFORM ITS CENTRAL PIEDMONT AREA INTO A COSMOPOLIS: MOONSHINE HAS BEEN REPLACED WITH WINE, AND TOBACCO WAREHOUSES NOW HOUSE ARTISTS AND COLLEGE PROFESSORS.

≫ DUKE FANS SHOW THEIR TRUE COLORS AT A BASKETBALL GAME AGAINST ARCHRIVAL UNIVERSITY OF NORTH CAROLINA.

- **Etymology of the State Name** Named for King Charles I of England by his son, King Charles II
- **Nickname** Tar Heel State
- **Motto** *Esse quam videri* (To be, rather than to seem)

- **Capital City** Raleigh
- **Population** 9.1 million
- **Area** 53,821 sq miles
- **Time Zone** Eastern
- **State Bird** Cardinal

- **State Flower** Dogwood
- **Major Industries** Biotechnology, textiles, furniture, banking
- **Politics** Blue state in 2008
- **Best Time to Go** May to October – outdoor summer concerts, warm nights and fireflies

HISTORY IN A NUTSHELL

One of the original 13 colonies, North Carolina was home to one of the USA's first English settlements (1587), the 12th state to join the Union (1789) and the last to join the Confederacy (1861). The Tar Heel State gained fame in the 18th century for its prominence in growing tobacco and rice, two crops that became highly dependent on slave labor in the eastern third of the state. North Carolina also had a large proportion of freed slaves, who were allowed to vote until 1835. Several prominent Civil War battles were fought on North Carolina soil, though many farmers in the state's west either remained neutral or actively supported the Union.

LANDSCAPE

North Carolina is divided into three distinct geological regions: the marshy eastern third with its tobacco and cotton farms and low-lying barrier islands; the rolling hills and flatlands of the central Piedmont region, dominated by all of the state's major cities, including Charlotte, Raleigh, Durham, Greensboro and Winston-Salem; and the western mountains, anchored by Mount Mitchell (6684 feet), the highest peak east of the Mississippi.

NATURAL BEAUTY

The beauty and relaxed attitude of the Outer Banks and Ocracoke Island have been drawing visitors since Blackbeard pillaged and plundered his way through this area in the 18th century. The Blue Ridge, Great Smoky and Appalachian Mountain ranges in the west of the state are some of the oldest mountains in the world and their weathered hills, tree-covered groves and dancing waterfalls bring leaf-peepers, snow-shoers and meanderers year-round, especially on the 200-mile swath of the Blue Ridge Parkway. Urban spots in the Piedmont are never more than an hour from a bucolic farm, family winery or wild river. North Carolina has the largest variation in climate east of the Mississippi, including the occasional hurricane. The state has four distinct seasons, though all of them are relatively mild.

NORTH CAROLINA REMAINS ADDICTED TO TOBACCO, GROWING MORE THAN ANY OTHER STATE.

PEOPLE

African Americans make up about a quarter of North Carolina's population and the state has the highest proportion (1.2%) of Native Americans east of the Mississippi. Hispanic, East Asian and South Asian immigration is growing rapidly.

CULTURE & TRADITIONS

North Carolina, bless its Southern heart, lives to be polite. Even an oil change will involve pleasantries about last night's basketball game. Religion is a way of life, from small-town mountain Southern Baptist churches to gay-friendly urban ministries. College basketball – most notably the Duke–Carolina rivalry – is an obsession in some parts, while Nascar rules in others.

TRADEMARKS

- College basketball
- BBQ
- Biltmore Estate
- Andy Griffith
- Tobacco fields
- Lighthouses
- Appalachian Trail
- Nascar
- Krispy Kreme doughnuts
- Blue Ridge Parkway

CUISINE

While sharing many similarities with other Southern states, North Carolina adds several distinct touches. It's the self-proclaimed BBQ capital of the world – Lexington, just northeast of Charlotte, specializes in western, tomato-based pulled-pork BBQ while the east prefers a vinegar base and chopped pork. The Yadkin Valley area's former tobacco farms have the perfect conditions to grow a new area favorite: wine. And, of course, North Carolina's favorite native dessert – Krispy Kreme doughnuts – is still best fresh out of the conveyor at one of its local shops.

ECONOMY

A shift to offshore manufacturing and downturns in the economy have been tremendous burdens to the local agricultural and textile industries. However, the economy of the cities and universities was a welcome replacement. The Research Triangle Park between Durham and Raleigh employs over 40,000 highly educated locals working in biotech, computer and medical research, not to mention the thousands employed by or studying at one of the Triangle's dozen universities. Charlotte might or might not be (depending on who has folded or been bought out recently) the second-largest banking city after New York.

URBAN SCENE

Several cities vie for top nightspot, including Raleigh, with five distinct nightlife districts, collegiate Chapel Hill just down the road, with its gritty nightclubs and vibrant music scene, and young and professional Charlotte, where the beautiful people sip cocktails in trendy bars.

REPRESENTATIONS

- *The Andy Griffith Show* (1960–68); the star's real-life home of Mount Airy was the inspiration for the fictional Mayberry
- *Bull Durham* (1988); the 'Hit bull, win a steak' sign from the movie is now a mainstay at the current Durham Bulls Athletic Park
- *On Agate Hill* (2006); novelist Lee Smith's chronicle of North Carolina life for a young girl after Reconstruction

DID YOU KNOW?

- The Raleigh-Durham area consistently appears as one of the country's top three most-educated cities, right behind Seattle and almost tied with San Francisco.
- Mount Airy's second-most-famous residents were Chang and Eng Bunker, the 'original' conjoined twins. The descendants of their 21 children still meet for an annual picnic.
- The only natural native habitat of the carnivorous Venus flytrap plant is the area within 100-mile radius of Wilmington.

NORTH CAROLINA LEGEND

In 1587 Virginia Dare became the first English child born on American soil at the Roanoke Colony in the modern-day Outer Banks. Soon thereafter, the colonists' governor, John White, took a ship back to England to gather supplies. He returned three years later to find a completely deserted colony. To this day, no one knows what happened. Twenty years later, Jamestown colonists reported seeing several Englishmen and a young maid assimilated into a local Native American tribe. Was this maid Virginia Dare? A DNA project is under way to determine the truth.

TEXT ALEX LEVITON

ESSENTIAL EXPERIENCES

- Lazing on a beach on Ocracoke Island
- Cheering at a Duke–Carolina basketball game
- Driving the length of the Blue Ridge Parkway
- Gallery- and organic restaurant–hopping in hippified Asheville
- Rafting Olympic-grade rapids at the US National Whitewater Center near Charlotte
- Catching a traditional or bluegrass jam session in the mountains
- Indulging in BBQ or pig pickin' at Hog Days in historic Hillsborough
- Visiting the Wright Brothers Memorial at Kill Devil Hills

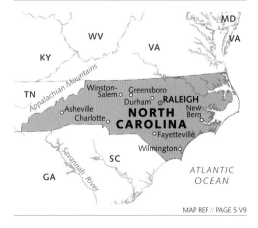

MAP REF // PAGE 5 V9

LOGAN MOCK-BUNTING // GETTY

⌃ LOCAL LEGEND DOC WATSON FLATPICKS BACKSTAGE AT THE MOUNTAIN SONG FESTIVAL IN BREVARD.

EROSION AT CAPE HATTERAS BRINGS THE OCEAN EVER CLOSER TO CIVILIZATION. ⌃

CLOG DANCERS TAP THEIR TOES AT A CULTURAL FESTIVAL. ⌃

SUNLIGHT PIERCES THE FOREST IN GREAT SMOKY MOUNTAINS NATIONAL PARK. ⌃

NORTH DAKOTA

THE LEAST-VISITED STATE, AND STILL RECOVERING FROM THE ACCENTS IN THE COEN BROTHERS' FILM *FARGO*, NORTH DAKOTA'S MODEST PLAINS ROLL PAST NATIVE AMERICAN SITES, BIG COW STATUES, OUT-OF-VIEW NUCLEAR-MISSILE SILOS, AND THE FETCHING THEODORE ROOSEVELT NATIONAL PARK.

⌃ FARMERS REST AGAINST A CLASSIC RED BARN IN AMIDON.

- **Etymology of the State Name** 'Dakota' is a Sioux word for ally or friend
- **Nicknames** Peace Garden State, Rough Rider State
- **Capital City** Bismarck
- **Population** 639,715
- **Area** 70,704 sq miles
- **Time Zones** Central, Mountain
- **State Bird** Western meadowlark
- **State Flower** Wild prairie rose
- **Major Industries** Agriculture, petroleum
- **Politics** Red state in 2008
- **Best Time to Go** June to August – North Dakota's winter temperatures are the lower 48's coldest

HISTORY IN A NUTSHELL

Lewis and Clark met their famed Shoshone guide Sacagawea at the makeshift Ft Mandan in 1804. The two Dakotas exist because Republicans wanted an extra senator in Congress, so in 1889 Dakota Territory was brought into the USA as two states (North Dakota is listed as the 39th state, one ahead of South Dakota). At statehood, half of North Dakota's quarter-million residents were foreign-born. A young Theodore Roosevelt, who came to hunt buffalo after his wife died, would later credit the state for toughening him up – and inspiring him to create the first national parks. North Dakota later flirted with several state-run enterprises (such as banks and mills) but quickly returned to more conservative, privately run policies.

LANDSCAPE

The glacier-made Red River Valley runs along the state's east border and turns into prairie and eventually the Great Plains of the Missouri Plateau in the west. In *Travels with Charley*, John Steinbeck noted how radically North Dakota changes across the Missouri River (green to the east, brown to the west), which runs north across its center then west: 'The two sides of the river might as well be a thousand miles apart.' North Dakota's continental temperature is almost unfairly hot and cold; summer temperatures can reach 100°F (38°C), while winter temperatures drop below zero (with average lows around -5°F/-21°C in January).

NATURAL BEAUTY

Though mostly flat lands peppered with silos and grain elevators, North Dakota has a few surprises. The most attractive areas are the two disconnected units of colorful rock formations at Theodore Roosevelt National Park: the south unit features a 36-mile scenic drive, near Medora (on I-94), while the more rugged north unit is reached by road or a 96-mile trail. Near the Winnipeg border, the Turtle Mountains – actually low hills made of glacial drift – are home to a Chippewa reservation, while US-83 follows the Missouri River, north and south of Bismarck.

SUE, THE WORLD'S LARGEST HOLSTEIN COW, STANDS TALL IN NEW SALEM. ≫

NORTH DAKOTA TOPS THE NATION IN SUNFLOWER PRODUCTION. ≫

PEOPLE

Nodaks are 94% white, many descended from Old World settlers who arrived in the late 1800s. Germans and Russians settled mostly in the south, while many Norwegians ventured north to towns such as Minot (rhymes with 'why not'). Nearly one in two North Dakotans claim German ancestry. The biggest minority are Native American groups – accounting for 5.5% of the population. Everyone's very religious (86% are Christian), with only 3% of the state not claiming a religion (the lowest percentage in the nation).

CULTURE & TRADITIONS

North Dakota borders Canada, but much of its day-to-day culture feels rather Wild West. Every May, Medora hosts a Dakota Cowboy Poetry contest; Dickinson unleashes the Roughrider Days festival (a nod to Teddy Roosevelt's days here) in July; and in September the capital, Bismarck, hosts the United Tribes Powwow, featuring 1500 dancers from local tribes.

CUISINE

German, Norwegian and Russian immigrants made a big impact on North Dakota meals, while cereal experimenters in Grand Forks created cream of wheat in 1893 (never mind its resemblance to Russian *farina*). In summer, dried venison or pork (and cheeses) fill 'summer sausage.' North-central Minot hosts the five-day Norsk Høstfest in October, serving Scandinavian specialties like *lefse* (Norwegian flatbread).

TRADEMARKS

- Big skies – they're bigger than Montana's
- Lewis and Clark sites, including Fort Mandan
- Sunflowers – North Dakota even beats Kansas in sunflower production
- Rugby, geographical center of North America

ECONOMY

With a bit more than half of the population still living in the countryside, agriculture runs the reins in North Dakota (its wheat production is the nation's highest), but there are sizable contributions from petroleum as well. North Dakotans earn an average $32,750 annually and enjoy one of the nation's lowest unemployment rates (3.3%).

URBAN SCENE

This is a state with few people, so don't expect a Manhattan. Two of North Dakota's main cities – Fargo and Grand Forks – huddle along the Red River border with Minnesota. Fargo in particular has a nice historic downtown with a recent boutique restoration of the 19th-century Hotel Donaldson, and the art-deco Fargo Theater. The capital, Bismarck, is quieter, despite the state government hubbub.

REPRESENTATIONS

- *Jesus Camp* (2006); documentary on a Pentecostal summer camp at Devils Lake, ND
- *Fargo Rock City* (2001); Chuck Klosterman relies on his North Dakota upbringing for this 'heavy metal odyssey'
- *Beyond the Bedroom Wall: A Family Album* (1975); the family saga of Poet Laureate Larry Woiwode, set in rural North Dakota

DID YOU KNOW?

- The movie *Fargo* (1996) is mainly set in Minnesota. Only the Paul Bunyan statue was shot in North Dakota.
- No one knows which Dakota was admitted to the USA first: to avoid rivalry, the official papers were shuffled then signed.
- For over three decades, famous North Dakotan Lawrence Welk led his 'champagne music' orchestra on TV with his clipped German American accent – though born in Strasburg, ND, he didn't speak English till he was 21.

NORTH DAKOTA LEGEND

Nodaks have a playful sense of humor regarding animals, evident in giant roadside buffalos and cows on I-94, and in some outright tall tales, including of a stray albino moose and a recently caught two-headed 'Franken-fish.'

TEXT ROBERT REID

ESSENTIAL EXPERIENCES

- Hiking or horseback riding across the badlands of Theodore Roosevelt National Park
- Snow-kiting across the rolling plains
- Stopping off at I-94 attractions – the 38-foot cow ('Sue') in New Salem, or the 28-foot buffalo in Jamestown
- Catching a movie or show at the historic Fargo Theatre

CANADA

Minot · Lake Sakakawea · Sheyenne River · Grand Forks · MN · Theodore Roosevelt National Park · MT · Dickinson · Mandan · **NORTH DAKOTA** · **BISMARCK** · Lake Oahe · Jamestown · Fargo · Red River of the North · James River · Missouri River · SD

MAP REF // PAGE 4 L3

⌃ ONCE A VAUDEVILLE PALACE, THE ART-DECO FARGO THEATRE NOW SCREENS ART FILMS.

RICHARD CUMMINS // LONELY PLANET IMAGES

A YOUNG COWBOY RUSTLES UP A FINE CHAPEAU. ≫

CHALKY CLIFFS AND WHISPERING GRASSES AWAIT AT LONELY THEODORE ROOSEVELT NATIONAL PARK. ≫

OHIO

PAY OHIO SOME RESPECT: IT'S THE NATION'S SEVENTH-MOST-POPULOUS STATE – STOCKED WITH ROLLER COASTERS, ROCK AND ROLL, APPALACHIAN PARKS AND PARTY ISLANDS – AND OHIO DECIDES THE NATION'S FATE WITH ITS POLITICAL VOTES.

≫ OHIO'S PARKS HIDE PLENTY OF SWIMMIN' HOLES.

- **Etymology of the State Name** Iroquoian for 'great river'
- **Nickname** Buckeye State
- **Motto** With God all things are possible
- **Capital City** Columbus
- **Population** 11.5 million
- **Area** 44,828 sq miles
- **Time Zone** Eastern
- **State Bird** Cardinal
- **State Flower** Scarlet carnation
- **Major Industries** Rubber, steel, consumer products
- **Politics** Swing state (blue in 2008)
- **Best Time to Go** June to August – for outdoor activities

HISTORY IN A NUTSHELL

Ohio's early native cultures were renowned builders of mounds and earthworks, and many examples of these still rise in the countryside. European settlers streamed into fertile Ohio following the Revolutionary War, and by 1803 it had enough people to become the 17th state. Ohio fought a war with Michigan in 1835 and 1836 – over Toledo, of all things. Hardly a drop of blood was shed and it was Ohio that emerged victorious. By 1850 Ohio was the third-most-populous state in the nation. Industry grew (steel in the north, pork processing in the south) and some families got rich (Rockefeller in the north, Messrs Procter and Gamble in the south). In recent years Ohio has played a pivotal role in deciding national elections – whoever has won the Buckeye State in the last few elections has also won the presidency.

LANDSCAPE

Lake Erie crowns Ohio, and the Ohio River races along the state's southern edge. The southwest is hilly and green in the pretty Ohio Valley, while the southeast kicks it up a notch with rugged hills and forests in the Appalachian Mountains. Fertile farming plains roll through Ohio's core and the flat northern rim along Lake Erie is part of a whopping snowbelt. There's less snow and more rain in the south, and summers are warm and muggy pretty much everywhere in the state.

NATURAL BEAUTY

The Bass Islands and Kelleys Island float in Lake Erie near Sandusky. Certain of Ohio's bays are party places for boaters, while other areas offer quiet beaches, bird watching, lighthouses and caves. Hocking Hills State Park in the Appalachian foothills is a favorite spot for rock climbers and hikers thanks to its sandstone cliffs, waterfalls and hemlock-shaded gorges. Prehistoric earthworks dot the land south of Columbus: Serpent Mound is the most captivating example of these structures – it's a giant, uncoiling snake that stretches over a quarter of a mile, and is thought to be a gift from the Hopewell people (circa AD 600).

THE CRAFT OF MOUNTAIN DULCIMER MAKING, AT THE OHIO STATE FAIR. «

PEOPLE

Most Ohioans are either white (83%) or African American (12%), with Hispanics and Asians splitting the remainder. A quarter of residents have German roots and about 13% are of Irish descent. Nearly half the state worships in Protestant churches (Baptists and Methodists lead the charge) and one in five is Catholic. Cleveland and Cincinnati have sizable Jewish communities and the nation's largest Amish population lives in northeastern Ohio.

CULTURE & TRADITIONS

In a nutshell, the north is more liberal, pro-Union and 'rust belt,' while the south is more conservative and rural. Southeast Ohio is part of the cultural region of Appalachia, with a rustic culture and accent akin to neighboring West Virginia. What unites these disparate forces? The buckeye, of course: a tree that grows throughout the state and whose nut is Ohio's beloved symbol.

TRADEMARKS

○ Buckeye nut

○ Wright Brothers – they lived and designed their aircraft in Dayton

○ Indian mounds

○ Burning rivers

○ Skyline chili

CUISINE

The north and south of the state each have their own specialties. If you're looking for a five-way, head south. We're talking about Cincinnati chili (Skyline brand preferred), which entails five ingredients: chocolate-and-cinnamon-spiced meat sauce ladled over spaghetti and beans, garnished with cheese and onions. It's thoroughly addictive, and junkies have been known to ship it across continents. Cleveland has the nation's largest concentration of Hungarians, Slovenes and Slovaks, so goulashes, stuffed cabbage and schnitzels are often heaped onto northern plates. Keep an eye out statewide for buckeye candy – a bite-sized peanut-butter ball dipped in dark chocolate so it resembles the killer nut.

ECONOMY

Ohio manufactures a lot, including steel, cars, airplanes and rubber products. Its farms yield eggs, hogs, dairy cows and sheep – enough of the latter to make Ohio the biggest wool producer east of the Mississippi River. Cincinnati-based Procter & Gamble is one of the world's hugest companies, and it's a good bet something in your pantry (toothpaste, tissues, detergent) came from this consumer-product giant. State incomes don't measure up to the national average, however: the state ranks 34th in household earnings, with 13% of residents living below the poverty line.

URBAN SCENE

It's all about the three Cs. Columbus is the capital and largest city, a pleasant enough place that has seen an upsurge in hip nightlife and has a vibrant gay and lesbian scene. Cleveland rocks, if you hadn't heard. It's Ohio's second-biggest city, an industrial place where the river once caught on fire from rampant pollution. Thankfully, the city cleaned up its act and now woos visitors with the Rock and Roll Hall of Fame. German-tinged Cincinnati makes a fine, slowpoke stop. Mark Twain said he wanted to be here when the world ends, as the city is always 20 years behind the times.

REPRESENTATIONS

○ *Winesburg, Ohio* (1919); Sherwood Anderson's novel evokes the loneliness and frustration of small-town America

○ *The Drew Carey Show* (1995–2004); TV series showing the shenanigans of working-class Drew and crew in Cleveland

○ *Rain Man* (1988); Tom Cruise and an autistic Dustin Hoffman ('I'm an excellent driver') road trip from Cincinnati to LA

○ *My City Was Gone* (1984); the Pretenders' Chrissie Hynde sings of disappointing changes in her home town of Akron

DID YOU KNOW?

○ Cedar Point Amusement Park has more roller coasters (17) than any other amusement park in the world.

○ Seven US presidents were born in Ohio (second only to Virginia, which produced eight).

○ Buckeye nuts are poisonous, except to squirrels.

OHIO MYTH

Ohio makes presidents, but it also kills them via 'Tecumseh's Curse.' Tecumseh was a famed Shawnee warrior from Ohio who William Henry Harrison defeated at the Battle of Tippecanoe. As revenge for Harrison's cruel treatment of the Native Americans, Tecumseh supposedly called down a mighty curse: Harrison would be elected president in 1840 but would die in office, and the same fate would befall every 'Great White Father' elected in a year ending in '0' (ie, every 20 years). Sure enough, Harrison caught pneumonia at his inauguration and died, and the curse resurfaced every 20 years to claim a victim, including Lincoln and Kennedy. Reagan finally broke the curse, though he barely escaped assassination in 1981.

TEXT KARLA ZIMMERMAN

ESSENTIAL EXPERIENCES

○ Feeling your stomach drop on a 120-mile-per-hour roller coaster looping 420 feet in the air at Cedar Point

○ Ogling Jimi Hendrix's Stratocaster or Neil Young's black-fringed jacket at the Rock and Roll Hall of Fame

○ Scarfing down Cincinnati chili after late-night cocktails

○ Browsing through a Holmes County Amish store for wind-up flashlights and non-electric waffle irons

○ Seeing the Ohio State University Marching Band form 'script Ohio' during a football game

⌃ MUSEUMS, MOSAICS AND THE AMTRAK STATION STUFF CINCINNATI'S 1933 UNION TERMINAL.

MAP REF // PAGE 5 T6

VISITORS PLUG IN TO THE LES PAUL EXHIBIT AT THE ROCK AND ROLL HALL OF FAME. ⌃

CORN COVERS 3 MILLION ACRES OF OHIO. ⌃

CHURNING STOMACHS ON ONE OF OHIO'S MANY ROLLER COASTERS. ⌃

OKLAHOMA

A REAL-LIFE COWBOYS-AND-INDIANS STATE, WITH CATTLE DRIVES AND OIL WELLS, OKLAHOMA IS HARD TO PEG – IT'S FILLED WITH GREEN OZARK LEFTOVERS FROM ARKANSAS TO THE EAST, AND WIDE-OPEN PLAINS BEGINNING HALFWAY WEST.

≫ YOU WON'T FIND A FRESHER STEAK THAN IN OKLAHOMA CITY'S STOCKYARDS, WHERE RANCHERS BUY AND SELL BOVINES.

- **Etymology of the State Name** Choctaw for 'red people' – a rough translation of 'Indian Territory'
- **Mottes** *Labor omnia vincit* (Labor conquers all things), Oklahoma is OK (after a much-mocked 1970s license-plate slogan)

- **Nickname** Sooner State
- **Capital City** Oklahoma City
- **Population** 3.6 million
- **Area** 69,903 sq miles
- **Time Zone** Central

- **State Bird** Mistletoe
- **Major Industries** Oil, manufacturing
- **Politics** Red state in 2008
- **Best Time to Go** June to August – festival season

HISTORY IN A NUTSHELL

At the time of statehood, in 1907, Oklahoma was mostly an afterthought territory where Native Americans had been relocated, most famously during the Cherokees' 1838–39 Trail of Tears. By the 1880s eager homesteaders ('Sooners') rushed across the lands after the USA gave the go-ahead to parcel out former Native American lands. In the 1920s there was a new reason to head to Oklahoma: oil. The Depression cruelly coincided with a dust bowl that sent many out-of-work Okies west to California.

LANDSCAPE

Mostly a flat state, Oklahoma's biggest hills – aside from the odd loner – cluster to the east, but the land steadily rises as it goes west, peaking at the Black Mesa (4973 feet). Weather forecasters get a bad rep here, with unpredictable storms rising out of nowhere, particularly spring tornadoes that zip through. Rainfall is heaviest in the southeast (50 inches annually), compared with the drier panhandle (about 15 inches).

NATURAL BEAUTY

The 54-mile Talimena Scenic Drive crosses the green Ouachita Mountains in the southeast, while in the southwest, the rugged Wichita Mountains Wildlife Refuge has roaming buffalo and prehistoric mountains with a scenic drive. North of Tulsa, the rolling hills of Osage County are lovely, including the bison-filled Tallgrass Prairie Reserve, near Pawhuska. Watch out for bugs – Latimer County alone has 3600 beetle species.

PEOPLE

Oklahoma is three-fourths white, a bit more diverse than its northern neighbours. It has more Native Americans per capita than any other state, making up about 7% of the population. Following the Civil War, many African Americans moved to Oklahoma, settling about 50 towns (13 remain). Oklahoma's Latin American and Asian American populations are growing substantially (each comprising nearly 6% of the population). Come Sunday, you'll find many Oklahomans at church, but you'll also see the occasional mosque and synagogue in bigger cities.

BIG, BAD STORMS SWOOP IN AND WALLOP THE TERRAIN. »

CULTURE & TRADITIONS

When not in church or chasing tornadoes, Oklahomans like getting outdoors – fishing in artificial lakes, attending crafts fairs (particularly in early summer) or hanging out at the mall. In smaller towns, you'll see small rodeo rings – one of the most memorable is the Boley rodeo, a 'black rodeo' held every Memorial Day weekend. Perhaps the most famous tradition occurs when Oklahoma University's football team scores and the pony-led 'Schooner Schooner' – tributing the Land Run of 1889 – charges the field in Norman.

TRADEMARKS

○ Country music! Garth Brooks, Reba McEntire, Toby Keith – all Okies

○ Conservative churchgoers

○ Tornadoes

○ The bombing of Oklahoma City's Alfred P Murrah Federal Building in 1995

CUISINE

A lot is said by Oklahoma's official state meal, passed by tax-paid legislators in 1988 – fried okra, squash, cornbread, BBQ pork, biscuits and gravy, corn, chicken-fried steak, pecan pie and strawberries. (The fried-catfish lobbyists are still steaming over their omission.) Meanwhile, El Reno, west of Oklahoma City, claims to be the birthplace of the 'onion burger' (with an annual festival on the first Saturday in May). Buffalo finds its way into chili or the famous BBQ sandwiches.

For something a little different, Oklahoma City's huge Vietnamese population run nearly a dozen authentic pho (noodle soup) shops.

DID YOU KNOW?

○ Oklahoma has more surviving miles of Route 66 than any other state.

○ In 1987 Tulsa-based evangelist Oral Roberts asserted God would 'call him home' if he didn't raise $8 million – he snared $9.1 million.

ECONOMY

Once the oil capital of the world, Oklahoma remains the country's second-biggest producer of natural gas and fifth-biggest of crude oil. Manufacturing (eg machinery, metal, food, printing equipment) makes up $40 billion annually, about 4% of the nation's total output – while the aviation and aerospace industry contributes about 150,000 jobs and $12 billion. That said, pay isn't high in Oklahoma; averages rank 40th in the country (about $46,000 per annum), while teachers (at about $32,000 annual salary) come in at 47th in the nation.

URBAN SCENE

Oklahoma's two main cities don't get along that well. For years, green, cosmopolitan Tulsa – near the oil wells and hills – brought in the money, with fine art-deco buildings and riverside mansions, while flatter, dustier state capital Oklahoma City focused on cows and state government. Things started to change after

Oklahoma City passed an ambitious one-cent sales tax to reinvent itself in the '90s, resulting in a rejuvenated Bricktown near downtown, an NBA team playing the new Ford Center, and yachts (and some water!) for the Oklahoma River.

REPRESENTATIONS

○ 'Oklahoma!' (1943); the official state song, lifted from the Rodgers and Hammerstein musical

○ *The Outsiders* (1983); shot in Tulsa, Francis-Ford Coppola's film version of Tulsan SE Hinton's 1967 book, helped launch the careers of Tom Cruise, Matt Dillon and, ah, Ralph Macchio

○ 'Oklahoma Hills' (c 1937); Okie Woody Guthrie's song became the state's folk song in 2001

○ 'Take Me Back to Tulsa'; a fiddle tune by Tulsa-based Bob Wills

OKLAHOMA LEGEND

Most agree that Vikings were the first Europeans to reach North America – but few are familiar with the claims of the little southeastern town of Poteau that Vikings discovered Oklahoma long before. The 12-foot-tall Heavener Runestone is carved in apparently Nordic script for 'Gnomel's Valley' and dates from AD 750.

TEXT ROBERT REID

ESSENTIAL EXPERIENCES

○ Bidding at a kept-real cow auction at the Oklahoma City Stockyards

○ Dining or sleeping in Frank Lloyd Wright's only skyscraper, the classy 19-storey Price Tower in Bartlesville

○ Detouring along patches of old Route 66 (an often overlooked stretch skips the toll between Oklahoma City and Tulsa)

○ Attending the three-day Red Earth Festival in June, one of the nation's biggest Native American powwows

○ Visiting great Western art collections at oilman Frank Phillips' summer home at Woolaroc (outside Bartlesville) or Gilcrease Museum in Tulsa

○ Flashing an upside 'horns' hand sign (anti-Texas Longhorn) at an Oklahoma football game in Norman

⌃ THESE KIOWA GIRLS AT A POWWOW ARE PART OF OKLAHOMA'S RICH NATIVE AMERICAN CULTURE.

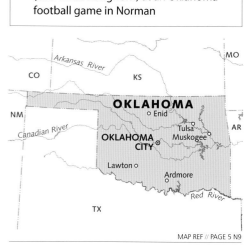

MAP REF // PAGE 5 N9

ROUTE 66 RAMBLES THROUGH OKLAHOMA FOR 426 MILES, STUDDED WITH PIT STOPS SUCH AS HILLBILLEE'S CAFE IN ARCADIA. ≫

BISON NIBBLE AT THE TALLGRASS PRAIRIE RESERVE NEAR PAWHUSKA. ≫

EASTERN GATE OF TIME AT THE OKLAHOMA CITY NATIONAL MEMORIAL. ≫

OREGON

OREGON IS A DIVIDED STATE, PHYSICALLY AND CULTURALLY. MOST RESIDENTS LIVE NEAR PORTLAND IN THE LUSH WILLAMETTE VALLEY, WHILE SPARSELY POPULATED AND POLITICALLY CONSERVATIVE EASTERN OREGON EVEN CONTAINS A FEW DESERTS. THERE HAVE BEEN TALKS (NONE TOO SERIOUS) OF SECESSION FROM FOLKS ON BOTH SIDES.

⌃ MEYERS CREEK BEACH IN PISTOL RIVER STATE PARK EXUDES QUINTESSENTIAL COASTAL SCENERY.

- **Etymology of the State Name** Unknown
- **Nickname** Beaver State
- **Motto** *Alis volat propiis* (She flies with her own wings)
- **Capital City** Salem
- **Population** 3.7 million
- **Area** 98,386 sq miles
- **Time Zone** Pacific
- **State Bird** Western meadowlark
- **State Flower** Oregon grape
- **Major Industries** Lumber, paper
- **Politics** Blue state in 2008
- **Best Time to Go** June to August – sunny days and summer festivals; March to May – for skiers

HISTORY IN A NUTSHELL

Native American tribes thrived in Oregon for hundreds of years but it wasn't until 1805, when two gents named Lewis and Clark strolled through the area, that Oregon was – literally – put on the map. Fur trappers of European descent arrived soon after and then, starting in 1841, the Oregon Trail brought thousands of hardy settlers out west. Statehood came in 1859 (Oregon was the 33rd state to join the Union), but folks were already well on their way. In the 25 years before the Transcontinental Railroad was completed in 1869, around half a million rugged men, women and children crossed part of the treacherous 2000-mile route with wagons and on foot, with almost 10% dying along the way. To this day, Oregonians are known for their self-reliant, pioneering spirit.

LANDSCAPE

Oregon is divided by the Cascade Range. The western third of the state is known for its beautiful beaches, rich farmlands and verdant coastal mountains. East of the Cascades is mostly high, arid desert. And, yes, it rains in Oregon, but not in all of it. While sections of the coastal mountains might receive 120 inches a year, the far eastern part of the state might receive only 6 or 7 inches. The part in between receives some of the heaviest snowfalls in the country – it's estimated that the craggy Cascades hold up to seven years' supply of water in their ice and snowpack.

NATURAL BEAUTY

The Oregon coast is dominated by isolated beaches (all public, a great source of pride to Oregonians), rocky basalt cliffs and quaint towns like Yachats, Newport, Florence and Lincoln City. The southern Cascades boast Crater Lake, North America's deepest lake, with crystal-clear water and a backdrop of snow-capped, ski-worthy jagged peaks. Plus, there are the trees – never-ending swaths of pine, hemlock, redwoods, aspen, apple, pear, chinquapin, fir and madrone. In fact, Oregon produces more Christmas trees than any other state.

MULTNOMAH FALLS, OREGON'S HIGHEST, CRASHES THROUGH THE COLUMBIA RIVER GORGE. ⌃

DON'T THINK IT'S ALL ABOUT BEER HERE – BOOKS ARE BIG BIZ AT POWELLS BOOKS. ⌃

PEOPLE

The population is concentrated along the Willamette River valley, from Portland to the collegiate towns of Eugene and Corvallis. Oregon is still a predominantly white state (around 90%) but has growing Latino and Asian communities. Mainly Christian, Oregon has one of the USA's largest Mormon (Church of Latter-day Saints) populations (over 100,000 members). Spiritualism has made Oregon the only state besides Hawaii where Buddhism is the second major religion.

CULTURE & TRADITIONS

Some say there are two distinct Oregon cultures: the granola crowd and the rural traditionalists. Each keeps a wary eye on the other. The latter prefer small-town values, guns and God while the former commune over post-consumer recycled protest signs at the Oregon Country Fair or festivals like Hempstalk, Faerieworlds or Plunderathon (Portland's annual underground festival for 'pirates, scallywags and grocery store clerks'). A newer, third, culture can often be located skiing down Mount Hood or wind-surfing the Columbia River Gorge.

TRADEMARKS

- Hippies
- Tillamook cheese and microbreweries
- Rain and trees
- Powell's Bookstore
- Oregon Trail
- Lewis and Clark
- Windsurfers
- Self-reliance

CUISINE

Oregon is known more for its agricultural traditions and sustainable farming than for any specific cuisine. From berries and apples in the west to hops in the Willamette Valley, wheat in the east and ranchers and dairy farmers throughout, fresh food is only a farm or two away from just about anywhere in the state. However, Oregon's most-loved culinary tradition isn't even edible: with more microbreweries per capita than any state, it's no wonder Oregon has attained a Zen state of mind known as 'beervana.'

ECONOMY

The focus of Oregon's economy has shifted from rural agriculture and lumber to computer- and research-based industries. The change hasn't happened quickly enough to save Oregon from having one of the country's top-five highest unemployment rates in recent years.

URBAN SCENE

With only three towns with a population of more than 100,000 (Portland, Eugene and Salem), 'dazzling urban scene' isn't the first thing that springs to mind. But Portland's Pearl District has quickly become a mecca for artsy types catching a band and a microbrew. Ex-warehouse district 'the Pearl' is plastered with art galleries, restaurants, loft conversions and locally owned boutiques.

REPRESENTATIONS

- *The Goonies* (1988); shot in film-friendly Astoria (also the location of *Kindergarten Cop*, *Overboard* and *Free Willy*)
- *One Flew Over the Cuckoo's Nest* (1975); Ken Kesey's 1962 novel about life in an asylum was filmed in a psychiatric hospital in Salem

DID YOU KNOW?

- Since 1975, the statewide Percent for Art Program has ensured that all public buildings with budgets of at least $100,000 allocate 1% of planned costs to public art.
- Oregon reportedly has more ghost towns than any other state.
- In 1973 Oregon became the first state to decriminalize marijuana; it continues to have some of the USA's most liberal cannabis laws.

OREGON LEGEND

Many Native American myths surround the ancient Bridge of the Gods, the land bridge that spanned the Columbia River Gorge until its collapse in the late 1600s. One such legend says that Mount Hood and Mount Adams were in love with the spirit of Mount St Helens. Erupting with rocks and lava didn't win her over but it did cause the earth to shake, annoying the Great Spirit, who destroyed the land bridge. Those broken pieces now make up the Cascade Falls, at present-day Bonneville Dam. A steel cantilevered bridge was built in 1926, named 'The Bridge of the Gods.'

TEXT ALEX LEVITON

ESSENTIAL EXPERIENCES

- Windsurfing the Columbia River Gorge
- Beer tasting at a microbrewery in Portland's Pearl District
- Renting dune buggies on the coast
- Skiing until 10pm in May on Mount Hood
- Catching *As You Like It* or *Macbeth* at the Oregon Shakespeare Festival in Ashland
- Admiring the urban planning of Portland from the tram, streetcar or MAX

ROBERTO GEROMETTA // LONELY PLANET IMAGES

⌃ WIZARD ISLAND RAISES ITS VOLCANIC HEAD FROM CRATER LAKE, THE NATION'S DEEPEST POOL.

WA
Astoria
Seaside
Columbia River
Tillamook Portland
Pendleton
La Grande
PACIFIC OCEAN
Newport **SALEM**
Albany
Cascade Range
Blue Mountains
Florence
Eugene
Bend
Reedsport
OREGON
Coos Bay
Malheur Lake
ID
Grants Pass
Upper Klamath Lake
Ashland
Klamath Falls
CA
NV
MAP REF // PAGE 4 D4

A GROUP TREKS OVER ELIOT GLACIER ON MOUNT HOOD, WHICH DRAWS ABOUT 10,000 CLIMBERS PER YEAR. ≫

PORTLAND IS DUBBED 'BEERVANA' FOR ITS WEALTH OF FRESH-BREWED NECTAR. ≫

LEE FOSTER // LONELY PLANET IMAGES

RAFTERS GO WILD FOR ROGUE RIVER RAPIDS. ≫

PENNSYLVANIA

THE BIRTH OF A NATION TOOK PLACE IN PHILADELPHIA, AND HISTORY IS CERTAINLY A BIG PART OF THE STATE'S MAKE UP, BUT PENNSYLVANIA HAS MORE TO OFFER, INCLUDING LARGE STANDS OF VIRGIN FOREST, ROLLING MOUNTAINS AND PASTORAL AMISH TOWNS UNOBSTRUCTED BY ELECTRICAL LINES.

⌃ THE SPRING AUCTION IN AMISH COUNTRY ATTRACTS LARGE CROWDS.

- **Etymology of the State Name** Latin for 'Penn's Woods'; after the state's founder, William Penn
- **Nickname** Keystone State
- **Mottes** Virtue, liberty and independence (official), America starts here (unofficial)

- **Capital City** Harrisburg
- **Population** 12.4 million
- **Area** 46,058 sq miles
- **Time Zone** Eastern
- **State Bird** Ruffed grouse

- **State Flower** Mountain laurel
- **Major Industries** Mining, steel, farming, tourism
- **Politics** Blue state in 2008
- **Best Time to Go** June – good weather; October – fall colors

HISTORY IN A NUTSHELL

Quaker William Penn founded Pennsylvania in 1681 as a 'holy experiment' respecting religious freedoms. European settlers quickly made it a prosperous colony and it contributed heavily to the Revolutionary War effort. 1787's constitutional convention took place in Philadelphia, where 11 years earlier the Liberty Bell tolled for the first reading of the Declaration of Independence. Pennsylvania was the second state to enter the Union, on December 12, 1787, and was the site of major Civil War battles, such as the one at Gettysburg. Over time the state's respect for religion attracted minority sects like the Amish and Mennonites, which still have a presence today.

LANDSCAPE

A hilly-to-mountainous state, much of Pennsylvania is part of the sedimentary Appalachian Plateau. The Appalachian range's Allegheny Mountains lie east of Pittsburgh, and its Pocono Mountains run from the state's south central to northeast. In the very far northwestern corner, the state meats the shoreline of Lake Erie in a lowland, farm-rich environment.

NATURAL BEAUTY

When settlers arrived they found a land covered in woods, and today Pennsylvania is still more than 50% forested. Spring blooms with abundant flowers in tended gardens and wildflower meadows, summer comes in a deep shade of green, and fall is ablaze with the vibrant reds, yellows and oranges of changing leaves. Allegheny National Forest, in the northwest, protects nearly 800 square miles of mixed northern broadleaf and conifer forests, reservoirs and rivers. In nearby Cook's Forest, virgin stands of white pine and hemlock soar to higher than 200 feet.

DID YOU KNOW?

- Pennsylvania is the only one of the original 13 colonies not to border the Atlantic Ocean.
- Hilly Pittsburgh has 300 sets of city-maintained stairs; lined end-to-end they'd reach higher than some of the Himalayas (26,000 feet).

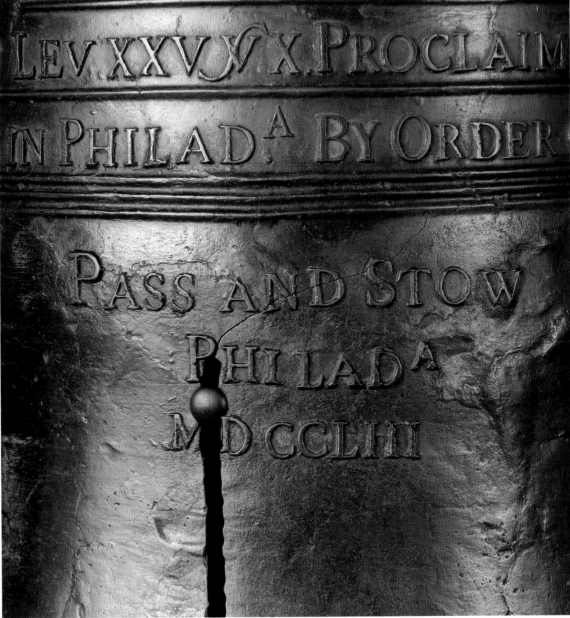

WHEN THE LIBERTY BELL TOLLS, IT SOUNDS AN E-FLAT. ≪

PEOPLE

The Pennsylvanian population is 11% African American, 4% Hispanic and 82% white. In the early 20th century, western Pennsylvania coal mines and steel mills attracted immigrants from Eastern Europe, and their descendants still make up a large part of the mix in that region. Though few Quakers live in the state today, their original religious tolerance is the reason that 115 faiths are now represented. Roughly 227,000 Amish live in Pennsylvania.

CULTURE & TRADITIONS

It's hard to miss the Amish buggies or old-fashioned clothing in Lancaster County and communities north of Pittsburgh. Men wear dark pants and coat, suspenders and a broad-brimmed hat. Women, who sew all the garments, don long, one-color dresses covered with white aprons, and a white bonnet when going out. Plainness is revered: buttons are banned for being fancy and photos are considered graven images (visitors should refrain from taking any that show peoples' faces). Discouraged from using power and machinery, Amish craftspeople make highly coveted handmade furniture and quilts.

TRADEMARKS

o Liberty Bell and Gettysburg

o Amish

o Benjamin Franklin and Andy Warhol

o Philadelphia cheesesteak and Hershey's

o Steel mills

o Groundhog Punxsutawney Phil

CUISINE

Heinz ketchup and condiments are produced in Pittsburgh, and Hershey's Chocolate takes up a whole town in central Pennsylvania, but it's Philly cheesesteaks that are the state's most iconic food. Thinly sliced and sautéed rib-eye steak is piled onto a crusty hoagie roll. Cheese Whiz (yes, the processed cheese spread) and cooked onions are the other traditional ingredients. Provolone and American are acceptable cheese substitutes, and some places may add mushrooms or peppers. Ordering in Philly requires the 'Whiz wit' system: saying the name of the cheese first, and then whether you want it 'wit' or 'witout' onions (delivered in your best blunt accent).

ECONOMY

Environmental constraints and foreign competition mean that steel production is not what it once was, but coal mining is still going strong. The medical and health service fields have been growing rapidly, and Philadelphia gets a large chunk of income from the tourist trade. Pennsylvania has the sixth-largest gross state product ($531,110) and the median household income is $43,174.

REPRESENTATIONS

o *The Deer Hunter* (1978); western Pennsylvanian steel workers get married and go into military service abroad in this movie

o *Groundhog Day* (1993); Bill Murray's character is forced to relive February 2 over and over again in small-town Punxsutawney

o Writer and environmental activist Rachel Carson and authors Louisa May Alcott, Willa Cather and Gertrude Stein all have Pennsylvanian ties

o *Witness* (1985); Harrison Ford goes under cover in Amish country to investigate a murder

o *Rocky* (1976); Sylvester Stallone's character fights his way back by training on the Philadelphia Museum of Art steps

URBAN SCENE

History is everywhere in Philadelphia, Pennsylvania's largest city (population 1.4 million). The 45-acre Liberty Park contains some of the nation's most cherished sites – the Liberty Bell, Independence Hall and Congress Hall. But Philly also has a vibrant urban entertainment and restaurant scene, and local theater productions often travel to Broadway. Hilly and green, Pittsburgh (population 311,000) is a city of ethnic enclaves and eateries at the confluence of the Allegheny and Monongahela Rivers. The Strip, a historic market district, contains trendy bars and restaurants galore.

PENNSYLVANIA LEGEND

Benjamin Franklin was larger than life: identifying electricity, founding a newspaper, helping to create the postal service, starting America's first circulating library… And in his spare time he invented swimming flippers, an efficient heating stove and daylight savings time. As a political leader Franklin assisted Thomas Jefferson in drafting the Declaration of Independence, attended the Continental Congress and became the fledgling nation's ambassador to France. And he did it all while dressed in simple Quaker clothing.

TEXT LISA DUNFORD

ESSENTIAL EXPERIENCES

o Ordering a 'Whiz wit' from the brash counter help at Geno's Steaks in Philly

o Riding the funicular up Pittsburgh's Mount Washington for a great city view

o Indulging in a chocolate bath spa treatment at the Hotel Hershey, in Hershey

o Standing beneath the cantilevered levels of Frank Lloyd Wright's Falling Water, looking at the waterfall under the house

o Watching groups of school children gather around the Liberty Bell

o Parking your car next to a horse-drawn buggy at a convenience store in Amish country

⌃ ORDER YOUR PHILLY CHEESESTEAK THE RIGHT WAY, OR RISK A POKE IN THE NOSE.

CANADA

Lake Erie

Erie

NY

PENNSYLVANIA

Scranton o

Pocono Mountains

Ohio River

Pittsburgh

o Altoona

Allegheny Mountains

Lancaster o

oHARRISBURG

Philadelphia o

NJ

WV

MD

MAP REF // PAGE 5 V5

GEORGE WASHINGTON SLEPT HERE, IN PRESENT-DAY BRANDYWINE BATTLEFIELD HISTORIC SITE. »

300-YEAR-OLD HOMES IN ELFRETH'S ALLEY, PHILADELPHIA. »

FIRST USED TO HAUL COAL, THE DUQUESNE INCLINE CABLE CAR NOW HAULS VISITORS TO A VIEW OVER PITTSBURGH. »

RHODE ISLAND

FLYING LARGELY UNDER THE RADAR OF FOLKS FROM THE OTHER 49 STATES, LILLIPUTIAN RHODE ISLAND HAS A FIERCELY IDIOSYNCRATIC PERSONALITY, A RIDICULOUSLY LONG COASTLINE, A COSMOPOLITAN CAPITAL AND A FUN-LOVING BEACH CULTURE.

⌃ UNSPOILED BLOCK ISLAND REMINDS MANY VISITORS OF THE GREEK ISLE OF RHODES.

- **Etymology of the State Name** From the Dutch *roodt eylandt* (red island), or from comparisons to the Greek island of Rhodes
- **Nicknames** The Ocean State, Biggest Little State in the Union
- **Motto** Hope

- **Capital City** Providence
- **Population** 1.1 million
- **Area** 1545 sq miles
- **Time Zone** Eastern
- **State Bird** Rhode Island Red

- **State Flower** Violet
- **Major Industries** Service industries, tourism
- **Politics** Blue state in 2008
- **Best Time to Go** May to September – especially August, for Newport music festivals

HISTORY IN A NUTSHELL

When Dutch explorers and Portuguese fishingfolk first spied this little corner of New England it was inhabited by the Narragansett, Wampanoag and Niantic tribes. Then English religious refugees from Massachusetts settled permanently in the area, followed by Quakers and Sephardic Jews (the latter established America's first synagogue at Newport in 1763). Rhode Island joined the Union as the 13th state on May 29, 1790, and immediately assumed a prominent role in the Industrial Revolution.

LANDSCAPE

The USA's smallest state is also one of the flattest, reaching its highest point at Jerimoth Hill (812 feet). Its geographic centerpiece is Narragansett Bay, dotted with islands and spanned by bridges. Large population centers cluster along the Blackstone, Seekonk and Providence Rivers north of the bay, and around Newport near the bay's mouth. Rhode Island enjoys somewhat milder winters than the rest of New England, thanks to its southerly location and maritime climate.

NATURAL BEAUTY

The coast is never far away in Rhode Island. Showcasing the state's watery beauty are a cluster of state parks at the mouth of Narragansett Bay and a long succession of beaches and national wildlife refuges running along the Atlantic Coast towards Connecticut. Broad, sandy Scarborough State Beach is one of the nicest. For wilder scenery, including red cliffs, a dramatic lighthouse and 25 miles of hiking trails, take the ferry to Block Island, a remote haven for birds along the Atlantic Flyway.

DID YOU KNOW?

- Rhode Island has more classic movie theaters per capita than any other state.
- Tiny Rhode Island is barely twice the size of Jacksonville, FL, yet its official name – Rhode Island and Providence Plantations – is the nation's longest.

QUAHOGS BRING A HUNGRY RUMBLE TO EVERY RHODE ISLANDER'S STOMACH. »

PEOPLE
Rhode Island has a higher percentage of Catholics (64%), Italian Americans (20%) and Portuguese Americans (9%) than any other state. Other common ethnicities include Irish (19%), French and French Canadian (17%), Hispanic (11%) and African American (6%).

CULTURE & TRADITIONS
Stick around Rhode Island long enough and you'll become familiar with the colorful local dialect, characterized by 'wicked strong' accents and a prodigious slang lexicon. A 'bubbla' is a water fountain, a 'cabinet' is a milkshake, and the city of Cranston is pronounced 'Creeanstin.' Other Rhode Island traditions include sailing, recreational fishing, and 'May Breakfasts,' festive spring fundraisers hosted by churches. On the downside, GMAC Insurance's National Drivers Test regularly reveals Rhode Islanders to be among the USA's worst drivers.

TRADEMARKS
- Tiny!
- Rhode Island Red roosters
- Newport's ocean-front mansions
- World Cup yacht racing

CUISINE
Rhode Island's culinary superstar is the giant quahog clam. Especially popular are 'stuffies': quahogs mixed with bread crumbs and other goodies and then stuffed back into the shell. Other specialties include clam cakes and Rhode Island clam chowder, made with clam broth rather than cream. Jonnycakes (white corn pancakes) are a traditional breakfast treat. Italian food is so ubiquitous that the Providence *Yellow Pages* don't list it as a separate ethnic category, and Portuguese influences also run deep – try the massive loaves of Portuguese Sweet Bread in Providence's Fox Point. Summertime favorites include Del's lemonade, an icy citrus slush sold from trucks along the state's beaches, and the Awful Awful, a milkshake from local chain Newport Creamery – drink three and the fourth is free! Lastly, there's the state drink: coffee milk, a blend of milk and coffee syrup so popular that it's even offered in kids' school lunches.

ECONOMY
The jewelry and textile mills that once flourished in the state have largely gone belly-up, giving way to a service economy based on government, education, health and business services. The US Navy is a big employer in Newport and summer tourism continues to be an important force. Rhode Island's income per capita ($39,710) and median household income ($53,570) are both slightly above the national average.

REPRESENTATIONS
- *The Case of Charles Dexter Ward* (1927); HP Lovecraft's macabre novella is set in (his home town of) Providence
- *Outside Providence* (1999); one of many Farrelly brothers' films featuring Rhode Island locations
- *My Rhode Island* (2003); cartoonist Don Bousquet's self-deprecating look at Rhode Island's quirky personality
- *Family Guy* (1999–present); the twisted TV series is set in the fictional town of Quahog

URBAN SCENE
The capital city Providence, filled with lovely tree-lined brick streets, historic homes and pretty white steeples, has been completely revitalized into one of New England's most dynamic cities. On College Hill, east of downtown, Brown University and Rhode Island School of Design keep the artsy/intellectual scene hopping, while neighborhoods such as Fox Point and Federal Hill brim with businesses reflecting their residents' Portuguese and Italian heritage. Open-air cultural events include ice skating, concerts and theater in the park, and WaterFire, a summer arts extravaganza featuring live music and bonfires lit on the local waterways. Rhode Island's biggest resort community is Newport, popular for its seaside mansions, surfing, yacht races and summer music festivals.

RHODE ISLAND LEGEND
Living legend and two-time felon Buddy Cianci has served six terms as Providence mayor, interspersed with assault and conspiracy convictions. At Cianci's first trial, the prosecution alleged that he threatened an amorous rival with a burning cigarette and a fireplace log. Cianci stepped down from office upon being convicted of assault, but rose from the ashes unscathed: after a stint as a radio talk-show host, he earned re-election in 1990, 1994 and 1998. Racketeering charges interrupted his career in 2002 but after five years in the slammer he returned to the airwaves with a new radio show. He has yet to throw his hat back in the mayoral ring.

TEXT GREGOR CLARK

ESSENTIAL EXPERIENCES

- Taking the ferry out to Block Island
- Listening to the waves and clanging buoys at sunset, Beavertail Point, Jamestown
- Eating Jonnycakes at the lunch counter beside the village green in Little Compton
- Checking out the mansions on the Newport Cliff Walk
- Watching bonfires shimmer on the river at WaterFire in Providence
- Discovering where the USA's Industrial Revolution started: at Slater Mill Historic Site in Pawtucket

MAP REF // PAGE 5 X4

THORNTON COHEN // ALAMY

⌃ NO BEACH VISIT IS COMPLETE WITHOUT A SWIG OF DEL'S FROZEN LEMONADE.

A MANSION LIKE THE ELMS CONSTITUTES A 'SUMMER COTTAGE' IN WELL-HEELED NEWPORT. »

QUAHOGGERS PLUCK SUPPER FROM THE SEA. »

THE NORTH LIGHT SHINES ON BLOCK ISLAND. »

TED HOROWITZ // CORBIS

SOUTH CAROLINA

THE FIRST STATE TO SECEDE FROM THE UNION AND SITE OF THE FIRST SHOTS IN THE CIVIL WAR, SOUTH CAROLINA STILL FEELS TIED TO ITS HISTORY IN A SPECTRUM OF WAYS. THESE DAYS, CHARLESTON'S HISTORIC STREETS AND ALLEYWAYS ARE ONE OF THE MOST POPULAR TOURIST DESTINATIONS IN THE USA.

⌃ THE COAST'S WHITE SANDY BEACHES BOOM WITH TOURISTS.

- **Etymology of the State Name** Named for King Charles I of England by his son, King Charles II
- **Nickname** Palmetto State
- **Motto** *Dum spiro spero* (While I breathe, I hope)

- **Capital City** Columbia
- **Population** 4.4 million
- **Area** 32,007 sq miles
- **Time Zone** Eastern
- **State Bird** Carolina wren

- **State Flower** Yellow jessamine
- **Major Industries** Livestock, automotive products
- **Politics** Red state in 2008
- **Best Time to Go** March to June – flowers in bloom and a lack of heat and humidity

HISTORY IN A NUTSHELL

The eighth of the original 13 colonies, South Carolina gained statehood in 1788. Already one of the wealthiest colonies when Britain attempted a siege during the Revolutionary War in 1780, the state (and especially Charleston) prospered mightily during the antebellum period. No other state depended upon African slaves and their agricultural knowledge quite like South Carolina, with its labor-intensive rice, indigo and cotton crops. The Civil War began when Confederate troops fired on Fort Sumter in Charleston Harbor in 1861. Some of the harshest Jim Crow laws were enacted in South Carolina and a few public schools weren't entirely desegregated until the 1970s.

LANDSCAPE

The state is divided into three separate regions – the famed beaches and Lowcountry, the midlands, and the western foothills. South Carolina's coastal area is home to beautiful beaches and endless marshes, while the midlands are mostly flat, with swaths of horse country, black-water swamps and forested patches of land. In the far west of the state, the area known as the Upcountry features rolling hills, jagged mountains and stunning waterfalls. The climate is mild in most of South Carolina, but subtropical summers can be unbearably hot throughout the state, hovering in the mid-90s in July and August.

REPRESENTATIONS

- Beach music (1950s); the music that inspired the 'shag' dance is now South Carolina's official state music

- *The Lords of Discipline* (1980); South Carolina's pre-eminent author, Pat Conroy (who also penned *Prince of Tides*), usually writes about lovingly dysfunctional South Carolina families, but detours here to his alma mater, Charleston's Citadel

- *The Colbert Report* (2005–present); on this TV program in 2007, native son Stephen Colbert announced his bid to run for president in 2008, but only on the South Carolina ballot

A MOSS-DRAPED LIVE OAK FRAMES DRAYTON HALL, A PLANTATION NEAR CHARLESTON. ≫

NATURAL BEAUTY

The marshlands of South Carolina rival any in Louisiana or Florida for beauty. Bald tupelos and cypress trees hang over gentle black-water swamps, wetlands and lakes throughout the state. The white sandy beaches of the low-lying resort islands and expansive coast, however, is what brings in millions of tourists each year.

PEOPLE

At the outset of the Civil War, South Carolina was almost two-thirds enslaved African Americans. Now numbering around 30%, many African Americans in the Lowcountry are Gullah, descendants of slaves who have preserved much of the language, food and culture from West and Central Africa. South Carolina is fiercely religious and over 92% of its people are Christian, one of the highest percentages in the United States.

CULTURE & TRADITIONS

Tradition takes on a new meaning around these parts. Whether it's Hoppin' John casserole on New Year's Eve or sipping lemonade on the porch of a *piazza* (the side porch of a Charleston home), South Carolinians like to preserve as much as possible of life in the olden times.

TRADEMARKS

- Battery Row mansions in Charleston
- Black-water swamps
- Myrtle Beach
- Gullah sweetgrass baskets
- Hilton Head golf
- Confederate flag
- Stephen Colbert

CUISINE

South Carolina's cuisine is Southern to the core – deep-fried, battered or fluffy – with a side helping of seafood. Any restaurant within 10 miles of a beach will offer South Carolina's favorite delicacy: she-crab soup. It's just what it sounds like – soup made from a female crab (using the roe). Boiled peanuts, the official state snack, can be found just about anywhere, including the annual South Carolina Peanut Party festival. Many popular dishes come from the West African Gullah tradition, including the rice-and-bacon dish, Hoppin' John. Some of the nation's best restaurants meld Southern tradition with fine dining in Charleston.

ECONOMY

Like many of its Deep South neighbors, South Carolina is one of the poorest states in the nation. Possessing the charms of historic Charleston, plus the allure of the resort islands and many popular beach destinations, the coast has become South Carolina's cash register. And while other states' auto industries are hanging by a thread, the BMW plant in Spartanburg is alive and well.

URBAN SCENE

With only two areas (Charleston and Columbia) with over 100,000 people, South Carolina doesn't have much of an urban scene. Much of the state's nightlife, culinary and cultural pursuits center around Charleston, which lands on just about every top-10 US tourist destinations list.

DID YOU KNOW?

- South Carolina, specifically Charleston, had the first library, museum and opera in the USA.

- In the beginning of the 19th century, Charleston had the largest Jewish population of any city in North America.

- Greenville's Bob Jones University holds one of the largest and most important sacred art collections in the USA (it's open to the public).

SOUTH CAROLINA LEGEND

One of South Carolina's most romantic legends is about a gold coin. Miss Queenie Bennett of Mobile gave George E Dixon, the captain of the *HL Hunley* submarine (the South's Civil War secret weapon), a gold coin in case he was ever captured. Dixon was shot in the leg at the Battle of Shiloh, but legend has it that the bullet bounced off the coin. When the Hunley was found years later, almost perfectly preserved on the ocean floor, there, slipped in Dixon's boot, was Queenie's gold coin. The coin was still dented, but had the inscription: 'Shiloh, April 12, 1862, GED, My life preserver.'

TEXT ALEX LEVITON

ESSENTIAL EXPERIENCES

- Strolling through the historic streets and Old Slave Mart of Charleston
- Golfing next to the beach on Hilton Head Island
- Rowing through black-water swamps
- Searching for seashells, fossils or shark teeth on Folly Beach
- Watching as thousands of fireflies flash in unison in the wetlands of Congaree National Park
- Shopping, sunbathing, seeing Broadway-style Southern entertainment or playing putt-putt along 60 miles of Myrtle Beach's Grand Strand
- Walking back in time through the mansion, gardens and slave quarters of the Middleton Place plantation

RICHARD NOWITZ / PHOTOLIBRARY

⌃ A GULLAH WOMAN CRAFTS A SWEETGRASS BASKET.

MAP REF // PAGE 5 U9

GATORS AND TURTLES AND BIRDS, OH MY! THEY LURK IN THE AUDUBON SWAMP GARDEN. »

CADETS GET IN LINE AT THE CITADEL, CHARLESTON'S FAMED MILITARY SCHOOL. »

SOUTH DAKOTA

THANKS TO HARLEY-DAVIDSONS, SIOUX TRADITIONS AND LOVELY POCKETS OF MOUNTAINS – INCLUDING A NOTABLE ONE FASHIONED INTO A PRESIDENTIAL 'GREATEST HITS' – SOUTH DAKOTA SEES MORE TOURISTS THAN ANY OTHER PLAINS STATE.

≈ MEN FACE A RESCUE TRAINING COURSE ON MOUNT RUSHMORE.

- **Etymology of the State Name** 'Dakota' is a Sioux word for ally or friend
- **Nicknames** Mount Rushmore State (but unofficially it's Sioux State or Harley Heaven)
- **Motto** Under God the people rule
- **Capital City** Pierre (pronounced 'peer')
- **Population** 796,214
- **Area** 77,121 sq miles
- **Time Zones** Central, Mountain
- **State Bird** Ring-necked pheasant
- **State Flower** American pasque
- **Major Industries** Hay, oats, tourism
- **Politics** Red state in 2008
- **Best Time to Go** June to August – festival season, especially August for the week-long Sturgis Motorcycle Rally

HISTORY IN A NUTSHELL

Picked up by the USA as part of the 1803 Louisiana Purchase, the South Dakota region remained mostly the domain of the Sioux until 1874, when Lt Col George Custer found gold in the Black Hills. War between the USA and the Plains Native Americans erupted in the 1870s but by 1877 increased numbers of US troops overwhelmed the Sioux, finally leading to their surrender. In 1890, a year after South Dakota became the 40th state, US troops attacked people at a Ghost Dance celebration at Wounded Knee, killing 250. Armed tribal leaders of the Oglala Sioux returned to the site in 1973 to protest, managing to hold federal agents off for 71 days.

LANDSCAPE

The jagged path of the Missouri River slices South Dakota into two distinct parts – the wetter, greener east and the more rugged west, with the startling buttes and rocky mountains of the sprawling 8000-sq-mile Black Hills. South Dakota's continental climate brings harsh winters (temperatures average 10°F/12°C in January) *and* summers (with July averages nearing 90°F/32°C).

NATURAL BEAUTY

South Dakota's greatest natural attractions cluster in the southwest of the state, notably the Black Hills' pine-topped mountains in Custer State Park and the lunar look of Badlands National Park, just east. The drive between the I-70 town Chamberlain and the capital Pierre offers stunning, timeless views of the Missouri River valley. Bald eagles, coyotes, elk, pronghorn, mountain lions and rattlesnakes are among the ample populations of nonhuman South Dakotan residents.

PEOPLE

Nearly nine in 10 South Dakotans are white, many linked with 19th-century settlers from Germany, Norway, Ireland or England. The biggest minority today is made up of Native Americans (nearly 9% of the population), most of whom live on frequently impoverished state reservations like the famous Pine Ridge Reservation (at 2600 square miles, it's larger than a couple of states).

A LAKOTA WAR DANCER DONS TRADITIONAL GARB AT THE CRAZY HORSE MEMORIAL. ⌃

CULTURE & TRADITIONS

Many Native American beliefs can still be seen in practice. Nearly 10,000 Native Americans come annually to Mato Paha (or Bear Butte mountain) to climb the rocky trail lined with prayer flags and pray to spirits. This Native American tradition is linked with 19th-century Sioux leader Crazy Horse's visions. On the noisier side of things, the Sturgis Motorcycle Rally attracts nearly half a million Harley fans annually. And a grislier tradition in this hunting-friendly state is hurling bloody carcasses of rival mascots, notably during South Dakota Coyote/South Dakota State Jackrabbit college games.

TRADEMARKS

o Mount Rushmore

o Harley-Davidsons in Sturgis

o Campy (and well-signed) Wall Drug Store

o The Corn Palace – a city convention center in Mitchell made from 275,000 ears of corn

o Wounded Knee

o Badlands National Park

o Crazy Horse

CUISINE

'Indian tacos' – fry bread with beef, beans and lettuce – make many menus around the Black Hills, Badlands and in reservation casino restaurants. On a slow day in Pierre, legislators passed the German-inspired *kuchen* (a sweet-dough coffee cake, usually made from apple) as the state dessert. The state bird, the pheasant, gets cooked up in many local styles, including roast pheasant in brandy and cream.

ECONOMY

Unusually for the Great Plains, tourism is a chief contributor to the state economy – visitors spend nearly $1 billion annually. Agriculture, finance and health-care industries – drawn by the lowest per-capita tax rate in the USA – provide other key players in the economy, though the state's gold revenue continues to fall (the largest mine, the Homestake, was closed in 2001). South Dakota's average annual salary is $27,000 but is much lower on reservations (where average annual salaries get as low as $3000).

URBAN SCENE

South Dakota doesn't do urban. Its biggest city, Sioux Falls (population 153,000), has a nice downtown by its falls, a huge hog-packing plant and a stunning number of slots casinos. More rewarding is Rapid City (population 60,000), the hub city for the Black Hills, with several historic buildings, hotels and museums (including the Sioux experience at the huge Journey Museum) in its pedestrian-friendly downtown.

REPRESENTATIONS

o 'Black Hills of Dakota' (1953); sung by Doris Day in *Calamity Jane*

o *Deadwood* (2004–06); HBO's swearing series of guts and gore set during the gold rush in them thar Black Hills

o *Starship Troopers* (1997); when Hollywood needs a scary outer-space bug-planet setting, they go to the Badlands

o *Dances with Wolves* (1990); Kevin Costner borrowed South Dakota's plains (and local Sioux costumes) for many of this epic's locations

o *Badlands* (1973); Terrence Malick's dreamlike period film about a murderous young couple

DID YOU KNOW?

o Construction for the massive Crazy Horse Memorial (100 times the size of the Rushmore heads) began in 1948 – after six decades, only the face has been finished.

o Many South Dakota side roads are pink, made from local pink-colored quartzite.

o Iowa outbid South Dakota to be the setting for a film called, uh, *South Dakota*, despite state senator Jim Lintz saying: 'We have more to offer than Iowa.'

o Sioux Indian costumes are often used to portray 'generic' Native Americans in Hollywood films.

SOUTH DAKOTA LEGEND

What to do when bugs attack? South Dakota has seen a few grasshopper storms, with millions coming in clouds, covering the ground 10 inches deep, ruining crops and creating havoc. After plagues hit Jefferson in 1874 and '75, a local priest put out three 'grasshopper crosses.' The next year's swarm skipped town – and haven't returned since, including one massive storm that affected surrounding areas in 1932.

TEXT ROBERT REID

ESSENTIAL EXPERIENCES

o Saluting the stone presidents at Mount Rushmore

o Driving through the otherworldly Badlands National Park, its name borrowed from the Sioux term *mako sica* (badland)

o Cycling the 109-mile Mickelson Trail, over an old rail line, through the Black Hills

o Visiting the somber Wounded Knee massacre site

RICHARD CUMMINS // LONELY PLANET IMAGES

⌃ THE WILDLIFE LOOP ROAD IN CUSTER STATE PARK ROLLS BY BUFFALO, ANTELOPE AND BIGHORN SHEEP.

MAP REF // PAGE 4 L5

IT'S JUST YOU, THE LONESOME WIND AND FLICKERING BIRDSONG WHEN HIKING IN THE DESOLATE BADLANDS. ☒

WALL DRUG'S BILLBOARDS BECKON THIRSTY TRAVELERS FOR MILES ALONG I-90. ☒

SHOWING OFF ITS BEST SIDE AT RAPID CITY'S DINOSAUR PARK. ☒

TENNESSEE

TENNESSEE DOES MORE THAN ANY OTHER STATE TO PROJECT AN APPEALING IMAGE OF SOUTHERN CULTURE TO THE WORLD, THANKS TO COUNTRY MUSIC, ELVIS, THE *GRAND OLE OPRY*, SOUL MUSIC AND A ROVING WILDERNESS THAT HARKENS BACK TO FRONTIER DAYS.

⌃ A WELL-ENDOWED SHOP SELLS DRESSES AT DOLLYWOOD.

- **Etymology of the State Name** Named after a Cherokee Indian village called 'Tanasi'
- **Nickname** Volunteer State
- **Motto** Agriculture and commerce
- **Capital City** Nashville
- **Population** 6.2 million
- **Area** 42,146 sq miles
- **Time Zones** Eastern, Central
- **State Bird** Mockingbird
- **State Flower** Iris
- **Major Industry** Manufacturing
- **Politics** Red state in 2008
- **Best Time to Go** Mid-June – country music fanfare in Nashville; mid-August – Elvis' death anniversary in Memphis

HISTORY IN A NUTSHELL

When it was admitted as the 16th state in 1796, Tennessee was home to Chickasaws, Cherokees and white settlers from east of the Appalachians. Scots-Irish farmers gravitated to the eastern part of the state, and Southern cotton planters claimed the west, each in turn pushing Native Americans out. Tennessee was the last state to join the Confederacy, the first Southern state to abolish slavery, and the first Confederate state to rejoin the Union. In the 1930s, the Tennessee Valley Authority introduced hydroelectric power, signifying the state's industrial growth. At around the same time, the popularity of country-and-western music put Tennessee on the popular culture map.

LANDSCAPE

Long, squat Tennessee encompasses a great variety of landscapes. The eastern extent cuts a jagged line through the Appalachian Mountains, and the state tumbles from there to the ridges and dips of the Great Valley. The terrain of Middle Tennessee includes the stony, river-slashed Cumberland Plateau and the broad sweep of the central basin. West Tennessee includes the flatlands of the Tennessee River Valley and the Mississippi's alluvial plain.

NATURAL BEAUTY

There are more species of tree in the Great Smoky Mountains National Park than in all of Europe. Add to that bears, white-tailed deer and 1500 species of flowering plants. Hikers can get away from the crowds by following part of the Appalachian Trail, which cuts through the Great Smokies and Cherokee National Forest before crossing the state line. From near Nashville, the Natchez Trace Parkway meanders through 450 miles of wooded hill country south to the Alabama border.

PEOPLE

Tennessee is 80% white, 16% African American and 3% Hispanic. Two-thirds of the population live in urban areas. Rural counties, particularly in the east, are less diverse; the great majority of African Americans live in the cities. Some 80% of the population is Christian, mainly Protestant.

A CLEAR VIEW FROM LOOKOUT MOUNTAIN OVER THE TENNESSEE RIVER NEAR CHATTANOOGA.

CULTURE & TRADITIONS

Tennesseans are generally friendly, conservative and proudly Southern. They favor dress-casual – ironed jeans and tucked-in shirts – which shows traditional Southern propriety has not gone by the wayside. Women favor big-hair styles. Getting outdoors is popular, but typically involves either hunting or watching motor sports. The state is home to three Nascar tracks, in Bristol, Nashville and Memphis. Country music *is* popular, but so is heavy metal, rhythm and blues, and hip-hop.

TRADEMARKS

- *Grand Ole Opry* and Nashville
- Elvis and Graceland
- Dolly Parton
- Memphis BBQ
- Stax Records and Soulsville, Memphis
- Jack Daniels and Moonshine
- Davy Crockett
- *Hee Haw*

CUISINE

Pork, greens, beans and corn bread about sums it up. Tennesseans favor a typical Southern diet, but have added memorable touches. Memphis BBQ, smothered in a spicy tomato-based sauce, is a standout. Many Memphis BBQ joints also feature the anomalous 'dry rub' ribs, which are patted with herbs and spices and slow-cooked. Sides sometimes include macaroni or spaghetti smothered in more irresistible 'Q sauce. Tennesseans also can't resist dunking everything into the fryer. In April the 'world's largest fish fry,' in Paris, TN, attracts 80,000 people, who consume five tons of catfish. Fried cornmeal (hush puppies) and fried fruit pies are also popular.

ECONOMY

Tennessee is more New South than Deep South, with modern industries now overshadowing agriculture. FedEx and AutoZone are based in Memphis, Eastman Chemical is in Kingsport, and Franklin is the North American base for Nissan. The state also produces textiles, cotton, beef and electricity. Tennessee is not a wealthy state: its income per capita is below $20,000.

URBAN SCENE

Memphis and Nashville don't seem like they're in the same state. The main difference is that Memphis is predominantly African American, while whites form the majority in Nashville. Memphis is a mecca for the urban blues, soul music, gospel churches and BBQ. That Elvis' crossover style emerged from here was no accident, for it was natural that a poor white boy in this town would pick up on black rhythm and blues. Nashville is the state capital and, more importantly, the world capital of country music. Music is *big business* here, and though it often seems that suited studio execs outnumber lovesick crooners, downtown still features traditional honky-tonks, along with modern country-politan clubs filled with line-dancing tourists. Both cities have NFL teams, and Memphis has an NBA team.

REPRESENTATIONS

- 'Tennessee Waltz'; the state song was penned by Redd Stewart and Pee Wee King in 1947
- *Hustle & Flow* (2005); a remarkably fresh film delving into Memphis' hip-hop scene
- *Mystery Train* (1989); a hip, mythological Memphis is still haunted by Elvis' ghost in this Jim Jarmusch film

DID YOU KNOW?

- The first atomic bomb was assembled in Oak Ridge in 1945.
- The world's first self-service supermarket, Piggly Wiggly, opened in Memphis in 1916.
- The Ku Klux Klan was born in Pulaski in 1865.
- Memphis' posh Peabody Hotel has a 'royal duck palace' on its roof, where live waterfowl live. During the day they are permitted to swim in a marble fountain in the hotel's lobby.

TENNESSEE LEGEND

Davy Crockett, Tennessee's 'King of the Wild Frontier,' was as much a politician as a frontiersman, and he served in the US Congress in the 1820s and '30s. In his autobiography, he quotes himself as telling the people of his district they could 'all go to hell' if they voted him out of office, which they did. When his constituents refused to go to hell, Crockett upped and left for Texas, where he died at the Alamo.

TEXT TOM DOWNS

⌃ ELVIS CROONED HIS FIRST HIT TUNE INTO THIS MICROPHONE, ON DISPLAY AT SUN STUDIO, MEMPHIS.

RAY LASKOWITZ // LONELY PLANET IMAGES

ESSENTIAL EXPERIENCES

- Honky-tonking on Broadway in Nashville
- Crooning into the mic at Sun Studio in Memphis
- Hiking Tennessee's portion of the Appalachian Trail, through Great Smoky Mountains National Park
- Wishing you could move into Graceland
- Lathering your lips with Memphis BBQ sauce

MAP REF // PAGE 5 R9

A FARMER AIRS OUT TOBACCO IN HIS DRYING BARN. ⤢

CRY A TEAR IN YOUR BEER AT NASHVILLE'S COUNTRY MUSIC HALL OF FAME. ⤢

TEXAS

SURE, TEXAS HAS BIG LAND AND BIG LONGHORNS, BUT IT IS SO MUCH MORE THAN THE STEREOTYPES; GREAT LIVE MUSIC, PALM TREES AND BEACHES, MEXICAN FIESTAS AND TASTY BBQ ARE ALL PART OF THE SUPERSIZED PACKAGE.

⌃ BLUEBONNETS AND BEEF: TWO TEXAS STAPLES.

- **Etymology of the State Name** From the Spanish territory *Tejas*, a corruption of the Caddo Indian word for 'friend'
- **Nickname** Lone Star State
- **Mottes** Friendship (official), Don't mess with Texas (unofficial)

- **Capital City** Austin
- **Population** 23.9 million
- **Area** 268,601 sq miles
- **Time Zone** Central
- **State Bird** Mockingbird

- **State Flower** Bluebonnet
- **Major Industries** Oil, gas and technology
- **Politics** Red state in 2008
- **Best Time to Go** February to April (earlier in the south, later in the north) – bluebonnets spring up but heat and humidity don't

HISTORY IN A NUTSHELL

Texas was part of Spanish territory in the Americas until Mexico won its independence in 1821. Shortly thereafter, independent Texans started scuffling with Santa Anna's territorial government. With a rallying cry of 'Remember the Alamo!' General Sam Houston eventually prevailed and the Republic of Texas was born. Nine short years after that auspicious beginning, in 1846, Texas opted to become the 28th state of the Union. Post–Civil War cattle drives helped create vast ranches, some of which still exist, but more than anything it's the boom-and-bust of the oil and gas industries that has shaped the state's recent history.

LANDSCAPE

The Rio Grande forms the southern border, where palm trees, citrus and vegetables are grown in subtropical heat. The Gulf of Mexico coast and sugar-sand beaches typify the semi-arid southeast; verdant hills and meandering rivers make up central Hill Country. Tall pine forests and swamps comprise the northeast, and wide, flat desert valleys alternate with mountain ranges (Guadalupe Peak at 8749 feet is the highest) in the way-far west. It gets pretty darn hot everywhere.

NATURAL BEAUTY

Texas' two national parks are in the west: Big Bend National Park encompasses the striking Chisos Mountains, with their desert flora and fauna, while the peaks of the Guadalupe Mountains National Park, to the north, are snow capped in winter and poppy covered in spring. Sixty miles of uninterrupted sand and dunes line the southern Gulf Coast's Padre Island National Seashore, where the endangered Kemp's ridley sea turtle nests.

DID YOU KNOW?

- King Ranch, in the southeast part of the state, is larger than Rhode Island.
- You can get a 72-ounce steak for free at the Big Texan in Amarillo if you eat it – and all the side dishes – in less than an hour.

EVEN COWBOYS PLAY THE BLUES, INCLUDING THIS SLIDE GUITARIST IN BANDERA. »

TEXANS DISPLAY THE LONE STAR FLAG EVERYWHERE, BARN ROOFS INCLUDED. »

PEOPLE

The second-largest state's population is hard to quantify, and differences are likely to be seen regionally. Officially, about 36% of the population is Hispanic, largely hailing from Mexico, but in cities such as San Antonio and El Paso, the percentage is closer to 60%. The remaining state population is roughly 48% white and 11% African American.

CULTURE & TRADITIONS

Again, regional characteristics prevail. Austin is alternative Texas, where 'keeping it weird' is as important as environmental integrity. Though the TV drama *Dallas* has long since been canceled, the Big D's culture is still about as upscale and image-oriented as the show depicted – big hair originated here. Conservative, casual Houston's oil and gas industrialites get together at clubby steakhouses, while San Antonio is the most Tex-Mexican of the bunch – annual celebrations like Cinco de Mayo and Fiesta take over the town. All across the state, one thing is true: football is sacrosanct, starting at the junior pee-wee league. College team rituals border on the occult and rivalries are serious business.

TRADEMARKS

- Big, big, big!
- 'God blessed Texas'
- Cattle ranches
- Cowboys
- Dr Pepper
- Corny dogs
- The Bush family
- *Dallas* and JR

CUISINE

You can certainly eat deep-fried favorites (chicken-fried steak, fried okra, fried Gulf Coast shrimp; heck, some places will even chicken-fry bacon) and Mexican food to your heart's content in Texas. But BBQ is king. Here it can refer to slow-smoked brisket, sausage or ribs. People passionately disagree about which joint serves the ultimate 'Q, but the best is usually found in Central Texas, where German and Czech settlers imported an Old World meat market tradition. To sauce or not to sauce is yet another question.

ECONOMY

Texas has the second-largest gross domestic product in the US – an economy just smaller than Mexico's. Fifty-eight of the top Fortune 500 companies are headquartered here, more than in any other state: names like ExxonMobil and ConocoPhillips are expected, but Dell Computers and AT&T also call the Lone Star State home. Airlines and aerospace account for a large part of the economy in Houston, as a result of Continental, Southwest and NASA Johnson Space Center. The median household income is $47,550, ranking 29th in the nation.

URBAN SCENE

Houston, a megalopolis that sprawls out instead of up, is the nation's fourth-largest city, with 2.1 million residents. But despite an interesting museum district, the culture and nightlife lag sadly behind that of other large towns in the USA. Dallas (with 1.2 million residents) is known for high art and a small alternative-music scene. It is similar in size to San Antonio (1.3 million residents), which has the famous Riverwalk entertainment area, and is packed with tons of restaurants and bars. But it's Austin, with a mere 709,890 people, that is undoubtedly the most entertaining. On every night of any given week the live-music capital swings, two-steps, slam dances and just plain rocks.

REPRESENTATIONS

- *Giant* (1956); the quintessential oil-rich ranch movie starring Elizabeth Taylor
- *Lonesome Dove* (1989); a Western miniseries based on Texas author Larry McMurtry's books
- *Dallas* (1980s); the world turned on the TV to see who shot JR
- *Friday Night Lights* (2004); Billy Bob Thornton starred in this movie about Texas high school football, before it became a TV series

TEXAS LEGEND

A classic tale of defiance, the battle of the Alamo looms large: 200 Texans defended the fortified mission against 1500 Mexican troops for 12 days, before they were overpowered and massacred on the 13th. Frontiersman Davy Crockett, colonel James Bowie (of Bowie knife fame) and Commander William Travis (who supposedly drew a line in the sand asking those who crossed to stand and die with him) have all grown larger than life through the story's retelling in song, literature and on the silver screen – both the Disney and John Wayne versions.

TEXT LISA DUNFORD

ESSENTIAL EXPERIENCES

- Eating melted-butter-tender barbecued brisket straight out of an open pit
- Boot-scootin' around a 100-year-old wooden dance floor
- Hiking past 2-foot-tall bluebonnets in Big Bend National Park
- Buying hand-tooled, inlaid leather boots – custom works of art for your feet
- Groovin' to those hard-rockin' blues at an Austin city nightclub
- Standing all four quarters chanting and whooping along with the yell leader at a Texas A&M Aggies football game

A YUCCA PLANT PREPARES FOR RAIN AT GUADALUPE MOUNTAINS NATIONAL PARK.

MAP REF // PAGE 4 M12

HOLGER LEUE // LONELY PLANET IMAGES

WILDFLOWERS BLANKET HILL COUNTRY FIELDS IN STONEWALL. »

STETSONS LINE THE RACKS AT PARIS HATTERS, SAN ANTONIO. »

THANKS TO HURRICANES, THIS IS THE THIRD INCARNATION OF BOB HALL PIER ON PADRE ISLAND. »

UTAH

ONCE SETTLED BY MORMON PIONEERS, UTAH'S CONTINUING CONSERVATISM IS TEMPERED BY OUTDOORSY TRANSPLANTS WHO'VE RELOCATED HERE TO HIKE WINDING TRAILS BENEATH REDROCK SPIRES AND CHALLENGE OLYMPIC-CALIBER SKI SLOPES.

≫ A HIKER TAKES A WALK ON THE WILD SIDE OF THE WAVE IN PARIA CANYON, SOUTHERN UTAH.

- **Etymology of the State Name** From the Ute word for 'home on a mountaintop'
- **Nickname** Beehive State
- **Motto** Industry
- **Capital City** Salt Lake City

- **Population** 2.6 million
- **Area** 84,904 sq miles
- **Time Zone** Mountain
- **State Bird** California seagull
- **State Flower** Sego lily

- **Major Industries** Coal mining and petroleum, light manufacturing, tourism
- **Politics** Red state in 2008
- **Best Time to Go** May or September – it's warm in the parks and cool in the mountains

HISTORY IN A NUTSHELL

'This is the place!' Brigham Young exclaimed when he and other Mormon pioneers arrived in Salt Lake Valley in 1847. Congress created the Utah Territory in 1850, but rejected the first five petitions for statehood because of the Mormon practice of polygamy. Once plural marriage was officially abandoned by the church, in 1896, Utah became the 45th state. Around the same time, Utah's rugged country served as the hideout for notorious Old West bad men and women, such as native son Butch Cassidy; and the last spike of the Transcontinental Railroad, which joined the East Coast to the West, was driven here. Throughout the 20th century the influence of the Mormon Church, today called the Church of Jesus Christ of Latter-day Saints (LDS), pervaded and Utah is still a conservative state.

REPRESENTATIONS

- *Mormon Country* (1942); writer William Stegner sheds light on Utah's religion and history
- More than 700 films (and more TV shows) have been filmed in Utah; the most iconic being the 1940s and '50s John Wayne Westerns
- *High School Musical I, II* and *III* (2006, 2007 and 2008); Zac Efron danced through East High School in Salt Lake City
- *Big Love* (HBO; 2006–present); follows the members of a polygamous Utah family
- *Red* (2002); a combination of poetry and political advocacy for the wilderness from native-born author Terry Tempest Williams

LANDSCAPE

Most of the state is high mountain desert, with an average elevation of 6000 feet. The southern section forms part of the Colorado Plateau, with stunning rockscapes eroded by wind and water, and sparse vegetation. To the north, the Wasatch Mountains dominate (King's Peak soars to 13,528 feet), with their pine forests and excellent skiing. Evaporation from the Great Salt Lake west of the mountains creates abundant, powdery lake-effect snow.

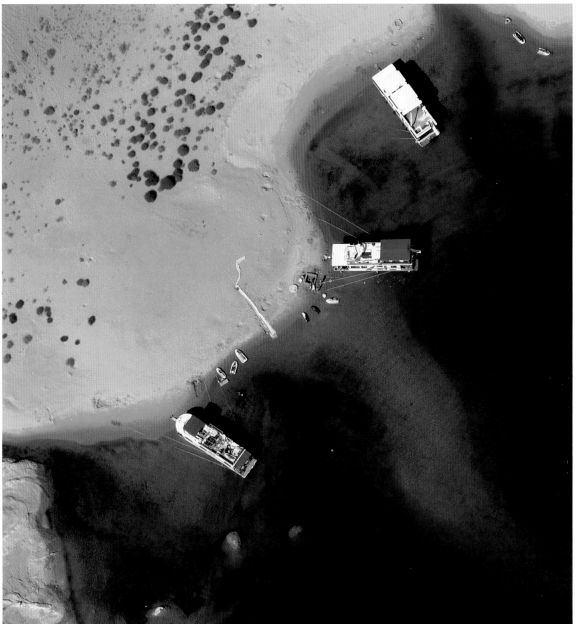

BOATS LAP LAKE POWELL'S SHORES IN GLEN CANYON NATIONAL RECREATION AREA. »

NATURAL BEAUTY

Twelve national parks and monuments and 41 state parks protect much of Utah's rugged beauty; 65% of the state is government owned. From A to Z: at Arches National Park red rock fins and overhangs defy gravity; in Bryce Canyon National Park there's a wondrous orange glow to the fanciful rock features and amphitheaters; vast winding canyons define the landscape in Canyonlands National Park; and even the roads are red (from asphalt using the local rock) in Zion National Park, where slot canyons and steep cliffs create dramatic vistas.

PEOPLE

There's evidence that LDS supremacy may be waning – only about 60% of Utah's population now claim Mormon church membership (the lowest percentage to date). That statistic doesn't equate to diversity however; 83% of the population are white. The state has the youngest population in the nation, with 26% under 18 and only 13% older than 65. Considering that almost 80% of residents live along the Wasatch front surrounding Salt Lake City, the low average population density (27 people per square mile) means that the hinterlands are pretty darn uninhabited.

ECONOMY

Unlike other faltering US state economies, Utah has held strong by going its own way in banking and other fiscal arenas. The median household income ($47,224) is $3000 above the national average. Construction and manufacturing employ a large sector of the population, as do tourism-related businesses.

CULTURE & TRADITIONS

There isn't a lot of nightlife outside the ski capital of Park City; the Mormon church still has a strong influence on the state's extremely polite populace. Its Words of Wisdom doctrine prohibits the use of coffee, tea, alcohol and tobacco. As a result, liquor licensing in the state is complicated; usually alcohol may only be served with food, and stand-alone bars are few and far between (coffee shops are quite common though).

TRADEMARKS

- Dinosaur fossils
- Red rock
- Delicate Arch
- Skiing
- Mormons
- Brigham Young
- Donny and Marie Osmond

CUISINE

Utah is not known for its food. Bland, generic US cuisine is the style of choice across most of the state. Salt Lake City and Park City, where upscale chefs experiment with 'nouvelle American,' are the exceptions. Utah does have a surprising number of microbreweries; Wasatch and Squatters Beers distribute statewide.

URBAN SCENE

Despite the fact that 2 million people live in the surrounding area, Salt Lake City has a surprisingly small-town feel. Consider it the Mormon equivalent of Vatican City. LDS's Temple Square is the biggest thing in town, but beyond the church walls a hint of liberal spirit, however slight, is evident in the eclectic dining options, coffeehouses and bookshops. When the trail beckons, brilliant hiking and skiing are only 45 minutes away. Neighboring Park City is a mountain ski village, but has the best nightlife and dining in the state, plus it co-hosts the Sundance Film Festival.

DID YOU KNOW?

- Natural Bridges National Monument (1908) is the USA's oldest National Park Service site.
- The nation's largest collection of fossils of the meat-eating allosaurus was found at the Cleveland-Lloyd Dinosaur Quarry in central Utah.

UTAH LEGEND

Nearly every small town in Utah claims some affiliation with notorious outlaw Butch Cassidy, born in Circleville in 1866. When reporters arrived at his boyhood cabin after the release of the movie *Butch Cassidy and the Sundance Kid* (1969), they met the outlaw's youngest sister. She claimed that Butch did not die in South America in 1908, but returned home for a visit after that date. Writers have been digging for the truth to no avail ever since.

TEXT LISA DUNFORD

ESSENTIAL EXPERIENCES

- Watching sunrise illuminate Bryce Amphitheater at Sunset or Sunrise Points
- Attending a movie premier at the Sundance Film Festival
- Touching a 150-million-year-old bone at Dinosaur National Monument
- Adventure touring in a 4WD across slickrock and sandstone outside Moab
- Swooshing down the groomers and bowls of a Wasatch Mountain ski resort
- Gazing up at the ethereal Salt Lake Temple lights in the moonlight
- Hiking knee-deep in water through the Narrows slot canyon in Zion National Park

PAUL KENNEDY // LONELY PLANET IMAGES

⌃ BRIGHTON SKI RESORT STOKES SNOWBOARDERS WITH ITS TABLETOPS, HIPS, RAILS AND JUMPS.

MAP REF // PAGE 4 G8

THE GREAT SALT LAKE DESERT COULD USE A DRINK. ⌄

CAROL POLICH // LONELY PLANET IMAGES

THE MORMON TABERNACLE CHOIR HAS RACKED UP FIVE GOLD ALBUMS SINGING TO THE HEAVENS. ⌄

DESOLATE BRYCE CANYON'S ANCIENT TREES AND ROCK SPIRES. ⌄

VERMONT

WHETHER SEEN UNDER BLANKETS OF SNOW, PATCHWORKS OF BLAZING FALL LEAVES OR THE EXUBERANT GREENS OF SPRING AND SUMMER, VERMONT'S BLEND OF BUCOLIC FARMLAND, MOUNTAINS AND THRIVING SMALL VILLAGES MAKES IT ONE OF THE USA'S MOST UNIFORMLY APPEALING STATES.

≪ SUGAR MAPLES CLOAKED IN FALL FINERY HUDDLE NEAR BARNARD.

- **Etymology of the State Name** From the French *vert* (green) and *mont* (mountain)
- **Nickname** Green Mountain State
- **Motto** Freedom and unity
- **Capital City** Montpelier

- **Population** 621,250
- **Area** 9614 sq miles
- **Time Zone** Eastern
- **State Bird** Hermit thrush
- **State Flower** Red clover

- **Major Industries** Tourism, agriculture, manufacturing
- **Politics** Blue state in 2008
- **Best Time to Go** May to October, December to February – avoid 'mud season' in late March/early April

HISTORY IN A NUTSHELL

For over a century after the Pilgrims landed, Vermont remained the impenetrable domain of the Abenaki people. In the 1700s New Hampshire and New York competed for this wild frontier, but in 1777 the fledgling Vermont Republic declared independence, laying down a groundbreaking constitution that abolished slavery, offered universal male suffrage and free public education. On March 4, 1791, Vermont joined the Union as the 14th state.

LANDSCAPE

From the Connecticut River (defining the state's eastern border) to the northwestern lowlands along Lake Champlain, Vermont's landscape is a sea of mountains. Flanking the Green Mountains' central spine you'll find the Taconics in the southwest and remnants of the White Mountains in the sparsely populated Northeast Kingdom. Long winters keep everyone bundled up from November through March, but summers are delightfully warm and not too humid.

NATURAL BEAUTY

Natural beauty lurks around every corner in Vermont, thanks to wise development decisions and a mountainous topography that changes color with the seasons. The Green Mountains form a distinctive backdrop, with 4000-plus-foot Camel's Hump and Mount Mansfield stealing the show. Outdoors enthusiasts can hike the ridgeline from Massachusetts to the Canadian border on the Long Trail or ski the valleys below on the 300-mile-long Catamount Trail. Other picture-worthy spots are Quechee Gorge and glacier-scoured Lake Willoughby. Vermont's iconic catamount (mountain lion) is long gone, but moose, deer, bears and foxes still make regular appearances, and the skies fill with honking Canada geese every spring and fall.

DID YOU KNOW?

- Vermont is one of four states prohibiting billboards.
- Vermont has more covered bridges and public libraries per capita than any other state.

TOY COWS ADD A TOUCH OF SURREALISM TO THE PASTORAL SCENE NEAR WOODSTOCK. «

PEOPLE

Vermont's population is predominantly white (97%) and English-speaking, but French surnames and Catholic churches testify to the sizable 19th-century influx of French Canadians who, with others of French extraction, account for 23% of Vermont's population. Nearly half of Vermonters (45%) have migrated from other states, and more claim no religious affiliation (34%) than in any other state.

CULTURE & TRADITIONS

Vermont long voted Republican, but a steady influx of flatlanders (folks from the less mountainous – and less conservative – states to the south) has turned the state 'blue' in recent presidential elections and helped spur Vermont's first-in-the-nation legislated same-sex marriage in 2009. The sometimes uneasy relationship between conservative old-timers and progressive newcomers is epitomized in the dueling slogans 'Take Back Vermont' and 'Take Vermont Forward,' but all Vermonters have worked together to keep downtowns, farms and family businesses alive, and many communities have successfully resisted the encroachment of suburban sprawl, mall culture and big-box stores. Outdoor activities are popular, even during the leafless months from November to March, when you'll find Vermonters skiing, snowboarding, deer hunting, ice fishing or maple sugaring.

TRADEMARKS

- Cows and cheddar cheese
- Fall leaves and skiing
- Apple cider and maple syrup
- Ben & Jerry's
- Gay marriage

CUISINE

Vermont is a locavore's paradise. In summer, fresh organic produce abounds at farmers markets and restaurants. Apple cider is king throughout the fall, while local meat and dairy products are mainstays year-round and creemee (soft-serve ice cream) stands are a favorite summer tradition. The abundant crop of microbreweries make some of the nation's tastiest ales.

ECONOMY

Vermont's four-season tourist industry thrives alongside economic mainstays, such as agriculture, quarrying and manufacturing. Vermont leads the nation in maple syrup production and boasts the world's largest deep granite quarry, Rock of Ages, in Barre. Despite losing two-thirds of its dairies in the past three decades, Vermont's venerable dairy industry remains New England's largest. A new generation of small farmers selling produce direct to restaurants, schools and farmers' markets is also helping revive the locally grown food economy. Vermont's income per capita ($37,446) and median household income ($49,907) lag slightly below the national average.

REPRESENTATIONS

- Robert Frost's poetry and Norman Rockwell's paintings
- Archer Mayor's series of detective novels
- *Snowflake Bentley* (1998); award-winning children's biography by Jacqueline Briggs and illustrated by Mary Azarian, of the Vermont photographer who revealed snowflakes' intricate beauty
- *Where the Rivers Flow North* (1978); Howard Frank Mosher's novella is set in Vermont's Northeast Kingdom

URBAN SCENE

'Urban Vermont' is something of an oxymoron. Burlington, the state's biggest city, barely reaches the 40,000 population mark, but it makes up in appeal what it lacks in size, with dazzling views of Lake Champlain and a pedestrian-friendly downtown. Montpelier, with 9000 citizens, is the smallest capital city in the USA – and the only one without a McDonald's – but bustles with energy thanks to a populace peppered with politicos, and chefs from the renowned New England Culinary Institute.

VERMONT MYTH

Every great lake needs a great lake monster, and Vermont's Lake Champlain is no exception. The native Abenaki called the monster Tatoskok, and French explorer Samuel de Champlain supposedly witnessed the serpentine form in 1609. Nowadays known as Champ to believers and nonbelievers alike, Champ has his own plaque and museum exhibit on the Burlington waterfront. The city's minor league baseball team – the Lake Monsters – sends a green-costumed Champ mascot to hug monster-smitten kids and dance on the dugout roof between innings.

TEXT GREGOR CLARK

ESSENTIAL EXPERIENCES

- Skiing the Catamount Trail, or hiking the Long Trail, Vermont's twin border-to-border recreation paths
- Riding the single chair lift – a relic unique in modern-day America – at Mad River Glen ski resort
- Getting lost under a canopy of fall foliage on one of Vermont's legendarily sinuous dirt roads
- Snowshoeing to a maple sugar shack and sharing stories around the steaming syrup evaporator
- Touring the Ben & Jerry's factory, or mingling with cows and sheep at one of Vermont's emerging artisanal dairies
- Attending the Tunbridge World's Fair, a traditional harvest celebration going strong since 1867

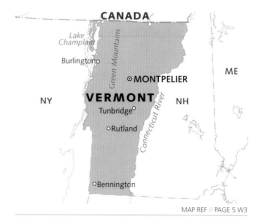

⌃ VERMONT SWEETENS THE NATION'S PANCAKES WITH ITS MAPLE SYRUP PRODUCTION.

DAVID FRAZIER // CORBIS

KILLINGTON RESORT TYPICALLY IS THE FIRST TO OPEN AND LAST TO CLOSE IN THE NORTHEAST EACH SEASON. ≫

CHEESINESS PERMEATES VERMONT; EVEN THE CALVIN COOLIDGE HISTORIC SITE HAS A FACTORY. ≫

PICTURESQUE FAMILY FARMS THRIVE IN VERMONT. ≫

VIRGINIA

ONE OF THE OLDEST, MOST ARISTOCRATIC STATES IN THE COUNTRY IS A BAROMETER OF THE NEW SOUTH, WHERE RURAL CONSERVATISM RUNS UP AGAINST INCREASINGLY INTEGRATED URBAN AMERICA. THESE DAYS DIXIE IS AS DEFINED BY CONSULTING AND CONTRACTING AS IT IS BY THE CIVIL WAR BATTLE SITES THAT PEPPER THE COUNTRYSIDE.

« HOUNDS SNIFF FOR CLUES DURING A FOXHUNT.

- **Etymology of the State Name** Named for Queen Elizabeth I, England's 'virgin queen'
- **Nickname** Old Dominion
- **Motto** *Sic semper tyrannis* (Thus always to tyrants), Virginia is for lovers (unofficial)
- **Capital City** Richmond

- **Population** 7.7 million
- **Area** 42,769 sq miles
- **Time Zone** Eastern
- **State Bird** Cardinal
- **State Flower** Dogwood

- **Major Industries** Federal government, high technology
- **Politics** Blue state in 2008 (the first time in 44 years)
- **Best Time to Go** April to June and September to October – weather is finest

HISTORY IN A NUTSHELL

The tidewater Native American kingdom of Tsenacommacah was displaced by several waves of remarkably inept settlers in the early 17th century (there were no farmers in John Smith's original Jamestown). Virginia quickly became one of the most important commonwealths in colonial America and birthed prominent leaders of the revolution. Its plantation elite helped spark secession (so they could keep their slaves) and ensured Richmond was the capital of the Confederacy during the Civil War. Since then the state has straddled a geo-cultural fault line – it remains a Southern stronghold but its DC-adjacent suburbs keep parts of it within the range of the Northeast Corridor.

LANDSCAPE

The coast comprises miles of flat marshland and peninsular 'necks' cut by rivers like the Rappahannock and the Rapidan. Hill-and-horse country dominates the central Piedmont Plateau, while the Shenandoah Valley and Blue Ridge highlands are defined by deep, wild mountains covered in galax, dogwood, bloodroot, black snakeroot, Virginia pine and bitternut hickory.

NATURAL BEAUTY

Eastern Shore marshland gives way to miles of buttery beach fronting the Atlantic Coast. The ever-expanding vineyards of the Piedmont give that upland country a Tuscany-comes-to-Appalachia vibe, while the indigo crest of the

Appalachians themselves defines the original US frontier. Don't forget Civil War battle sites; these preserved spaces hold the greatest remaining examples of 19th-century US countryside.

TRADEMARKS

- Skyline Drive and the Blue Ridge Parkway
- Civil War sites
- Jamestown
- George Washington, Thomas Jefferson and six other presidents
- The Pentagon
- Ella Fitzgerald

COAL MINED IN THE SOUTHWEST COUNTIES CHUGS TO GREAT LAKES STEEL MILLS. »

PEOPLE

Northern (and increasingly, Central) Virginia is a muddle of whites, African Americans, Latinos and Asians (including one of the largest Vietnamese communities on the East Coast). Loudoun County is one of the fastest growing in the nation, thanks to both massive immigration and residential spillover from the DC suburbs. Richmond is a more traditionally Southern city, divided between white and black, though a fast-growing immigrant influx is adding brown to its palette. Much of rural Virginia is made up of white or black small towns scattered around the hills and the wiry farming and exurban country of Southside, Virginia (south of the James River, east of the Blue Ridge).

CULTURE & TRADITIONS

Northern Virginia is DC-suburban. It resembles both spread-out sun-belt cities like Atlanta and the immigrant-heavy Eastern seaboard. Fredericksburg marks the ham-and-biscuit line where the South, as a cultural entity, truly begins. Dixie society and aristocracy (plus country black culture, which is far more laid-back than African American enclaves in the Northeast) is exemplified in cities like Richmond, and rural areas are as culturally conservative as the deepest South. The Atlantic Coast is dominated by naval bases and military families.

CUISINE

Traditional Virginia cuisine is up-country Southern, consisting of ham, spoon bread, biscuits and corn bread set off by the state legume, the Virginia peanut. On the coast, seafood (particularly fish and oysters) is added to the menu, while fare like soybeans and pintos characterize mountain diets. There's also an incredible ethnic menu on offer in Northern Virginia; office workers with deep Dixie roots are more likely to scarf pho (Vietnamese noodle soup) or takeout from a Peruvian chicken shack than hoe into ham and peas.

ECONOMY

Fairfax and Loudoun Counties have vied for years for the highest median income in the USA. Much of Northern Virginia is well educated and well off, many employed as staff for the federal government, within the military, for high-tech firms or in service sectors that work for all of the above. On the downside, there is an urban black underclass in Richmond and deep-seated poverty in rural parts of the state.

REPRESENTATIONS

- *Notes on the State of Virginia* (1781), by Thomas Jefferson; one of the defining works of US colonial literature, establishing a freshly written voice for a newly emerging country
- *The Silence of the Lambs* (1991); the FBI scenes were filmed in Virginia
- 'Straight Outta Virginia' (2003), by Timbaland; what any self-respecting commonwealth native yells in da club

URBAN SCENE

Alexandria and Arlington are Washington, DC, suburbs, full of ethnic enclaves and middle-class amenities, and Richmond, a more traditionally Southern city, is slipping into the bubble of the Boston–DC corridor. The state capital is beginning to balance Dixie architecture and monuments with a hip student scene and immigrant influx. Charlottesville, home of the University of Virginia, is a quintessential Southern college town: stately, brick-laned and hopping at night.

DID YOU KNOW?

- Over 100,000 Americans were killed in a 10-mile radius surrounding Fredericksburg during the Civil War.
- Eight presidents were born in Virginia.
- Norfolk is the world's largest shipping yard.
- Virginia has had three capital cities (Jamestown, Williamsburg and Richmond).

VIRGINIA MYTH

John Smith and Pocahontas were never romantically tied; when they met he was 28 and she was roughly 12. Their love was a myth that cast the colonization of the New World in romantic terms – the native falling for the foreign soldier. Pocahontas did eventually marry John Rolfe, for which she was ostracized by her people, the Powhatans, who were later wiped out by disease and her adopted English countryfolk.

TEXT ADAM KARLIN

ESSENTIAL EXPERIENCES

- Trucking down Skyline Drive or the Blue Ridge Parkway
- Eating New Southern cuisine or hot soul food in Richmond
- Strolling through Charlottesville's student society
- Visiting Manassas Battlefield Park – one of the most beautiful rural landscapes in the eastern USA
- Following the 'Crooked Road,' a country, bluegrass, old-time music trail through southwest Virginia
- Tracing Robert E Lee's final retreat from Petersburg, through Southside Virginia, to Appomattox Courthouse

ANNE GRIFFITHS BELT // GETTY

⌃ THE GARDENS OF ARLINGTON NATIONAL CEMETERY ARE A HOT SPOT FOR WATCHING FOURTH OF JULY FIREWORKS.

MAP REF // PAGE 5 V8

RUSTIC VISTAS LIE JUST A STONE'S THROW FROM THE HUSTLE OF WASHINGTON, DC. ⊗

DENNIS JOHNSON // LONELY PLANET IMAGES

ALEXANDRIA'S OLD TOWN DISTRICT INCLUDES MORE THAN 4000 HISTORIC BUILDINGS. ⊗

THE FIFE AND DRUM CORPS MARCHES THROUGH WILLIAMSBURG. ⊗

WASHINGTON

THE NORTHERN AND SLIGHTLY MORE URBANE HALF OF THE PACIFIC NORTHWEST, WASHINGTON IS MOST FAMOUS AS HOME TO SEATTLE, BUT MUCH OF THE STATE REMAINS RURAL, WITH STUNNING AGRICULTURAL AND FORESTED LAND. THE SEATTLE AND TACOMA AREAS HAVE BEEN TRANSFORMED BY COMPANIES LIKE AMAZON, BOEING AND, OF COURSE, MICROSOFT.

- **Etymology of the State Name** Named for the first US President, George Washington
- **Nickname** Evergreen State
- **Motto** *Al-ki* (Chinook word meaning 'bye and bye')

- **Capital City** Olympia
- **Population** 6.5 million
- **Area** 71,303 sq miles
- **Time Zone** Pacific
- **State Bird** Willow goldfinch

- **State Flower** Coast rhododendron
- **Major Industries** Computer software, agriculture, aircraft manufacturing
- **Politics** Blue state in 2008
- **Best Time to Go** July to September – best weather, fresh produce and festivals

HISTORY IN A NUTSHELL

When Washington was divided from the Oregon Territory in the 1850s there were a mere 4000 pioneers, fur traders and enterprising merchants living within its borders. Downtown Seattle was covered in trees as tall as 400 feet. Over the next 60 years Washington gained statehood (in 1889; it was the 42nd state) and several rail lines, making travel to the isolated outpost easier and more desirable. During this time it also experienced the short-lived Klondike Gold Rush. It wasn't until the Boeing Aircraft Company established its headquarters (now in Chicago) in Seattle during WWI, and later employed tens of thousands of workers during WWII, that the state established itself as a hotspot for innovation and educated workers.

NATURAL BEAUTY

The Cascades Loop scenic highway route passes through an assortment of Washington's most scenic charms – rich forests, pioneer villages and mountain vistas. The lush San Juan Archipelago is a sort of hippie Caribbean of the Northwest, a chain of islands populated by artists, retired Microsofties, weekenders and killer whales (orcas). Glacial Mount Rainier in the center and volcanic Mount St Helens in the south satisfy the cravings of those looking for vertical beauty, while the dry southeastern part of the state is colored with wineries and apple orchards.

LANDSCAPE

Geographically (and culturally), Washington is two vastly different places. East of the Cascade Range the landscape is high, dry desert where passing tumbleweeds aren't uncommon. The coastal western half of the state is dominated by a temperate rain forest, filled with spruce, pine and Douglas fir trees. Annual rainfall on the Olympic peninsula can reach 12 to 14 *feet* in some locations and the Cascades are one of the snowiest places on earth (snowfall exceeded 1144 inches on Mount Baker in the 1998–99 season).

PEOPLE

Seattle, like most of the rest of the state, is predominantly (over 85%) white, though Washington has one of the largest Asian populations (7%) in the country. Although the history of Washington has been heavily influenced by the Chinook and other Native American tribes, Native Americans currently make up less than 1% of the population. Washington is primarily Christian but has one of the USA's highest percentages of people identifying as nonreligious.

CULTURE & TRADITIONS

Whether it's a pink-haired art-school student making your half-caf, low-foam latte in Seattle or your truck-driving roller-coaster mate at the Washington State Fair in Puyallup,

Washingtonians are a friendly bunch. Washington has had a reputation of radicalism that goes back to its agrarian roots, still seen in its residents' commitment to political and community activism and their dedication to preserving the land.

TRADEMARKS

- Starbucks
- Seattle Space Needle
- Mount St Helens
- Rain
- Microsoft
- Apples and cherries
- Puget Sound

CUISINE

Washington has a dedication to all things fresh, organic, local and sustainable, and the burgeoning wine industry is the country's second largest (behind California). From apple farms in the east to oyster beds in the west, the state has a commitment to low food miles, shown in the number and popularity of local farmers markets. There is no better homage to all foods Washingtonian than The Herbfarm restaurant in rural Woodinville, where the five-hour, nine-course dinner features dozens of local ingredients.

A FERRIS WHEEL KEEPS ON TURNIN' UNDER SEATTLE'S SPACE NEEDLE. »

ECONOMY

Lumber, agriculture and fisheries used to rule the economy. However, the changing face of US business has been kind to Washington. Some of the most popular Fortune 500 companies in the USA, including Costco, Nordstrom and Amazon, claim Washington as their headquarters. In 1979, a whiz kid named Bill Gates moved his little start-up back from Albuquerque to his native Seattle. Microsoft – the most profitable company on earth – has produced thousands of millionaires and several billionaires. The trickle-down theory bodes well for Washington; many of these millionaires have a typical Washingtonian commitment to social and ecological concerns and have poured millions into local schools, universities, museums and the environment.

URBAN SCENE

There is only one place in Washington considered to have a true urban scene: Seattle.

Jet City still manages to feel like a small town divided into close-knit neighborhoods, while at the same time retaining cosmopolitan touches like international restaurants, music clubs, yoga studios and chic boutiques. Since grunge invaded in the early 1990s, the music and club scene has been legendary. Recent revitalization efforts have spruced up the downtowns in Tacoma and, especially, Spokane.

REPRESENTATIONS

○ *Sleepless in Seattle* (1993); Seattle's Pike Place Market and houseboat community feature prominently in this iconic Tom Hanks/Meg Ryan romantic comedy

○ Grunge (1990s); Nirvana and Pearl Jam exemplified the music, and flannel and unkempt hair exemplified the style

○ *The Absolutely True Diary of a Part-Time Indian* (2007); poet and novelist Sherman Alexie grew up on the Spokane Reservation, also home to *Diary*'s 14-year-old protagonist

○ *Twin Peaks* (1990–91); TV drama set in a fictitious Washington town but filmed in Snoqualmie and North Bend

DID YOU KNOW?

○ Seattle has the northernmost latitude of any city in the contiguous USA, at 47.6 N it parallels the very northern tip of Maine.

○ Washington has been home to some of the country's most notorious serial killers, including Ted Bundy, Robert Yates and the Green River Killer.

○ In 2004 Washington became the first state to simultaneously have a female governor and two female senators.

WASHINGTON LEGEND

On November 24, 1971, a man who called himself Dan Cooper (later referred to by the media as DB Cooper) boarded a commercial flight from Portland to Seattle. He handed a flight attendant a hijacking note demanding $200,000 in $20 bills, and four parachutes. Cooper received his requested booty during a forced refueling stop, and later jumped out of the plane over southern Washington. Although there were several suspects throughout the years, and $6000 worth of the marked $20 bills was found near the banks of the Columbia River in 1980, Cooper was never found, identified or heard from ever again.

TEXT ALEX LEVITON

≫ ONE OF THE LOCAL PERKS IS A COFFEE SHOP ON EVERY CORNER.

LAWRENCE WORCESTER // LONELY PLANET IMAGES

ESSENTIAL EXPERIENCES

○ Fishmongering at Pike Place Market

○ Kayaking past orcas through the San Juan Islands

○ Sipping a cappuccino at one of what seems like 77.4 million coffee shops

○ Ascending the Space Needle for a panoramic view of Seattle, the Puget Sound and Mount Rainier

○ Hiking Mount Rainier

○ Wine tasting in and around Walla Walla, the state's northwest or near Yakima

○ Snowboarding the pristine powder of Mount Baker

CANADA

San Juan Islands · Bellingham · Mount Baker

Port Angeles · Port Townsend · Everett · Grand Coulee Dam

Puget Sound · Bremerton · Seattle · **WASHINGTON** · Spokane

Aberdeen · Tacoma · Wenatchee

Willapa Bay · **OLYMPIA** · Ellensburg · Pullman

Mount St Helens · Mount Rainier National Park · Yakima

Longview · Kennewick · Walla Walla

Columbia River

OR

MAP REF // PAGE 4 E3

FLOWERY MEADOWS LEAD THE WAY TO GLACIER-STRIPED MOUNT RAINIER. ⌃

MICHAEL HANSON // AURORA PHOTOS // CORBIS

ORCAS LEAP AMONG THE SAN JUAN ISLANDS, DRAWN BY JUICY SCHOOLS OF SALMON. ⌃

WASHINGTON'S BOUNTIFUL FARMERS MARKETS DESERVE A SMILE. ⌃

WASHINGTON, DC

THE USA'S CAPITAL IS ITS OWN LITTLE ENTITY: FEDERALLY FUNDED, LOCALLY RUN, AND LACKING A SEAT IN CONGRESS AND THE ABILITY TO TAX MOST OF THE PEOPLE WHO WORK THERE. IT'S A SMALL TOWN THAT'S A CITY THAT'S A NATIONAL CAPITAL

- **Etymology of the District's Name** The city is named after George, 'DC' stands for District of Columbia (after Columbus)
- **Nicknames** DC, the Nation's Capital, Chocolate City
- **Population** 588,292

- **Mottoes** *Justitia omnibus* (Justice for all); Taxation without representation (unofficial)
- **Area** 69 sq miles
- **Time Zone** Eastern
- **State Bird** Wood thrush

- **State Flower** American beauty rose
- **Major Industry** Running the country
- **Politics** Blue district in 2008
- **Best Time to Go** March to May – cherry blossoms; June to August – swelter and intern parties

HISTORY IN A NUTSHELL

Regional rivalries between the new not-so-united states led Congress to carve a federally run capital from 10 square miles of Maryland and Virginia farmland in 1791. During the Civil War freed slaves became the basis of the capital's population, and their descendants watched the city burn during 1968's race riots. Forty years later a new chaos broke out – celebrations over the election of Barack Obama.

ECONOMY

Only 14% of DC residents work for the federal government. The rest are employed in universities, think tanks and policy centers, or in the service sector that supports these civil servants. DC has the lowest unemployment rate of the 40 largest US metro areas but has one of the nation's largest number of residents below the poverty line. Washington's inability to tax the DC-employed incomes of Maryland and Virginia residents is a major financial handicap.

PEOPLE

'Chocolate City' is still 56% African American, but gentrification has pushed poorer groups into Maryland's Oxon Hill and Berwyn Heights. DC's old row houses (and new condos) are filling with the young and moneyed. Peppering everything are immigrant enclaves from Ethiopia, El Salvador, Sudan, Pakistan and the Bahamas. DC's white middle and upper classes tend to concentrate in leafy Upper Northwest, although young professionals are moving into hip 'hoods like U Street and Columbia Heights.

TRADEMARKS

- The White House
- Smithsonian Institution museums
- The National Mall
- Cherry Blossom Festival
- Duke Ellington

CULTURE & TRADITIONS

Washington has traditionally been split between a conservative, buttoned-down corporate culture and its black neighborhoods. This dichotomy is now overlaid by ambitious young students and staffers, and the capital's reputation has morphed into one where folks work hard, party harder and support an increasingly excellent arts, music and foodie scene.

CUISINE

DC's dining scene has blown up over the past decade – its number of starred restaurants is incredible given its size. That said, there's also a surfeit of good, cheap places, from soul food to *pupuserías* (places that sell Salvadoran tortillas) and, of course, the excellent, ubiquitous half-smoke, the local, meatier version of the hot dog.

TEXT ADAM KARLIN

ESSENTIAL EXPERIENCES

- Walking the Mall, from the Capitol to the Lincoln Memorial
- Eating Ben's Chili Bowl at 3am, after a night out in U Street
- Catching a Redskins game, preferably in winter
- Taking in a burger, a beer and some senator spotting on Capitol Hill
- Exploring 'America's attic' – the excellent Smithsonian Institution

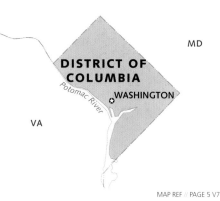

MAP REF // PAGE 5 V7

THE VIETNAM VETERANS MEMORIAL IS A PLACE FOR REFLECTION. »

WEST VIRGINIA

WITH A SOMETIMES CONFUSING LOVE OF MOUNTAINS, MINING, GOD, GUNS, LIBERTY AND LABOR UNIONS (IN PRETTY MUCH EQUAL MEASURE), PLUS ONE OF THE MOST DISTINCT REGIONAL CULTURES IN THE COUNTRY, WEST VIRGINIA MARKS THE DEFINITIVE EDGE OF THE EASTERN SEABOARD AND THE HEART OF THE APPALACHIAN SOUTH.

≈ THE MOUNTAINEERS OF WEST VIRGINIA UNIVERSITY BUST ONTO THE FOOTBALL FIELD.

- **Etymology of the State Name** In honor of Elizabeth I, Virgin Queen of England
- **Nickname** Mountain State
- **Motto** *Montani semper liberi* (Mountaineers are always free), Wild and wonderful (tourism slogan)
- **Capital City** Charleston
- **Population** 1.8 million
- **Area** 24,231 sq miles
- **Time Zone** Eastern
- **State Bird** Cardinal
- **State Flower** Rhododendron
- **Major Industries** Coal, small-plot agriculture, chemical products, tourism
- **Politics** Red state in 2008
- **Best Time to Go** September to November – foliage and crisp air

HISTORY IN A NUTSHELL

Prior to European settlement, this stretch of the Appalachians was known for mound-building native cultures. Following settlement, western Virginia, populated by German and Scots-Irish small landholders, was long distinct from eastern Virginia, ruled by an aristocracy of plantation and slave owners. Many Appalachian settlers had pressed for a state of 'Westsylvania' since the American Revolution, and when Virginia seceded from the Union, its northwestern counties seceded from Virginia. Mineral wealth was the economic engine of the state for years, while the labor movement – mining unions versus mining companies – became its defining sociocultural struggle.

LANDSCAPE

West Virginia is the only state to be entirely located within the gorgeous Appalachians. This land manages to be at once rugged yet slightly user-friendly. There's a flinty, undeniable toughness to the range, but it's also carpeted in dark green forests, which makes it feel less imposing than the younger Rockies. The Allegheny Plateau covers the western two-thirds of the state.

DID YOU KNOW?

- West Virginia has the USA's oldest median age.
- It introduced the USA's first sales tax, in 1921.
- The USA's first spa town, still famous for its mineral water, is Berkeley Springs, WV.

- The state is nearly three-quarters forested and has the highest average altitude of any state east of the Mississippi.

REPRESENTATIONS

- *October Sky* (1999); Jake Gyllenhaal and Chris Cooper star in this movie about real-life rocket scientist and coal miner's son Homer Hickam
- *Matewan* (1987); John Sayles' masterpiece on labor wars in the West Virginian coal country, filmed near the New River Gorge
- 'Take Me Home, Country Roads' (1971); the signature song of both John Denver and West Virginia

A CLIMBER SCALES THE FLINTY APPALACHIANS. »

NATURAL BEAUTY

West Virginia is known for its looks. Vermont might claim the 'Green Mountain State' nickname, but West Virginia deserves it. Between the George Washington National Forest (one of the largest tracts of public land in the eastern USA), the winding red path of the Chesapeake and Ohio Canal, some of the most spectacular portions of the Appalachian Trail, and the weird, wet moors of the mountain swamps of the Canaan Valley, this is some of the best nature North America has to show off.

PEOPLE

It's pretty homogenous here: 94% white and only 1.3% foreign born. Most of the white folk are descended from Germans and Scots-Irish farmers, although immigrant alliances (and tensions) defined much of West Virginia's unionization struggle (in the early 20th century). John Brown's raid and attempted slave revolt at Harpers Ferry sparked the Civil War, but African Americans still only make up 4% of the population. Almost 90% of West Virginians identify themselves as Christian, with most of the rest listing 'nonreligious.'

CULTURE & TRADITIONS

West Virginian culture is characterized as liberty-loving, with a focus on reverence for God, gun rights and freedom from government regulation. All this is represented by a 'Live free or die' ethos. While mountain culture, one of the USA's most enduring, overlays the state with bluegrass music and smoky up-country accents, there are major geographic divisions. Southern West Virginians identify with the American South, the state's north feels like part of the Pittsburgh–Ohio rust belt and the eastern panhandle is the prettiest edge of the greater Washington, DC, metro area.

TRADEMARKS

- Appalachian Mountains
- Coal mining
- The Hatfields and the McCoys
- Bluegrass and old-time music
- The West Virginia University Mountaineers and their rowdy fans

CUISINE

People eat Southern in West Virginia, but it's a Southern influenced by the limited resources of the mountains, Germanic culture and the need for food that kept during long periods of isolation. Pickling is popular, especially of cabbage and beans; and pinto beans and corn bread topped with salt ham or bacon is perhaps the most distinctive local dish (that or the evil 'slaw' hotdog – a wiener with chili and coleslaw). Wild game is delicious and plentiful; there's a good chance the venison on the table was prancing through the woods not long ago.

ECONOMY

West Virginia ranks near (often at) the bottom of the national median income scale. The state has a relatively enormous amount of operator-owned small farms, but these aren't the wished-for organic plots of apartment yuppies – they're hardscrabble, rarely profitable and speak to endemic rural poverty. Heavy industry is common, within Pittsburgh's economic orbit, and the state remains the nation's highest coal producer. Tourism, of the adventure and outdoorsy sort, is increasingly becoming the economic backbone of many parts of the state.

URBAN SCENE

Charleston, with 50,000 citizens, is the biggest city around but it's the north's Morgantown, which houses West Virginia University, its associated arts scene (including the cultivation of many mountain traditions) and a relatively diverse population, that is probably the state's most interesting city. With that said, West Virginia is a place where small-town culture – laced with mountain warmth and a strong sense of independence – defines its populated centers.

WEST VIRGINIA MYTH

'Take Me Home, Country Roads' is not really about West Virginia. Well, sort of: the song was inspired by the small roads of western Maryland, but the regions' scenery overlaps so much only a nitpicker would notice.

TEXT ADAM KARLIN

ESSENTIAL EXPERIENCES

- Tailgating for a West Virginia University football match with Southern Comfort at Mountaineer Stadium
- Having your car struggle up the umpteenth gorgeous hill
- Hiking. Anywhere.
- Visiting the Mystery Hole, at Ansted, where gravity and good taste are a figment of your imagination
- Scoffing the goods at Biscuit World: a fast-food chain based in Nitro and usually paired with Gino's Pizza and Spaghetti
- Listening to bluegrass music at the Purple Fiddle, in Thomas

⌃ A DULCIMER PLAYER PICKS A TUNE AT CHARLESTON'S VANDALIA GATHERING FOLK FESTIVAL.

MAP REF // PAGE 5 U7

COAL IS BIG BUSINESS BUT IT ISN'T PRETTY, AS SHOWN BY REFUSE AT THIS RACINE MINE. ⨠

HISTORIC HARPERS FERRY PLAYED A PIVOTAL ROLE IN LAUNCHING THE CIVIL WAR. ⨠

WISCONSIN

WISCONSIN IS CHEESY AND PROUD OF IT, BUT BEYOND THE COW-SPECKLED FARMLAND AND ARTISANAL HUNKS LIES A BIG OUTDOOR PLAYGROUND OF SHIMMERING ISLANDS, LAKEFRONT BEACHES, FORESTED TRAILS AND GOOD-TIME BASHES TO HELP CELEBRATE IT ALL.

≈ THE POSTER CHILDREN FOR THE DAIRY STATE ARE A SERIOUS, MILK-MAKING BUNCH.

- **Etymology of the State Name** French corruption of a Native American word for 'river that meanders through something red'
- **Nicknames** Badger State, America's Dairyland
- **Motto** Forward

- **Capital City** Madison
- **Population** 5.6 million
- **Area** 65,503 sq miles
- **Time Zone** Central
- **State Bird** Robin

- **State Flower** Wood violet
- **Major Industry** Agriculture
- **Politics** Blue state in 2008
- **Best Time to Go** June to August – festival season

HISTORY IN A NUTSHELL

Lead was Wisconsin's first boom industry, drawing miners from nearby states and from as far away as Cornwall in the 1820s. The miners were called 'badgers' for their subterranean activities, and the moniker stuck as a descriptor for the state. In 1832 the Black Hawk War's final battle took place in western Wisconsin, where militias killed 60 Native Americans as they tried to cross the Mississippi River to safety. Wisconsin entered the Union in 1848 as the 30th state. Soon after, immigrants poured in – from Germany, Switzerland and Scandinavia most notably, bringing their cheese-making and beer-brewing skills with them.

LANDSCAPE

Lake Superior crowns the island-fringed north, while Lake Michigan splashes the state's eastern breadth, providing plenty of beachfront. The Door County peninsula juts like a thumb to the far east, slapped by the frosty waters of Green Bay, Lake Michigan and the treacherous Death's Door Strait. Boreal forests and glacial lakes fill the North Woods but it's the hilly southwest that's Wisconsin's claim to fame. Here, in what's known as the Driftless Region, glaciers did not flatten the landscape as elsewhere but left hills, valleys and limestone-rich soil – poor for crop farming, but perfect for roaming dairy herds that produce sweet milk. The state gets snowed under in winter; summers are brief and cool.

NATURAL BEAUTY

Rustic barns, spotted cows and sun-bleached hay bales flash by, pretty as a picture, throughout Wisconsin. In the north, windswept beaches and cliffs comprise the 21 nuggets of the Apostle Islands National Lakeshore. Most of this wooded archipelago is uninhabited and reachable only by kayak or National Park Service ferry. Door County's rocky coastline, picturesque lighthouses, cherry orchards and 19th-century villages make it a more romantic escape. And though the first thing that may come to mind at the mention of 'Wisconsin Dells' is kitschy water parks, the name actually refers to an extraordinary sandstone gorge on the Wisconsin River. The endangered whooping crane honks in nearby wetlands.

THE MOD MILWAUKEE ART MUSEUM IS A CITY ICON. ⌃

GREEN BAY PACKERS FANS ARRIVE EARLY AND BUNDLE UP AT LAMBEAU FIELD. ⌃

PEOPLE

Wisconsin's population breaks down to 86% white, 6% African American, 5% Hispanic, 2% Asian and 1% Native American. Eleven Native tribes live here – more than in any other state east of the Mississippi River. About half of all Wisconsinites are Catholic or Lutheran. The majority have German or Scandinavian roots, similar to neighboring Minnesota.

CULTURE & TRADITIONS

Wisconsinites are a social bunch. Every Friday they gather in pubs or churches for the traditional 'fish fry,' a meal of beer-battered cod, walleye or perch, with french fries and coleslaw, to celebrate the end of the work week. The food is hearty, sensible and communal – much like Wisconsinites themselves. Tailgating provides a similar festive atmosphere. Locals attending a Brewers baseball or Packers football game bring portable grills to the parking lot and fire up bratwurst-laden feasts to share. Even bars are a family affair – teens are allowed in as long as mom or dad is there and says it's OK.

CUISINE

Simple heartland food – meat, potatoes and lake fish – goes down the gullet in most parts. Cheese adds to the palette of course, particularly artisanal and farmstead creations and squeaky curds. An impressive foodie/locavore scene has been active in Madison for years; it's the location of one of the country's largest farmers markets. Milwaukee is famous for its German-influenced cuisine, ie sausages and beer.

ECONOMY

It's probably no surprise to learn Wisconsin is the nation's top cheesemaker. It pumps out 2.4 billion pounds of cheddar, gouda and other smelly goodness each year – a quarter of America's hunks – plus milk and butter. Not as well known is that Wisconsin is the nation's leading cranberry producer, or that it rates among the top 15 states for industrial output. Engines and shovel hoists aren't as glamorous as Harleys and Miller beer (both brands were invented and are still made here), but they all add cash to local coffers. Tourism rounds out the main industries. Wisconsin's household income hovers right in the middle of the US pack at $50,600.

TRADEMARKS

o Dairy cows and cheese!

o Breweries (including Miller) and beer-cooked bratwursts

o Dells water parks

o 'Cheesehead' Green Bay Packer fans

URBAN SCENE

While Milwaukee's reputation as a working-class town of brewskis, bowling alleys and polka halls lingers, attractions like the Calatrava-designed art museum, badass Harley-Davidson Museum and stylish eating and shopping 'hoods have turned Wisconsin's largest city into a surprisingly cool place. In summertime, festivals let loose downtown every weekend. Granola crunchers and gastronomes sip free-trade coffee and cycle to work side by side in Madison. The small, beloved capital wins kudos for everything from most ecofriendly city to most walkable, best for road-biking and most vegetarian city in the USA.

REPRESENTATIONS

o *Happy Days* (1974–84); the Fonz, Richie Cunningham and friends lived in 1950s Milwaukee in this TV comedy series

o *Laverne & Shirley* (1976–83); *Happy Days* spin-off – Laverne and Shirley also lived in 1950s Milwaukee, working as brewery bottle-cappers

o *Little House in the Big Woods* (1932); Laura Ingalls Wilder's children's book about a family living in a Wisconsin forest cabin in the 1870s

DID YOU KNOW?

o The Green Bay Packers are the only community-owned team in the NFL.

o Milwaukee earned its 'nation's watering hole' nickname in the 1880s when Pabst, Schlitz, Blatz, Miller and 80 other breweries made suds here. Only Miller and a few microbreweries remain.

o Milwaukee's phone book has more German-ish names beginning with 'Sch' than Munich's.

WISCONSIN MYTH

Be careful in the North Woods. If you see a horned, flame-snorting beast with large fangs and green eyes, three claws facing forward and one pointing backward, wafting a scent of buzzard meat and skunk perfume – run. The ferocious Hodag roams the area around Rhinelander. It was first captured in 1896 and shown at the local fair. Admittedly, that Hodag proved to be a hoax, but sightings are still reported.

TEXT KARLA ZIMMERMAN

ESSENTIAL EXPERIENCES

o Biting into a squeaky-fresh cheese curd at a dairy

o Partying at a good-time Milwaukee festival with an icy local brew in hand

o Kayaking through forlorn sea caves in the Apostle Islands

o Polka dancing at a Friday-night fish fry

o Donning a foam-rubber cheese-wedge hat for a Packers game

MAP REF // PAGE 5 P4

⌃ A LIGHTHOUSE DOTS WISCONSIN POINT NEAR THE TOWN OF SUPERIOR.

BEER FLOWS FROM PLENTIFUL TAPS IN MILWAUKEE, ONCE THE NATION'S BREWING CAPITAL. «

VOLKMAR K. WENTZEL // GETTY

DRUMLINS, AKA MOUNDS OF GLACIAL DRIFT, POCKMARK THE LANDSCAPE; SOME ARE LINED WITH WISCONSIN'S CASH CROPS. «

A CHEESEMAKER SALTS WHEELS OF SWISS IN MONTICELLO. «

WYOMING

THE LEAST POPULATED STATE IN THE UNION, WYOMING IS SINGULAR AND ADVENTUROUS, A FRONTIER STATE THAT STILL ESCHEWS TIES AND SUITS FOR A COWBOY HAT AND BOOTS ANY DAY. AND WHILE THE STATE IS FAMOUS FOR ITS WINDS AND PLAINS, THERE ARE ALSO PLENTY OF BIG-TIME MOUNTAIN VIEWS.

≪ THE MOON MOVES IN FOR A CLOSE ENCOUNTER WITH DEVIL'S TOWER.

- **Etymology of the State Name** It either means 'at the big river flat' in the Munsee language or it's named after the Wyoming Valley in Pennsylvania
- **Nickname** Equality State, Cowboy State
- **Motto** Equal rights

- **Capital City** Cheyenne
- **Population** 522,830
- **Area** 97,818 sq miles
- **Time Zone** Mountain
- **State Bird** Western meadowlark

- **State Flower** Indian paintbrush
- **Major Industries** Mining, tourism, some farming and ranching
- **Politics** Red state in 2008
- **Best Time to Go** June to September – Indian paintbrush blooms on steep mountainsides

HISTORY IN A NUTSHELL

The history of this large Western state is one of movement and transition. The Crow, Lakota, Arapaho and Shoshone peoples were the major stakeholders in the region before white explorers ventured in. And while Wyoming didn't see the major mineral strikes other Western states did (and consequently never saw a major population boom) it was an ideal place for frontierspeople to move westward – the Oregon Trail and Union Pacific Railroad all passed through here, as does today's massive east–west corridor, the I-80. This is also a place of firsts: the first national park at Yellowstone was established in Wyoming in 1872, and it was the first state to allow women's suffrage.

Wyoming gained statehood on July 10, 1890, becoming the 44th US state.

LANDSCAPE

Numerous mountain ranges collide in Wyoming to form the spine of the Rocky Mountains. The rest of the state is a high-altitude windswept sea of grass and ranchland that slopes gently down to the Great Plains.

NATURAL BEAUTY

Much of the state's natural treasures, including jagged mountains, geyser fields and wide-open prairie, can be appreciated in the national parks, forests and monuments, including the 2.2-million-acre Yellowstone, 300,000-acre Grand Teton, and smaller areas like Devil's Tower and Fossil Butte. Believe it or not, this is still the land where the buffalo roam. They're joined by foxes, wolves, elk, moose, and black and grizzly bears.

PEOPLE

Wyoming is considered by most to be the USA's most sparsely populated state. Around 94% of the state is white, Hispanics make up about 5%, and Native Americans comprise 1%. And in a state that values individual freedom above anything else, it's not surprising that more than 20% of state residents claim zero religious affiliation. And Protestants account for more than 50% of the state's Christians.

AN ELK WONDERS WHERE HIS FELLOW WILD THINGS ARE IN YELLOWSTONE NATIONAL PARK. »

CULTURE & TRADITIONS

Cowboy culture is alive and well throughout this state, which was founded by frontierspeople. It can be witnessed at the stock shows and in the country music halls. It's particularly apparent out on the range, where real cowboys and cowgirls still stand tall in the saddle, driving those 'doggies' to better pastures. And being a Rocky Mountain state, Wyoming is also home to a fair amount of mountain 'dirtbag' types, the kind of people that don't bat an eye at class V rapids, 5.12-grade climbs and 40-degree ski slopes. The one thing that these diverse characters can agree on is to live and let live.

CUISINE

This is beef country. And any meal is best served medium-rare. There are also good game dishes, like elk and deer, and a fresh-caught trout sizzled over an open fire is something special.

TRADEMARKS

- Yellowstone National Park's Old Faithful Geyser
- Cowboy hats worn by honest-to-goodness cowboys
- Ski bums
- Devil's Tower (shown in *Close Encounters of the Third Kind*)
- Dick Cheney and Jackson Pollock (both born here)

- Wind
- Pick-up trucks
- Barbed wire

ECONOMY

With so many incredible national parks and forests, and a few impressive ski areas, tourism makes up a large part of the economy, bringing in more than $2 billion yearly of the state's $27.4 billion annual state product. Digging for coal, oil, natural gas and uranium are also big. A bunch of sweeping ranches are testament to Wyoming's enduring claim of being cattle country.

URBAN SCENE

There are a few spots for urban cowboys to get their groove on but the only real cultural centers are Cheyenne, Casper and Laramie, which has a sizable university. While some fine arts can be found in these towns, most of the culture is cowboy-centric.

REPRESENTATIONS

- *Shane* (1953); one of several Westerns that were filmed here
- *Brokeback Mountain* (2005); set here but filmed in the Canadian Rockies
- *The Laramie Project* (2002); half-documentary, half-drama telling the story of the murder of a gay college student in Laramie

DID YOU KNOW?

- The Old Faithful Geyser in Yellowstone shoots up to 8400 gallons of boiling water skyward in a 150-foot eruption that happens about every 90 minutes.
- Jackson Hole Ski Area gets about 450 inches of snow a year, and has 2500 acres of skiable terrain.
- The Yellowstone Caldera, also known as the Yellowstone Super Volcano, last erupted some 640,000 years ago.

WYOMING LEGEND

No US monolith inspires the way Devil's Tower does. This massive 1267-foot geological oddity 'engendered an awful quiet in the heart of man' (writer N Scott Momaday), and inspired President Theodore Roosevelt to declare it a national monument more than 100 years ago. The fissured tower was also a sacred place for many Plains Indian tribes, who called it the Bear's Lodge. One lovely legend from the Kiowa tells the story of seven young women being chased by a bear. The girls jumped onto a rock, which began to grow skyward. The bear fell short and scratched its claws into the rocketing monument as it fell toward the ground. While the women escaped the rapacious claws of the bear, they were stranded on the rock and eventually became the stars of either the Big Dipper or the Pleiades (depending on who retells the tale).

TEXT GREG BENCHWICK

COWBOYS SADDLE UP AT THE CODY NIGHT RODEO.

ESSENTIAL EXPERIENCES

- Taking the 'tram' at Jackson Hole, your heart in your throat, your knees a-jitter and your sights set on some of the USA's steepest inbounds skiing terrain
- Attending a rodeo, such as Cheyenne Frontier Days, or heading out to a dude ranch to help bring the cattle home
- Climbing one of many mountains
- Rafting through Wind River Canyon
- Camping for a week in the Yellowstone backcountry, your only pals the local elk, grizzly bear, wolf and deer
- Sliding over the snow on a dogsled, snowmobile or one-horse open sleigh

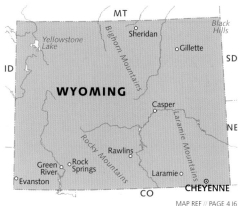

MAP REF // PAGE 4 I6

TANGERINE DREAM – THE YELLOWSTONE RIVER SLIPS THOUGH THE HAYDEN VALLEY AT SUNSET. ⌃

MORNING GLORY HOT SPRING BLOWS COLORFUL ⌃
BUBBLES IN YELLOWSTONE.

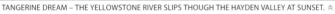

THE HOME WHERE THE BUFFALO ROAM IS ANTELOPE FLATS, SHADED BY THE TETONS. ⌃

THE TERRITORIES

The USA extends well beyond 50 states, deep into the Pacific and Caribbean, where a handful of scattered islands comprise its territories. If you're talking 'location, location, location,' these places deliver: deserted beaches, balmy breezes, turquoise water and all the other tropical clichés. But to be honest, the 'location' the USA originally wanted them for was strategic – the military used them for bases and supply stops (and sometimes to test bombs).

Today the military presence is lessened, if not altogether gone, and the territories have set up their own governments. These operate like US state governments, with a popularly elected governor, legislature and local judiciary. Each territory also sends a delegate to the US House of Representatives, although the delegate has no vote. Most territory residents are US citizens, with the same rights and privileges except they're not allowed to vote in US elections.

FORT SAN CRISTÓBAL FORT LOOMS OVER THE CANDY-COLORED HOMES IN SAN JUAN'S LA PERLA. ⌃

LOOKING LIKE A TANGERINE, AN ORANGE BALL SPONGE FLOATS IN CONGO CAY NEAR SAINT JOHN. ⌃

PUERTO RICO

CAPITAL SAN JUAN
POPULATION 4 MILLION
AREA 3515 SQ MILES
OFFICIAL LANGUAGES SPANISH, ENGLISH

Spain ruled Puerto Rico for 400 years, bringing slaves for sugar-cane plantations, and swirling the population into a native, European and African mix. The USA took possession in 1898 after the Spanish-American War, but the archipelago still very much has a Latin-Caribbean cultural scene – *mojitos* and salsa music, 16th-century walled forts and men clacking dominoes while sipping island-grown coffee. It's estimated more Puerto Ricans now live Stateside than on the island, and every once in a while the cry goes out for Puerto Rico to become the 51st state. Stay tuned regarding the territories' most powerful player.

US VIRGIN ISLANDS

CAPITAL CHARLOTTE AMALIE
POPULATION 109,840
AREA 136 SQ MILES
OFFICIAL LANGUAGE ENGLISH

Floating beside Puerto Rico, the Virgin Islands span 50 land masses (and that's just the US ones; several British Virgin Islands mingle next door). The main three are cruise-ship mecca Saint Thomas; Saint John, two-thirds cloaked in park land and beaches, ripe for hiking and snorkeling; and Saint Croix, with sugar plantations, old forts and great scuba diving. The USA paid Denmark $25 million in gold for the Virgins in 1917. West Indian culture remains the islands' strongest influence: calypso and reggae rhythms swirl through the air, and curried meats and mango-sweetened microbrews fill the tables.

A SENTRY POST WATCHES FOR GHOSTS OF GALLEONS PAST AT FORT SOLEDAD, UMATAC. ≫

GUAM

CAPITAL **HAGÅTÑA**
POPULATION **175,877**
AREA **209 SQ MILES**
OFFICIAL LANGUAGES **ENGLISH, CHAMORRO**

Hovering just south of the Marianas, Guam was a Spanish colony until US forces took it in the 1898 Spanish-American War. The US Navy set up a base and has been there ever since, except for two years during WWII when Japan occupied the island. The military and tourism, the latter mostly from Japan and Korea, form Guam's economic backbone. The north (where the navy is) has swaying palms, cliffs and caves. The south is more about sleepy villages, volcanic hills and waterfalls.

WILL IT BE SNAPPER OR GROUPER FOR DINNER ON SAIPAN BEACH? ≫

NORTHERN MARIANA ISLANDS

CAPITAL **SAIPAN**
POPULATION **86,616**
AREA **184 SQ MILES**
OFFICIAL LANGUAGES **ENGLISH, CHAMORRO, CAROLINIAN**

The Marianas' 14 islands stretch over 300 miles in the Pacific. The USA claimed them from Japan during WWII, and they have the dubious distinction of being where American B-29s flew from to drop the atomic bombs on Hiroshima and Nagasaki. Locals live on six islands (Saipan, Rota and Tinian are the main ones), where they farm, strum ukuleles, BBQ and chow down on taro and fish dishes. Tourism hasn't caught on (not for lack of beauty) but the apparel manufacturing industry has.

BLUE SKY MEETS BLUE WATER BESIDE VOLCANIC-PEAKED OFU ISLAND, AMERICAN SAMOA. ≫

AMERICAN SAMOA

CAPITAL **PAGO PAGO**
POPULATION **64,827**
AREA **76 SQ MILES**
OFFICIAL LANGUAGES **ENGLISH, SAMOAN**

American Samoa – the only occupied part of the USA in the southern hemisphere – drifts far in the Pacific Ocean, in the neighborhood of Fiji and Tahiti. Germany, Britain and the USA all had early claims on Samoa, and in 1899 they signed a treaty to partition the islands. The eastern-most ones became American Samoa. The territory has seven islands: five are forested, volcanic-peaked beauties, where blue seas lap palm-studded beaches in a guileless Polynesian idyll; the other two are coral atolls. Tuna canneries comprise the main industry and brawny NFL players are one of the biggest exports.

BLACK NODDIES AGREE: MIDWAY ATOLL'S WILDLIFE REFUGE IS SOMETHING TO SEE. ≫

MIDWAY ISLANDS

POPULATION **40**
AREA **2.4 SQ MILES**

Sometimes called Midway Atoll, these tiny dots of sand sit halfway between California and Japan. The islands became the USA's first offshore acquisitions when annexed in 1867. Midway looms large in military history, notably as the location of a 1942 battle between the US and Japanese navies that marked a turning point in WWII and the decline of Japanese power in the Pacific. The US Navy used the islands until 1993, with a peak population of more than 3500 personnel. Today the islands form a national wildlife refuge for seabirds, dolphins, monk seals and green sea turtles.

OTHER ISLANDS

The USA's territories also include several uninhabited islands. In the Caribbean, steep-cliffed Navassa lies between Jamaica and Haiti; the isle is disputed, as Haiti also claims it. In the Pacific, the USA maintains a group of atolls, islands and reefs that form the Pacific Remote Islands National Monument, whose thriving marine habitat is home to sharks and millions of nesting seabirds. The group includes Kingman Reef, which emerges only in low tides; nearby Palmyra Atoll; Johnston Atoll, which was the site of nuclear blasts; and Howland, Baker, Jarvis and Wake Islands.

THE AUTHORS

As well as contributing to the state and regional sections, several authors wrote the introductory and end matter sections of this book: Karla wrote The USA at a Glance, The USA By Theme and The Territories, Greg wrote the National Parks of the West road trip, Sara wrote the Route 66 and Highway 1 road trips, Gregor wrote the New England road trip, Tom wrote the Great River Road trip and Adam wrote the Blue Ridge Parkway road trip. Karla also coordinated the writing of this book.

KARLA ZIMMERMAN

When she's not home in Chicago watching baseball, er, writing for newspapers, books and magazines, Karla is traveling. The lifelong Midwesterner has been snowed on in Minnesota, stepped in pig doo in Indiana and watched sausage-racing in Wisconsin. Internationally she's traveled to more than 55 countries and published stories on Prague, Cape Verde and Vietnam, among others. She has coauthored several Lonely Planet guidebooks covering the USA, Canada and the Caribbean.

GREG BENCHWICK

Greg has rumbled in the jungles of South America, walked across Spain on the Camino de Santiago and challenged the spires, peaks and rivers of Colorado and Utah. He specializes in adventure and sustainable travel and has written more than a dozen guidebooks. When he's not on the road, Greg develops his new-media company www.monjomedia.com.

SARA BENSON

Midwestern by birth and Californian by choice, Sara has traveled extensively to every state except Alaska – but she dreams of heeding the call of the Great White North just as soon as she can. An author of dozens of travel and nonfiction books, Sara has contributed to many Lonely Planet travel guides. She also works as a national park ranger.

GREGOR CLARK

Gregor Clark's love of travel and languages has taken him to 50 countries on five continents and to all 50 states. He developed an early fondness for New England, skating on frozen ponds in Washington Depot, CT, and seeing his first shooting star in Vermont's Green Mountains. Now a Vermont resident, Gregor has contributed to Lonely Planet's New England Trips as well as guides to Brazil, Portugal, Italy, Argentina and California.

TOM DOWNS

A native Californian, Tom has been traveling throughout the USA ever since he got his driver's license, and he has been writing about his journeys for more than a decade. His family roots drew him to the northern Plains, while blues, jazz, BBQ and sultry weather attracted him to the South. Once, during a month-long road trip, he traveled the entire length of the Mississippi, exploring each state that touched the great river.

JIM DUFRESNE

Jim has a passion for two things, sunsets and shoreline, the result of living his entire life in Alaska and Michigan, the two states with the most coastline. In Alaska, Jim was the first sportswriter to win a national award from Associated Press. In Michigan, Jim has never resided more than an hour's drive from a Great Lake. Jim's other Lonely Planet titles include Alaska and Hiking In Alaska.

LISA DUNFORD

Lisa learned to sign room-service bills early, as her father's hotel-industry career moved the family from Chicago to New York, Dallas, Pittsburgh… After college and a stint abroad she settled in south Texas and became a features department editor, writer and restaurant reviewer. Since turning freelance, Lisa has two-stepped across Texas, rock climbed in Utah and eaten far too much deep-dish pizza in Chicago for Lonely Planet.

ADAM KARLIN

Adam Karlin was born in Washington, DC, and raised on the banks of St Mary's River, MD. After graduating from college he worked at newspapers from Olympia, WA, to Key West, FL. Then Lonely Planet made the mistake of hiring him, sending him as far afield as the Andaman Islands and the Kenyan coast. Closer to home, he's written or contributed to several guidebooks on the Eastern seaboard, including Miami, Florida, Mid-Atlantic Trips, Washington, DC and other titles.

ALEX LEVITON

Californian by birth and Southern by homeownership since 2003, Alex lives part-time in a tobacco warehouse loft in Durham, NC. In 2008 she road tripped throughout her adopted region for The Carolinas, Georgia & the South Trips. She's spent over 20 years traveling throughout the Pacific Northwest with her brother Scott, who lives on a houseboat in Seattle's Lake Union.

ROBERT REID

Robert Reid is an American. Raised in Oklahoma, he's lived and worked all over the globe, including in Vietnam, London, Melbourne and Lonely Planet's sweet Oakland office. Since 2003 he's been based in Brooklyn, where he has updated 21 (and counting) Lonely Planet guidebooks and created his own free guidebook to Vietnam (www.reidontravel.com).

REGIS ST LOUIS

A Hoosier by birth, Regis grew up in a sleepy town where he dreamed of big journeys across America and beyond. After studying Russian in Moscow, he set out on a life of travel. He's crossed the USA by bus, train and automobile, and has traveled six continents. Regis has contributed to numerous Lonely Planet guides, including New York City, New England and USA. He lives in Brooklyn. Regis wrote Introducing the USA at the front of this book.

INDEX & STATE ABBREVIATIONS

THE USA BOOK
SEPTEMBER 2009

PUBLISHER Chris Rennie
US PUBLISHER Brice Gosnell
ASSOCIATE PUBLISHER Ben Handicott
COMMISSIONING EDITOR Suki Gear
DESIGNER Gerilyn Attebery
PROJECT MANAGER Jane Atkin
LAYOUT DESIGNER Margaret Jung
COORDINATING EDITOR Kirsten Rawlings
CARTOGRAPHERS Wayne Murphy, Marion Byass, Sophie Reed, Ross Butler
MANAGING EDITOR Sasha Baskett
MANAGING LAYOUT DESIGNER Sally Darmody
ASSISTING LAYOUT DESIGNERS Paul Iacono, Cara Smith, Indra Kilfoyle, Nicholas Colicchia
ASSISTING EDITORS Daniel Corbett, Gina Tsarouhas, Laura Gibb
IMAGE RESEARCH Rebecca Dandens, Aude Vauconsant, Sabrina Dalbesio, Naomi Parker
PRE-PRESS PRODUCTION Ryan Evans
PRINT PRODUCTION MANAGER Graham Imeson

THANKS Shahara Ahmed, Mo Elkhalloufi, Laura Jane, Rachael Nusbaum

PUBLISHED BY
LONELY PLANET PUBLICATIONS PTY LTD
ABN 36 005 607 983
90 Maribyrnong St, Footscray,
Victoria, 3011, Australia
www.lonelyplanet.com

Printed through Colorcraft Ltd, Hong Kong
Printed in China

ISBN 978 1 74104 732 5

Text © Lonely Planet 2009
Photographs © Photographers as indicated 2009

PHOTOGRAPHS
Many of the images in this book are available for licensing from Lonely Planet Images.
www.lonelyplanetimages.com

LONELY PLANET OFFICES

AUSTRALIA
Locked Bag 1, Footscray, Victoria, 3011
Phone 03 8379 8000 Fax 03 8379 8111
Email talk2us@lonelyplanet.com.au

USA
150 Linden St, Oakland, CA 94607
Phone 510 250 6400 Toll free 800 275 8555
Fax 510 893 8572 Email info@lonelyplanet.com

UK
2nd fl, 186 City Rd, London, EC1V 2NT
Phone 020 7106 2100 Fax 020 7106 2101
Email go@lonelyplanet.co.uk

PHOTO CREDITS

Front cover // Colorado River canyon, Grand Canyon National Park, Arizona; Momatiuk - Eastcott // Corbis. **Inside front cover** (from left) Statue of Liberty; Mark Newman // Lonely Planet Images. The 131st Kentucky Derby; Steve Boyle // Corbis. **Back cover** (from left) American diner; BWAC Images // Alamy. Field with red barn; Panoramic Images // Getty. Jazz band members, New Orleans; Mike Kepka // Corbis. Yearling brown bears; Mark Newman // Lonely Planet Images. **Inside back cover** (from left) Players in dugout; Moodboard // Corbis. Navajo elder; Dallas Stribley // Lonely Planet Images. **Spine image** Colorado River canyon, Grand Canyon National Park, Arizona; Momatiuk - Eastcott // Corbis **p2** (from left) Chile harvest, Chimayo, NM; Craig Aurness // Corbis. Bayou swamp with cypress moss; Nathan Benn // Corbis. Bison on prairie, Badlands National Park, South Dakota; Jake Rajs // Getty. **p3** Marching girls in International District Parade, Seattle; Lawrence Worcester // Lonely Planet Images. **p6** (from left) A banjoist perfoms in Lexington, KY; Kevin R Morris // Corbis. Surfboards, Waikiki Beach, HI; Richard I'Anson // Lonely Planet Images. Hawai'i Volcanoes National Park; John Elk III // Lonely Planet Images. **p7** Statue of Liberty; Mark Newman // Lonely Planet Images. **p28** Adina Tovy Amsel // Lonely Planet Images. **p30** Greig Cranna // Photolibrary. **p32** Angus Oborn // Lonely Planet Images. **p34** Eric Meola // Getty. **p36** Macduff Everton // Corbis. **p38** Frans Lanting // Corbis. **p40** Panoramic Images // Getty. **p49** Mark Newman // Lonely Planet Images. **p55** David Tipling // Lonely Planet Images. **p107** Macduff Everton // Corbis. **p151** Gareth McCormack // Lonely Planet Images. **p159** Thomas Winz // Lonely Planet Images. **p167** Mira // Alamy. **p235** Richard Cummins // Lonely Planet Images. **p239** Richard Hamilton Smith // Corbis